"Arnold."

I froze in my tracks. Where had that sound come from? I was the only person in the house, but I could swear someone had said the bird's name.

"Arnold!"

There it was again—the same word, in a slightly different tone. It sounded a lot like me when I was scolding him.

I pinched myself. It hurt and I was awake. No doubt about it, Arnold was saying "Arnold." He was saying his name as clearly as I would, in the varying tones of voice I'd used.

Strangely, it was the first sound he had ever uttered. Never so much as a "peep" or a "squeak" or a note of song had crossed his beak previously.

ARNIE, THE DARLING STARLING

Margarete Sigl Corbo
and
Diane Marie Barras

Illustrated by Leslie Morrill

FAWCETT CREST • NEW YORK

*Warm-hearted, gentle people
inspire more than they ever realize.*

For Mary Jane and Patsy,

*and Big Sue,
who first said, "Dare to Dream"*

i Flowers were the only things I'd planned to rescue that day. Already annoyed with myself for having gotten a late start, I was in no mood to tolerate interruptions. Yet, before I could even begin work, I had to contend with an intruder in the garden. Looking up at me from the middle of a patch of daisies, his beady eyes demanded, rather than beseeched, attention. Leaning my hoe against the side of the house, I crouched to get a closer look. Impudently, he continued to glare at me. Considering his helpless, hopeless predicament, considering that a moment before I had almost squashed him out of existence with my big foot, he should have been begging for help. But begging is not the way of his kind, apparently; certainly it wasn't *his* way.

At that first encounter, he was merely a familiar springtime dilemma: a baby bird fallen from the nest, his chances of survival doubtful. I looked down at him with disgust. Never had I seen an uglier, more alien-looking creature. He didn't have a single feather or bit of fuzz on his body yet. The bright sunlight shone through his translucent pink skin, outlining his innards as clearly as though they were fixed on X-ray film. His belly protruded roundly; like a balloon pumped as full of air as possible, it looked likely to burst at any moment. Aside from that, he was incredibly scrawny, appearing too insubstantial to be alive. His head was balanced precariously atop a flimsy shoestring of a neck. He stared at me past a conical, tightly shut infant beak, his darkly bright eyes insisting, "Take me home. Immediately!"

Little did I realize, at that moment, what he meant by "home." I stared up at the one I thought he meant and sighed. Tiny tufts of nesting straw protruded from the narrow opening between the rafters and wall of my house, an opening that had been tightly sealed against just such an intrusion. I wondered how his parents had managed to peck through the louvered aluminum vent covers. I could hear his brothers and sisters cheeping loudly up there, but the bird on the ground remained strangely silent.

With mounting distress, I wondered how I was going to get him back where he belonged. The birds had chosen to build their nest in the very least accessible spot—a niche, between rafters, that was only a few inches tall. I doubted very seriously if I could reach it from inside the house. On the other hand, the nest was at least twenty feet above the ground, and I didn't have a ladder that would reach so high. It seemed there was little choice; I would have to carry him through the attic and hope it would be possible to reach the nest from inside.

I'd better hurry, too, I thought with irritation. Spring weather had already given way to the typical sultry heat of summer in southeast Texas. At ten o'clock on that mid-May morning it was already ninety-four degrees Fahrenheit, and I really did want to finish my outdoor chores before the mercury climbed much higher.

"Let's get you home right now, Bird," I said. Gingerly, I scooped the hapless little creature into my hand. He snuggled up immediately, resting his chin on my thumb and closing his eyes contentedly. Strange. Wild baby birds usually struggle in fright at the human touch. Such trusting dependence was moving, but best ignored. I strode off purposefully to do what must be done. Clutching the little bird lightly, I carried him up the stairs to my living quarters. When I closed the door behind me, he stirred slightly and wiggled deeper into my hand. "Don't get too comfortable, Bird," I said. "You'll be home very soon."

The air-conditioned house was a welcome relief, making the hot job ahead of me seem even more unpleasant. Reaching the bird's nest would not be easy. Except for a short, narrow walkway and small storage area, there was no floor in the attic. I would be forced to walk on the narrow wooden joists—no simple task for my rather large, clumsy feet. The sooner the job was done, the less time I'd have to worry about it, though.

I set up the ladder and climbed it to the attic entrance. Then, holding the hatchling protectively against my chest with one hand, I struggled with the other to lift the trap door that sealed the four-foot-square access hole. Taking two more steps up, I paused midway through the entrance while my eyes adjusted to the dimness. Through the vents at the far side of the attic, the sun beckoned like distant lights in a dark cave. The air was still, heavy, lifeless, devoid of odor. It was even hotter than I had expected. My little ward stirred again, lifting his head with a jerk, and looked around alertly. "Almost there," I said.

As my eyes adjusted to the darkness, the forty feet I had to traverse to reach the nest appeared to stretch endlessly. Carefully, carrying the little mote of life with utmost tenderness, I stepped from joist to joist. The ventilators near the peak of the roof whirred, alternately admitting then blotting out sunshine as they turned. It created a dizzying strobe-light effect. I tottered, weaved, faltered, clutching futilely at empty air for support. Closing my eyes, I took a quick, deep breath and held it, barely managing to maintain my footing.

The little bird strained in a seeming attempt to help me. I cooed nonsense sounds to calm his fears—and mine. He settled quietly into my cupped hand again, tucking his head deeply into my palm. "I'll have you home soon," I said, hoping I would be able to fulfill the promise. But the closer I moved toward the nest, the smaller appeared the space in which it was located.

The sloping roof forced me to hunch lower and lower as I tiptoed delicately along, clinging to a rafter. Each completed step was a minor triumph. Looking up to judge how far I had to go, I rammed my head into the protruding point of a roofing tack. My precious cargo squirmed in agitation at my yelp of pain. "It's nothing, Bird," I lied. "I'll have you home as soon as I quit seeing stars."

I completed the harrowing journey partly on knees and the one free hand, then in an inching crawl from point to point, toes and elbows providing locomotion. The Fiberglas insulation grabbed at my clothing and bare skin, clinging, tickling, itching annoyingly. The rough wooden edges of the upright joists scraped my flesh cruelly as I slid over them. Finally, I reached a point where the space between roofing board and joist was so narrow that I could go no further. The nest was still out of sight, and the oblong of light where I knew it to be seemed distant. Discouraged to think I'd come so far and had failed to reach my destination, I rested and wondered what I should do next.

In the quiet of the attic, I suddenly realized that the urgent cheeping had ceased, and now only rustling noises came from the nest. My presence must be frightening the hatchlings there. The little bird in my hand wiggled. It seemed as though he was trying to escape my grasp so he could walk the rest of the way on his own. Well, maybe he could—if I could just get him close enough, over that last joist and into the space where the nest had been built. Stretching my arm full length, I took careful aim, silently wished the hatchling good luck, and tossed him toward his siblings with a snap of my wrist. There was a muffled thud, followed by an increase in the rustling noises. I had hit the mark, and the little bird was safely back where he belonged.

Satisfied, I wormed my way backward until I could stand again. Basking in the pleasure it had given me to return the baby bird to his nest, I walked confidently from one narrow board to another until I reached the attic entrance. I hummed as I climbed down the ladder and lowered the trap door.

Now that I'd taken care of the bird's problem, I could resume the task I'd barely begun when I found him. Armed with hoe and cultivator, I returned to the flower bed to do battle against encroaching grass and weeds. I was determined to save the struggling daisies.

Among which, once again, was nestled the baby bird. I stared at him in disbelief. After all that effort! Maybe I had tossed him too hard, overshooting the nest, though I could have sworn... His unblinking glare commanded as before: *I told you to take me home!* Once again, the daisies would have to wait.

I tried to return him to his nest three more times that day. Not once did I see the adult birds, which made me worry that my presence was preventing them from feeding the entire brood. After the fourth attempt, I looked down at the hatchling with some annoyance. "What's going on here, Bird? Am I throwing you too hard, or are you jumping out of the nest on your own? We can't keep this up forever, you know." He looked up at me without so much as a blink.

It suddenly occurred to me that he was getting nothing to eat. He would starve at this rate. "Well, what do you think I should do, Bird? Shall I take you home once more?" His eyes bored into me, saying it was time for the nonsense to end, time for more meaningful effort to begin. He seemed to take it for granted that I would accept full responsibility for his welfare.

I'd never had much luck helping birds I'd found in his circumstances, though. I hated the thought of failing again. Cuddling him against my chest, I felt the incredibly fast throb of his heartbeat, so different from my own. I looked down at him and sighed. What choice did I have?

"Well, little one, you've become quite a challenge. I'm not the greatest bird-mother who ever lived, but I'll do my best until you're strong enough to make it on your own. I guess you've found yourself a temporary home with me."

I could have sworn he smiled.

ii The little bird was strange from the very beginning. He continued to stare his demands in silence,
keeping his beak tightly closed. That beak had not
opened, not emitted a sound, since the first moment
of our acquaintance, and that could be a problem. If
he wasn't going to cry out, I'd never know when he
was hungry. And, with his beak so tightly shut, I'd
never be able to get food into him. Whether he wanted
to or not, though, he was going to eat, I resolved. But
what should I feed him? Since he wasn't talking and
his species was undetermined, his dietary needs were

anybody's guess. I took inventory of my pantry and refrigerator and decided to try canned corn, raw steak, and orange juice. They should do. After all, every bird's diet consists primarily of grain, protein, and fruit, doesn't it?

I opened the can of corn, minced the meat, poured the orange juice into a dish, and settled at the breakfast bar with my guest. My three cats, never well mannered and ever curious, gathered round at a not-discreet distance, settling in comfortably to watch the show.

Far from being intimidated by his audience, the star attraction enjoyed the attention. Despite the fact that he must certainly be starving, he seemed more interested in making friends with the cats than in the feast I was offering. No amount of cajoling could persuade him to open that tightly clenched beak. His head swiveled constantly as he took in the details of his new surroundings.

Suddenly, I laughed aloud, realizing that his actions reminded me of my daughter as a child. At the dinner table, she'd always been just as interested as he in everything *except* the painstakingly prepared contents of her dinner plate. She'd considered every mealtime an annoying interruption to more important activities, while I'd felt duty-bound to ensure that she ate every morsel of her nutritionally balanced meal. Despite the fact that she'd tried my patience sorely, and I hers, during those daily ritual stubborn standoffs, she had eaten when hungry and developed quite laudably.

This newly adopted child would do no differently. I would be patient and outstubborn him if I had to sit there for the next week and tempt him with every single food item in the house. As though he'd read my mind and was satisfied that he'd established his right to self-determination, he abruptly ceased reconnoitering, stared at me up the tilted angle of his beak, and snapped the orifice open.

Hastily, I popped in a tidbit of the steak. He spat

8

it out, yet opened his beak for more. I tried a kernel of corn. That, too, was rejected. When his beak opened again, I stuffed corn and meat together and aimed them down his gullet with the tip of my smallest finger. This time, I was rewarded with a swallow. Next, using an eyedropper, I gave him some of the orange juice, being extremely careful to dole out no more than he could swallow. He drank and ate and ate and drank until I thought his belly would pop. Then he stopped as abruptly as he'd begun, blinked twice in appreciation, squatted down, tucked his head into his shoulders, and fell asleep.

He would live! I knew now he would live. A warm glow of triumphant satisfaction spread over me. I would be nature's assistant, foster bird-mother, rescuer of the hapless helpless unloved ugly little hatchling. What a smugly good feeling! The cats smirked: *Um-hum, he's getting you well trained already. And you're smug about it?* What a dumb feeling. What on earth was I to do with him now? With three cats in the house!

Samantha, the diminutive black one, crept nearer, sniffing curiously at the sleeping infant, keeping an eye on my reaction. Following his mother's lead, Vagabond also ambled closer to the little bird, mischief dancing in his large, amber eyes. Their curiosity was natural, normal, and tolerable, so long as they understood that this was a guest, to be treated with respect. Close inspection was permitted; touching was verboten. They understood the rules and stayed a whisker away.

Such brazen, plebian behavior was not for Mitzi, though. With a disdainful sniff, she left our little gathering. Mitzi is the eldest cat, the one my daughter refers to as "the Palm Beach snob." Usually, she slinks arrogantly through life in her calico fur coat, her nose too high in the air to pay heed to the commonplace happenings of the world. She's a fraud, though. Whenever she thinks no one will notice, she forgets about dignity, acts as foolish as a kitten, and earns the playful nickname Mip-Mip. That sort of conduct, however, is reserved for very private occasions. She'd be mortified if anyone outside of the family knew of her secret self. Mip-Mip would return to indulge her own curiosity once the rabble had departed.

For now, I was left with the two commoners to ponder the future of the little bird who had thrust himself uninvited into our lives. I considered Vagabond's character and Samantha's background, and I knew that they couldn't be trusted to maintain their respect for the baby bird without my looming presence.

While not deliberately malicious, Vagabond didn't have an ounce of gentleness. He'd been such a bumbling clown as a kitten that I'd begun calling him Bundy, reserving his proper name for scoldings, but now he looked and acted more like a football player. Though he was sleek and ebony like his mother, it was hard to believe that his eighteen pounds of brawn had sprung from Samantha's delicate six-pound body.

Of course, it was no wonder that Sammie was tiny; she'd spent her first half-year in the wild, existing off the land when she couldn't get into garbage cans. A neighbor had fed her dinner scraps, primarily pasta and salad, and allowed her to stay in the garage during her first pregnancy. Then the neighbor had moved without a thought for the creature that had become so dependent upon her benevolence.

Samantha had tried to be a good mother, I think. But, abandoned in the garage with five demanding infants when she was little more than a kitten herself— how could she produce milk for them when *she* was starving? By the time I'd become aware of her plight, Samantha was gone, perhaps fleeing the horror of having four of her offspring starve to death because she'd been unable to provide them with nourishment. Vagabond had been her fifth kitten—how could I not bring him home after I found him starving all alone in that garage?

When I next saw Samantha, weeks later, she was pregnant again. She couldn't have weighed two pounds at our second encounter, half of that the weight of those well-developed fetuses that dragged her swaying belly to the ground. Her coat had faded with malnutrition from dingy black to dingier brown. She was in the process of stalking a bird when I spied her, but the bird had eluded her easily. She toppled over and lay panting beneath my mulberry tree.

I almost broke my neck running down the stairs with a can of cat food. Unlike the wild animal she should have been, she didn't budge an inch. Her eyes regarded me with apathy, a look that quickly changed to gratitude when I set the food in front of her. She gobbled the tuna, then promptly threw it up and ran away as though ashamed at her body's rejection of my offering.

Though I continued to put food out for her, I absolutely refused to get to know her, to allow any closeness to develop. It was my hope that she'd get strong enough to go somewhere else. I had no desire for, no use for, another cat. I'd had one cat already when I adopted her son, and there was no room in my life for a third. But how could I not feed her after seeing her condition? And, as I fed her, she grew on me. No matter how I tried to talk myself out of it, I knew deep down that I'd have to take her in.

All right, one more cat—but *not* her litter. In one fell swoop, I'd seen to it that she was aborted, given a hysterectomy, and declawed. Dear, sweet, gentle, loving, and lovable Sammie has since devoted her life to showing her gratitude. Unfortunately, neither her gratitude nor her apparent tameness guaranteed that her predatory nature wouldn't return in the right circumstances.

As I thought about the cats and wondered how to

ensure the little bird's protection from them, a friend popped in and added to the weight of my thoughts.

"What have we here now?" Dee asked, taking in the two nosy cats, the sleeping hatchling, and my doleful expression—doleful because I was beginning to realize the responsibility I had assumed.

"You won't believe how he happens to be here," I responded, and proceeded to tell her about my eventful morning.

"Have you named him yet?" she asked.

"Of course not. He's just a wild bird. He doesn't need a name. He won't be staying. As soon as he's strong enough, I'll throw him out to fend for himself. He just needs a little help until he can fly."

"Ha!"

"You'll see," I said in reply to her skepticism. I would not name the bird. That would be getting too personal; making an emotional commitment; asking for heartbreak when it was time to turn him loose. After all, he was nothing more than a wild bird, for goodness' sake!

Dee persisted. "Hmmm. Look at that tiny head. His body's huge by comparison—like a weight lifter's. Why, he looks like Arnold Schwarzenegger. Why don't you call him Arnold? It would fit."

"It will *not* fit! He does not get a name. I will not think of him in terms of a name. That would personalize him too much. I will not get personal this time. I'll just toughen him up, then out he goes."

I really meant it, too.

iii Before I could toughen him up, however, he would have to survive infancy. That first feeding was only the beginning of the struggle to keep him alive. Like a premature baby, he clung to life precariously during our first few days together and required constant attention.

His first bed was a cardboard box that had originally contained cowboy boots. Poked full of holes for ventilation and padded with strips of newspaper and soft facial tissue, it seemed an ideal nest. He slept peacefully in it beside my easy chair as I read the newspaper and watched television that evening. When I retired for the night, I carried the box with me and placed it on the far side of my bed. Sentimentally, I thought that my presence might ease his loneliness and fright if he awoke on this first night away from his parents and siblings.

Checking up on him one last time before turning out my light, I was shocked at the ice-cold feeling of his body, at his feeble response to my touch. It seemed life was ebbing from him. In the nest, he would have had the combined body heat of his parents and brothers and sisters all huddled together to keep him warm. I picked him up and cuddled him against my body, enfolding him with both of my hands. He squirmed a bit, then snuggled quietly against me. His coldness penetrated my nightshirt like an ice cube. I hugged him closer. Gradually, my warmth seeped into him, but it was ridiculous to think I could hold him all night that way. Reluctantly, I put him back into the box and covered him with a pair of wool socks. Then I put the lid back on the box, scooted it closer to my pillow, and draped it with a beach towel. The cats sniffed over the setup, then settled at the foot of my bed. I fell into an uneasy sleep.

Waking in predawn darkness a few hours later, my first thought was of the hatchling. I turned on the bedside lamp so I could check on him. The beach towel was in disarray, the lid was off of the box, and Samantha sat alertly peering down into the makeshift nest. My heart quickened. "Samantha, you wouldn't dare!" I said. She looked at me and cocked her head as if to say, *How could you think such a thing of me?* The baby bird lay unharmed on top of the wool socks, looking up at Sammie as though they had been interrupted in the middle of an interesting conversation.

As I leaned over to look at him, he swiveled his head toward me, and his beak popped wide open. I smiled. "Time for your four o'clock feeding, Bird? I'm wide awake anyway, so you might as well have an early breakfast." When I picked him up out of the box, I was distressed anew at the iciness of his flesh. If his body temperature couldn't be maintained he would surely catch pneumonia. Once again, I held him closely, warming him with my body, cupping him protectively with one hand while holding my coffee cup with the other.

I was beginning to feel we would all be better off if he simply went to sleep and didn't wake again, though. It would certainly make life easier for me. He was so time-consuming! As those treacherous thoughts crossed my mind, he squirmed around in my hand, took a deep breath, then curled into a new sleep position. Looking down at him, I thought again how incredibly homely he was—and how trustingly dependent, and endearing. How could I not do my best to keep him alive? There had to be a way to keep him warm. There had to be!

With Sammie curled up in my lap, the bird snuggled near my heart, and the sun peeking above the horizon, I fell asleep sitting up and dreamed of the blue April skies filled with gracefully soaring eagles. They were joined in the sky by a pink, featherless little hatchling, valiantly flapping his useless wings with all his might, trying to attain their lofty heights.

This time when I woke, haunted by that vision of the little one struggling so hard, I knew exactly what to do. This wasn't the first tiny infant I'd had to rescue from unkind fate and protect from members of my household. There had been Hansel, the rat, for instance. The white-and-sable product of generations of laboratory breeding, he had been earmarked in babyhood as a future meal for a pet python. Hansie's breeder had been in a hurry to dispose of him, a last remnant of a home business venture gone sour. When I'd heard what was to become of him, my heart had melted for that little rat, making him suddenly seem the sweetest furry thing I'd ever seen. I'd never been fond of rodents, but in the two years he'd lived with me, Hansel had become one of the most endearing pets I'd ever known. Though I'd thought it would be necessary to protect him from Mitzi, the two of them had become quite attached to each other. Frequently, they curled up together for a nap or romped in a game of chase. Alas, Hansie had been rescued from the maws of a snake only to be plagued through most of his life by cancer.

He was only a fond memory now, but the cage in which he'd lived was stored in the attic. I dragged it down, laid newspaper in the bottom, and carefully centered the bird's boot-box nest within it. With the lid snapped in place, the wire enclosure looked like an ideal way of protecting the foundling from the cats. To keep him warm, I placed a small lamp next to the cage, turned it on, and draped a blanket over the entire contrivance. The heat from the light bulb would be retained by the blanket and keep the bird as toasty as he would have been under the wings of his parents.

It was touch and go for the next few days. I often thought he would certainly die soon. At least one of the cats kept him company at all times, lying patiently beside the tented cage like relatives standing vigil at a sickbed. Gradually, his body temperature leveled off and he gained strength. Downy fuzz began to cover his naked body, and feather shafts protruded here and there through his skin. The down softened his boniness, making him look almost cute, but the feather shafts destroyed the effect. His body appeared riddled with dozens of arrows. "Maybe your mother kicked you out of the nest because you're so ugly, Bird," I commented once, then hastened to add, "But don't worry about that. We love you. Remind me to tell you the story about the ugly duckling someday. Maybe you'll turn into a beautiful bird, too." He looked more ridiculous each day, however, as the shafts began to open at the ends to permit the emergence of wispy feather tufts.

Although I made it a point to feed him regularly, I was able to go about my normal routine in the first few days. He was secure from harm within the cage, and it wouldn't do at all for me to hover over him. The less I had to handle him, to be with him, the better. I was determined that I would not become attached to him. Born to the wild he'd been, and to the wild he belonged. I felt duty-bound to free him as soon as possible.

As his strength increased, he became much more active. The boot box became obsolete as a nest, for he refused to stay inside of it. Each time he climbed over the edge of the box, he fell the rest of the way out, usually landing on his head. Thinking of that fragile string of a neck now hidden beneath a fine covering of gray feathers, I removed the box from the cage before one of those falls could result in disaster.

Like any developing infant, he slept less and less and spent most of his waking hours exploring his world. I walked into the house one day to find him in the middle of the living room floor, at least ten feet from his securely closed cage. Evidently he'd squirmed through the bars to wander about on his own. As he hopped and fluttered in what seemed a joyful dance, all three cats watched with great interest. They were so close, he must surely have felt their breaths hot on his back. Bundy looked poised to leap at any moment.

"Vagabond! Samantha! Mitzi!" I bellowed. "Get away from him! Now! Don't you touch one feather on his head, you hear me?" I clapped my hands vigorously as I yelled, my heart pounding as loudly as my heavy, hurried footsteps across the room. All four animals looked at me with annoyance, seemingly united in the feeling that I was interrupting a mutually enjoyable pastime.

Scooping the bird up in my hand, I knew something had to be done to prevent him from crawling through those bars again. I used window screening to line the inside of the cage, securing it to the bars with a weave of fishing line. But he hated the reinforced enclosure and fluttered frantically to indicate his feelings.

"You're going to be the death of me yet, Arnold," I scolded him. The name had stuck after a few days; it came more radily to the tongue than "Bird" did. One can't possibly hand-feed a living creature without talking to it, and in the talking, one must use a name. I'd surrendered to the inevitability of Arnold as an appellation. It was more convenient, even if it was only temporary. Once he was set free, his fellows would probably call him something like "Twiple" or "Chirple" or whatever birds call each other.

His progress was a joy to watch, and I found myself spending more and more time with him, holding him, talking to him, petting him. As though he felt I was being too intimate, however, he hated it more each time I touched him. He began to struggle out of my hands immediately after I lifted him from the cage. I'd had pet birds before and knew how lovingly touchable they could be, so I concluded that Arnold's untouchability was caused by his wild origins. It was not right to keep him confined to a house with only cats and a human being as companions. He belonged with his own. My resolve became ever stronger. As soon as he learned to pick up food and eat it, out he would go.

Unfortunately, his feeding habits were a major stumbling block to my plans for him. Totally dependent on hand-feeding, he would not consume a crumb of anything that was not physically placed inside his mouth. He came to me willingly for that service, his beak wide open and demanding when he was hungry. It was a situation I intended to remedy quickly. I placed little dishes of corn beneath his beak, refrained from offering him any by hand, and allowed him to become hungrier by the hour. All of it was to no avail. Like a recalcitrant child, he played with his food. Using his beak, he pushed it around inside the dish, then shoveled it out of the container.

Exasperating as he was, however, I had to laugh at his antics. Once the corn was out of his dish, he would shove it until it was just where he wanted it to be; back away; and walk in circles around it. He would eye it suspiciously, as though it might attack him; approach it again, one cautious centimeter at a time; then charge toward it with beak open, jamming his mandibles firmly against the floor on either side of that tidbit of food. He would stand there without moving a muscle for long minutes afterward, his parted beak forming a te-pee over the kernel of corn, looking for all the world as though he expected it to hop into his mouth. He didn't seem to realize that all he had to do was close his beak to grasp it. Eventually, he would give up and walk away without eating. He repeated the act over and over until I gave up and fed him once more by hand.

Thinking he might respond better to natural foods, I filled his dish with birdseed. He loved it! It was such fun to shove the little seeds around in the dish with his beak; such a delight for him to bounce on the rim of the dish until it tipped and spilled the contents. And the seeds were so tickly underfoot as he swept them onto the carpet for me to clean up. Not for one second did he consider them edible, however.

Wild berries, gathered from my hedgerow, were equally appreciated. They rolled as well as marbles. To give him credit, Arnold did test their palatability. Parting his beak and placing it firmly to either side of the berries, as he had done with the corn, he waited with that attitude of expecting them to hop into his mouth. After he walked away from them repeatedly, I concluded that he didn't like the berries either.

No matter what I tempted him with, he would not pick up anything to eat on his own. Nervously, I began to wonder if I was going to have to continue hand-feeding him for the rest of his life. "What did I get myself into when I picked you up out of that daisy patch, Arnold?" I wailed repeatedly. Invariably, he responded by cocking his head to the side and looking at me as if I were crazy. It seemed he did, indeed, expect me to be his faithful slave for as long as he chose to remain with me.

His horizons were expanding ever more, though, and I had faith he would eventually ask for his freedom. He walked all over the house, waddling with a jerky gait that reminded me of Charlie Chaplin as the little tramp. He followed me everywhere I went, exploring boldly, but only as long as I was in plain sight. The hodgepodge strewn on kitchen and bathroom countertops was a special delight to examine, and he loved sliding around on the slippery Formica surfaces. Though he couldn't fly, he used his extended wings like parachutes to slow his descent to the floor when he tired of the heights and wanted a stroll on the carpet.

Nonchalantly, he walked among the cats, strutting regally as though he were king and they his subjects. They were so intrigued by him that they froze like statues, barely seeming to breathe when he was near. Whiskers twitched and eyes rolled wildly when he hopped up and walked along their backs, but they retained that rigidly self-imposed discipline while I broke out in a cold sweat. Someday he would have to learn that birds cannot normally get away with treating cats with such arrogance.

I permitted him to remain outside the cage, to wander about at his will, whenever I could be nearby to watch over him. I'd never had the opportunity to observe a bird growing up before, and I found his daily development fascinating. I became so enchanted with watching him that I didn't realize he was quickly becoming a spoiled brat.

But the day arrived when I could no longer afford the luxury of spending so much time with him. My

daughter and grandson and friends of theirs were coming to visit me for summer vacation, and there were a million things I needed to do before they arrived. Time had flown quickly while I'd been sitting around with Arnold. A glance at the calendar jarred me into the realization that if I didn't quit spending every spare minute with him, my visitors would find my place a shameful mess.

Why, in just a few days, my daughter and grandson would arrive! We hadn't seen each other in years, and so much had happened in that time. Suddenly, I had nervous flutters of excitement. My feelings seemed to communicate to the four animals, for they were all unusually frisky. While the cats played chase, Arnold wisely avoided the game and stayed near me, busily prancing all over my armchair and my person, pecking and prying and probing with his beak. "You know, you're going to have to stay in your cage now while I get my work done, Arnold," I told him. "You'll be free to go wherever you want soon enough, but for now I'm going to have to confine you. It's for your own good, you understand." He looked attentive as I talked and seemed to accept what I said.

Trouble began the next morning, however, when I put him into the cage immediately after his breakfast feeding. He was accustomed, by then, to a long playtime in the morning, and darn if he was going to give that up without a fuss! He ran frantically about the floor of his cage, fluttering and flapping his wings in great agitation, hopping high into the air over and over again, slamming his body against the sides of the enclosure, banging the screening with his beak. Fortunately, he hadn't found his voice yet, or certainly he would have been screaming his lungs out, too. I watched in amazement. I'd never seen a bird throw a temper tantrum before. Surely he was going to hurt himself! He kept it up and kept it up, punishing his body meanly, his new feathers rapidly becoming as tattered as my nerves, until I could endure it no longer.

I gritted my teeth, steeled my resolve, and walked away from the cage, intending to do some work outdoors. The cats, who had run from three separate directions to investigate the commotion, stared after me. Their expressions clearly told me how surprised they were at my unusual cruelty. Realizing he had allies, Arnold increased the intensity of his protest demonstration.

"It's a perfectly good, comfortable cage," I said defensively. "It's much larger than most birdcages. What does he expect for guest accommodations? There is absolutely no reason for Arnold to act that way!"

It was really exasperating. He made me feel like an ogre. And yet, he demanded so much of me that it seemed I didn't have time for anything else anymore. Frequently regretting the fateful moment I'd decided to tend the daisies, I had been fighting off murderous thoughts of sending him back to nature before he was ready to fend for himself.

I was so proud of the fact that he'd survived at all, however, that I was really looking forward to showing him off to Hanna and Travis. In fact, the little bird figured very heavily in my plans for the next few weeks; helping to prepare Arnold for survival in nature would be an interesting summer project for my grandson. Of course, if I wanted to show him off to my visitors, I had to prevent him from battering himself to pieces against the sides of the cage, as he seemed so intent upon doing at the moment.

Well, I sighed, all I really had to do outside was mow the lawn. And that would just have to wait. Arnold was a living, breathing, warm-blooded, feeling animal, infinitely more important than a chore I hated anyway.

Relenting, I opened the top of the cage, leaned down so he could hop onto my hand, and placed him on the kitchen countertop. He glared at me in stern reprimand before marching off to rip my paper towels to shreds within their holder, an annoying prank at which he'd become quite adept.

"Your manners are terrible, Arnold," I observed. "You'd better clean up your act for my company, you hear, or I'll be forced to put you out on your ear." As usual, he ignored my scolding. He had me wrapped right around his little talon, and he knew it.

iv I spotted the headlights of Hanna's Triumph just as I heard the toot-tooting of her car horn. The car whizzed past the driveway without slowing. I was mystified. Surely my daughter had seen the driveway; after all, the house and grounds were illuminated as brightly as the Washington Monument by double flood-lights attached to the eaves at all four corners.

"Hanna!" I yelled out the bedroom window through which I'd been nervously watching for her arrival. "Hanna, you're here. This is the place! Hanna!" The car slowed at the corner, then whipped around it to roar down the intersecting road past the front of the house.

I had turned on the floodlights so she would be delighted, astonished, impressed by the sight of the towering building surrounded by rolling lawn and stately old trees. I thought it all very beautiful and was so proud of the accomplishment it represented that I expected my daughter to burst at the seams with similar pride in her mother.

The last time she'd visited me I had just arrived in Texas myself. I was living in a rented apartment, and had planned to stay no longer than a couple of months while looking over possible real estate investments. Living there permanently had been the furthest thought from my mind.

I had come from California, where I'd just finished dissolving a business partnership. As a result of that, I had a bit of money to invest. I realized the years were creeping up on me and was looking for a way to parlay my modest nest egg into a comfortable retirement fund.

Despite a continuing friendship, my husband and I had terminated our marriage after more than twenty years of growing in different directions. I had been headed for our family home on Cape Cod, but it was a time of many crossroads in my life, and I had no strong sense of direction.

As it happened, I drove from California to Texas during the early days of the "oil crisis." Despite all the talk in the news about the shortage of oil in the world, there seemed to be oil wells everywhere I looked. A dream took root and grew as I waited in gasoline lines along the way—the dream of black gold.

I'd decided to use my nest egg to buy some reasonably priced Texas acreage, which I envisioned as sitting atop an undiscovered pool of oil. If I picked land in the right place, I had faith it would be only a matter of time before someone came knocking on my door and asked for permission to erect an oil rig in the back yard; they'd find oil the minute the drill bit broke dirt, of course.

In the following year, however, my simple plan had mushroomed incredibly. I'd entered into another partnership with three dear friends. Though I'd eyed several large tracts of undeveloped land strictly with my original concept in mind, I wound up with a smaller piece of suburban commercial property. While I was waiting for the oil well to come in, the partnership would develop the surface of the land. Step by step, we would erect a small shopping center and apartment complex. An ice cream and sandwich seemed like a realistic starting point. Above the shop we could have our first apartment. High on hope, but short on capital, we planned to build it ourselves. On the day the slab foundation was poured, we inscribed into the wet cement the words "We Dare to Dream." It seemed so appropriate then.

We labored together through summer's sultry heat and vicious insect attacks, through winter's bone-numbing cold and drizzling rain. Our lives became a blur of endless seven-day work weeks. Exhausted, we fell into countless petty disputes that destroyed the spirit of friendly cooperation. The project began to eat us alive. Like a marriage worn down by hardship and weakened by faltering commitment, the partnership fell apart. Two of the friends decided to bow out.

When that happened, the building towered thirty feet high, but it wasn't nearly completed. The wood siding for it was stacked neatly on the concrete floor. Framing timbers stood bare within the emptiness of the skeletal structure. I viewed it as a grotesque, mocking monument to our delusion.

I had pledged everything I had to the venture. So had one of the other partners. The mistake could not be undone. Possessed by stubborn pride, the two of us shrugged and proceeded like automatons, finishing enough of the building to open the business. The shop went over well, but every fledgling business demands a large chunk of soul. We had burned ourselves out on the building and had no soul left to give. One Monday morning after a particularly exhausting weekend, my partner and I had a long talk. It took only the first five minutes of that talk to reach the decision that we were going out of business. Neither of us ever regretted that decision.

Now I resided above the defunct sandwich shop in the building's second-floor apartment. It remained but an empty shell for a long while after I moved in. Indescribably weary, I lived there without much caring about my surroundings. Occasionally, sparks of life prompted me to chip away at the mountain of unfinished work, but the flame did not last. I isolated myself from people most of the time.

When I found the baby bird among the daisies, I was still only making feeble attempts to return to normal. With the coming of Arnold, however, I began to climb up out of my despair. Maybe it was time's natural healing that did it, but he deserved a lot of the credit. Much more presumptuous than the cats, he demanded that I give of myself far beyond the simple service of feeding him. I needed something like that to draw me out of my self-absorption. Despite his total dependence on me, he was consistently cocky. The challenge he represented, his attitude, his personality and mannerisms—everything about him touched feelings inside of me that had been long dormant. I was so proud that I'd been able to keep him alive. My sense of humor began to return, and my spirit. I regained proper perspective of the important things in life. Looking at the building now, I saw it as a monument to prodigious accomplishment.

When I learned my daughter and grandson were coming from Florida for a visit, I decided I had to make my living quarters look more like a home than an indoor campground. I goaded myself back to work. While the cats ran away and hid, Arnold clung to me during most of the noisy sawing and hammering. Since he continued to throw temper tantrums when I put him inside the cage, keeping him with me was the only way I could get anything done at all without feeling cruelly neglectful. Stretching himself mightily from his vantage point on my shoulder or head so he could get a better look at what was going on, he enjoyed the abnormal activity. Though it was difficult to hammer or saw because he kept hopping onto my hands, I managed. His insistence on sticking so close to me was heart-warming, and his companionship was welcome.

I didn't accomplish everything I'd set out to do before the arrival of my visitors, but I was satisfied that the place was presentable. Anxiously surveying everything as I waited for them to arrive that evening, I felt quite smug. Surely my daughter would understand what an accomplishment the building was. My still-tender ego needed the balm of her approval.

And here she was, finally. She'd taken the detour around the corner so she could get a really good look at the entire layout; and she was laughing in pleased astonishment. That laugh told me more eloquently than all the words in the world that she liked what she saw.

"I don't believe it, Mumma. I just don't believe it! You told me it was a sandwich shop. I expected a little shack. This is enormous. It's fantastic! Where's the oil well?"

"I'm still waiting for that," I said with a laugh. "All things in their own time. Isn't this enough to satisfy you?"

"Enough? For once in my life I'm speechless. Give me a chance to absorb it all before I pile on the praise."

"You go ahead and absorb all you want. Where's my handsome grandson?"

Six-year-old Travis was still in the back seat, rubbing the sleep from his blue eyes. His hair was bleached white by the Florida sun, his nose freckled and peeling. His friend Kyle was just beginning to stir. The boys looked enough alike to be brothers, although Kyle's eyes were gray and his coloring golden bronze, darker than Travie's. Hanna and Kyle's mother, Joanne, had driven the boys to Texas, where they would be staying with me for the summer.

"Do you understand now how hard it is having a mother like Margarete?" Hanna said. "I swear, Josie, trying to keep pace with my mother is my burden in life."

The black cloud of depression that had almost suffocated me departed for good. I had needed the flattery. Tears gathered in my eyes as I hugged my daughter. "Let's get the boys and go inside before the mosquitoes drain us all dry. I have something very, very special to show all of you."

The boys were so sleepy we had to half-carry them up the stairs. The sight of Arnold in his cage brought them wide awake, however. Travie had always held a special love for animals, and it appeared his best friend shared the same interest. Each of them gathered a black cat into his arms. Mitzi trotted up for a perfunctory greeting, then went her own way. The boys sat beside the cage in its corner niche and peered through the bars with an intensity matched by Arnold's as he craned his neck to look curiously up his beak at them. I lifted him out of the cage onto the floor so they could be more intimate.

"Does he talk?" Travie asked.

"No, he's only a wild bird."

"Does he sing?" Kyle wanted to know.

"No, he doesn't sing, either. As a matter of fact, he hasn't made a sound since the day I found him." I told them Arnold's story with great elaboration.

"I'm so glad you boys are here. I need someone to catch bugs and dig up worms for him to eat. That's something I can't do for him. Will you do that for me while you're here?"

"Yeah! You bet! That'll be fun."

"Me and Kyle are the best bug catchers in the whole state of Florida!"

"Kyle and I," his mother corrected automatically, but was ignored.

"What does Arnie like best: beetles or spiders or crickets?"

"Arnold likes steak best, and that's not natural. We have to teach him to like bugs. So far, I've had to teach him everything he knows about being a bird, and he has to learn a great deal more."

"He must be pretty smart if he likes steak better than bugs," Kyle said. "Can we teach him to do tricks, Margarete?"

"Arnie already knows how to do one trick," Travie said, pointing downward. Arnold was sitting on Travis's bare foot, inserting his beak between my grandson's toes and prying them apart with his mandibles. "He knows how to tickle people!" Travie laughed happily, being very careful not to move the foot on which Arnold perched.

"Okay, you two, it's bedtime," Hanna commanded. "You can play with the bird and the cats tomorrow."

"Aw, do we have to?" Travie protested. "We are on vacation, you know."

"Yes, you have to. You're both exhausted from the drive. To bed, to bed. Where to, Mumma?"

"My room," I pointed. "There's a mattress on the floor for Kyle, and my bed's big enough to share with Travie. Let me tuck them in." I scooped up Arnold and put him back into the cage. His usual protest began immediately.

"Let him stay out, Mumma. I'll make sure the cats don't get him."

"You don't have to worry about the cats. Strangely enough, they've all become friends. He will be happier if he can stay with us until we've all settled down, though." I lifted Arnold out and placed him on the back of my chair. He smirked his triumph, then hopped his way over to the couch. Waddling over to a place behind Joanne's head, he grabbed a few strands of her long hair with his beak, stepped back and pulled, looking at though he were engaged in a game of tug of war. Startled, she turned quickly to look at him, freeing her hair from his grip. Not to be bested, Arnold hopped onto the top of her head and began parting her hair with his beak. Joanne looked toward the top of her head and giggled. "You're quite a character, bird." I reached to take him off her head. "He's okay, Margarete," she said. "Leave him there."

"Er, he's not potty trained, you know," I cautioned.

"Oh. Oh well, my hair needs washing anyway."

"Well, he's not that messy. A Kleenex cleans it all up nicely. If you change your mind, get Hanna to take him off your head."

Walking into the bedroom, I found that the boys were already asleep. I arranged their covers and tiptoed back into the living room in time to catch Arnold stealing a cigarette from my open package. Gripping the filter in his beak, he strutted around with the cigarette jutting in front of him, looking for all the world as though he were waiting for a light so he could smoke it.

"I see your bird shares your vices, Mumma," Hanna said dryly. "It's bad enough that you're ruining your own health. Did you have to corrupt an innocent little bird, too?"

"Corrupt him? That bird's part of the conspiracy to reform smokers. He's trying to make me quit by stealing them all. Arnold! Drop it, Arnold. Give it here. Arnold!" Knowing what he would do next, I lunged toward him, trying to grab the cigarette.

More nimble than I, he ran beyond my reach, clutching his prize possessively. Sensing an ally, he trotted across Hanna's lap, not stopping until he was safely on the couch between her and Joanne. Keeping one eye on me, he swung his beak back over his shoulder, holding the cigarette as if he were a baseball player readying his bat for the pitch. Then he swung it with all his might, as if taking a wicked cut at a fast ball. Connecting solidly with the back of the couch, the cigarette snapped in half. Not satisfied with semidestruction, Arnold shook his head vigorously from side to side and up and down. He slammed and banged and bashed the cigarette, ripping the paper again and again, shredding the compacted tobacco, demolishing the offensive object. He dropped the filter then and probed with his beak at the tattered remnants on the couch. He'd done the job thoroughly. The rubble was unrecognizable. He stared up at me defiantly, then glanced from side to side at Hanna and Joanne.

"He's smiling," Joanne said. "He really looks like he's smiling!"

"Of course he's smiling," said Hanna. "Score one for the bird. Maybe he's a secret agent for the American Cancer Society."

I sighed. "Maybe he is. He does that to me all the time."

"I'm beginning to like this bird," my daughter said.

After one victorious look in my direction, Arnold spread his wings and parachuted to the floor. Strolling nonchalantly, he looked around for something else to do. The cats watched him with only moderate interest.

"Shall we have a glass of wine?" I asked my guests.

"I thought you'd never ask!" said Hanna. "After this trip, I need all the relaxation I can get. Bring on the vino!"

The three of us settled down for conversation. I lifted Arnold back onto my chair, just to be on the safe side in case one of the cats, Bundy in particular, decided to be rambunctious. Our glasses of wine sat on tables within easy reach as we talked. There was so much to catch up on—all those things that never seem to get said over the telephone.

Engrossed with one another, we didn't pay much attention to the quiet little bird who walked and hopped from one glass to the other, dipping his beak in for a little sip here, a little sip there, several sips from that one. Tra-la-la! Tra-la-la! Sip. Sip. Sip. He felt our excitement, I suppose. Celebrating with us, Arnold was having his own good time. He waddled about for just one more round. Sip. Sip. Sip-sip-sip.

"What's wrong with the bird, Margarete?" Joanne's voice was shrill with alarm.

Arnold was in the middle of the floor, lying on his side. One wing was outstretched, looking for all the world as if it were broken. He spun in slow circles. His beak opened and closed with tiny gasps. His eyes were glazed. Distress emanated from every feather.

"He drank some of my wine," Joanne said. "I didn't think to stop him. Do you suppose it hurt him?"

"And he drank some of yours, Mumma. And some of mine. I think your bird's drunk."

The little lush sprawled on the rug, too inebriated to stand, incapable of so much as a stagger. If not for the support of the one wing, he would have been flat on his back. He blinked rapidly, trying to focus his eyes. A string of spittle formed between his parted mandibles. Managing to stop his head from swaying, he fixed me with his blinking gaze, his eyes pleading for help.

Hanna and Joanne started laughing. "It's not funny," I said. "He could die of alcohol poisoning."

Arnold hiccupped, forced himself to his feet, splayed both wings for balance, and staggered toward me. Collapsing at my feet, he looked up at me, hiccupping. When I reached to pick him up, he wrapped his wings around my hand like a drowning victim grasping a life preserver. Cooing soothingly, I cradled him to me. He nestled close against my body. I could feel his pounding hearbeat slow to normal. He'd be all right—as soon as the hiccups stopped and he sobered up.

"Congratulations, Mumma," Hanna said. "You've found yourself a really cute pet."

"He's not a pet," I corrected. "He's just a wild bird. A wild bird could never become tame enough to be a pet."

The wild bird hiccupped one last time and snuggled into a sound sleep.

$\mathcal{V}$ "Arnold."

I froze in my tracks. Where had that sound come from? I was the only person in the house, but I could swear someone had said the bird's name. I'm still dreaming, I thought, and reached for my toothbrush.

"Arnold!"

There it was again—the same word, said in a slightly different tone. It sounded a lot like me when I was scolding him.

"Arnold!"

I pinched myself. It hurt, and I was awake. I couldn't

fall back on a dream to explain away what my senses would not accept. No doubt about it, Arnold was saying "Arnold." He was saying his name as clearly as I would say the word, in the varying tones of voice I'd used. Strangely, it was the first sound he had ever uttered. Never so much as a "peep" or a "squeak" or a note of song had crossed his beak previously. The implications were staggering.

"Coffee. I need coffee," I mumbled. I stepped out of the bathroom and skirted around the aviary that had come to dominate the living area. Staring at Arnold in disbelief, I held my breath, waiting for him to repeat the sound.

As was his habit, Arnold hopped down from his nighttime perch until he was at bird's-eye level with my hands and the automatic-drip coffee machine. Bundy hopped onto the countertop at my other side, as was his own morning habit. I seemed destined to be overseen every morning by these two chauvinistic males who had little faith I could make coffee without their supervision.

"Arnold?" He tilted his head to one side, inquiring if I had understood. He pecked at his screening to make certain of my undivided attention. "Arnold," he repeated smugly.

"Did you hear that, Bundy?" I asked. "We have a talking wild bird on our hands. Can you beat that?"

Bundy's response was to jump off the counter. All he cared about at the moment was breakfast. Arnold was an old fixture within the house now and didn't interest him anymore.

"Arnold," the bird said again.

Oh, how I wished for a witness—someone, anyone, to corroborate what I was hearing. Hanna, Joanne, and the boys were off exploring the Lone Star State, however, and wouldn't be back for a week.

"Arnold. Arnold? Arnold!" Reveling in the discovery of his voice, he was experimenting with different sounds of the same word. I watched in fascination as the feathers bobbed at his throat, as his beak opened and closed. Cocking his head to one side and then the other in a thinking pose, he appeared to be trying to get the feel of the word before saying it again. "Arnold. Arnold!" He said it once with his beak tightly shut, the next time with his mandibles parted, though all of the sound was being created within his throat.

"Absolutely amazing! Ouch!" Bundy had nipped me on the back of the leg, his favorite ploy for attention. He stared up at me with exasperation in his eyes. Mitzi and Sammie were posted at their dishes, their expressions clearly accusing me of ignoring them for too long. After all, it was breakfast time. Dutifully, I dished out their portions, then reached for the coffee pot. Only then did I realize I'd been so distracted I hadn't even poured the water into the machine yet. I quickly corrected the oversight.

"Arnold, you've certainly turned this day topsy-turvey," I commented as the water began to hiss and gurgle.

"Arnold!" he said proudly.

Eager to hear more, I stood next to his cage and reflected upon the weeks since he had joined the household. The day I'd found him among the daisies seemed an incredibly long time ago now, though he was barely two months old. I had tried very hard during that time to prepare him for a return to the wild.

As soon as his body was covered with feathers, I had taken him outside for flying lessons. He had made a few attempts on his own before, but the inside of a house was no place for a bird to learn how to use his wings. Within such confined spaces, there were entirely too many obstacles to navigate, and Arnold had managed to encounter them all with his head. After knocking himself silly a few times, he'd reverted to using his wings as mere parachutes. If he was ever to learn to be a respectable bird, I would have to do what I could to teach him the art of his ancestors.

Easier said than done, of course. I didn't know very much about flying myself. I discarded the notion of flapping my arms as an example and threw him high into the air with the shouted instruction "Fly or dive, kid!" After one feeble flutter, he dived. I winced at his ineptness as he plunged beak-first with tightly furled wings, and I cringed when he hit the ground. His body proved far more resilient than it looked. Barely taking the time to shake off the jarring effects of the crash-landing, he rolled to his feet and broke into a run. Obviously terrified of the big, strange new world, he came waddling through the grass to huddle trembling at my feet. I steeled myself, picked him up, and tossed him again—and again—and again—until, finally, he flapped his wings in true flight, struggled upward, and landed awkwardly on a lower branch of my mulberry tree.

My smile of triumph quickly became a grimace. On the branch, Arnold tottered, teetered, lurched forward! "Curl your toes, er, talons, fool! Grab hold of that branch, or you'll fall. Curl your dumb toes!" Shouting useless instructions, I watched helplessly as he fell. It had never occurred to me he might need lessons in perching as well as flying. Shaking, stunned, the wind knocked out of him, he hugged the ground as though determined never to leave it again.

"I guess the glories of flight aren't all they're cracked up to be, Arnold," I said as I picked him up. Soothing him with my voice, I brought him inside the house. My own resolve was shaken as much as his confidence. He wasn't ready for his freedom yet, and neither was I.

We went back to square one: lessons in the art of perching. Since human toes can't possibly curl like those of a bird, any more than human arms can achieve the lift necessary for flight, teaching by example was

39

out of the question. I tried showing him with my fingers, curling them around a broom handle, but he didn't make the connection. To him, my fingers represented a beak, the means of delivering food to him. It was the obvious connection for him to make, of course, and no reflection on his intellect.

Arnold wasn't dumb, just confused. Though they are primarily designed for perching, his feet by then had become accustomed to flat surfaces. He'd used them to pace the floor of his cage, to walk along on the rug, to slide around the slippery surface of the breakfast bar, to cling to the arm of my chair. His feet had never contacted anything suitable for perching. He didn't know how to curl his talons, to grip with them. Perhaps it would have been instinctive under normal circumstances, but his instincts had been smothered by his abnormal living conditions. Before he could learn the new, he must be made to unlearn the old. He must not be allowed to walk those flat surfaces any more than absolutely necessary, and he must be taught to use his talons correctly.

Arnold spent a great deal of time on his back for the next few days. Lying in my hand, hating every moment of the experience, he squirmed in protest as I smacked objects against the bottoms of his feet. First, I used small branches, but they were awkward and often broke. Next, I tried a pencil, but it was too thin for him to grip properly. Finally, a nice, fat, wooden dowel proved just right.

Smack! Smack! Smack! I slapped the bottoms of his feet over and over again, trying to make him curl his talons, to grab the object so it wouldn't keep smacking. It must have stung. I felt like a school teacher of old, cracking knuckles with a ruler to correct improper behavior. It was horrible for both of us, but it worked.

He finally decided that the only way to keep that hated object from descending in punishment again was to prevent it from ascending, to seize it and hold it still. He reached out with his toes, grabbed, and held on for dear life.

With one hand holding the dowel, I righted Arnold's body and released him, leaving him with only the dowel for support. Poised precariously, he perched! Only for a brief moment, however. His talons worked properly, grasping the dowel as they should, but his equilibrium failed. He toppled over to hang upside down, clinging to the dowel, staring at me through spindly legs with the most bewildered expression I've ever seen on any creature.

The cats, ever a rapt audience, blinked in commiseration with Arnold. They, too, were mystified by my conduct. Rather than risk similar treatment, they watched from a safe distance, ready to run if I made a move toward them.

"I don't like this any more than you do," I said lamely, "but he has to learn somehow."

Arnold lost his grip with one foot and dangled lopsidedly by the other. He uttered not one sound of indignation. His silent, bewildered stare was a thousand times more jarring than a scolding. Unless I wanted to enslave myself to him forever the way I had been doing, though, we both had to extend our patience and persistence a bit more. The lesson continued.

The next time, just as he began to fall, I jerked the dowel sharply downward. The abrupt movement caused him to flutter his wings in alarm, which helped him to maintain an upright position. He wobbled a bit, but each time he began to fall I jerked the dowel downward. He fluttered his wings each time and remained perched.

It was a cinch after that. He progressed much like a human infant first learning to walk. He was awkward and took a few spills, but then gamely tried again and again. Spurred on by initial success, Arnold persisted and made himself work at it until he got it right.

Soon he was perching everywhere: on my finger,

on the backs of chairs, on curtain rods and towel racks and the edges of lampshades. Once he could perch, flying was no problem. At last he could go anywhere he wanted to go, when he wanted to do so. Arnold had found his version of freedom, and he loved every minute of it.

It became impossible to persuade him to stay in the rat cage. He could fly! He could perch! He'd discovered the joys of birdhood! He would be confined no longer. When I attempted to capture him to return him to the cage, he gladly used the excuse to lure me into a game of chase. He almost always won the game, too. He came to me for feedings, for conversation, for protection when Bundy wanted to play, and for closeness. But he read my mind each time I thought of putting him back into that enclosure he had grown to hate.

I took him outside again, thinking it might be time to free him, but instead of flying away, he ran from my shoulder to the back of my neck. There, he clung to the collar of my blouse and hid under my hair. When I reached for him, he squirmed closer, flattening himself into the crevice between my collar and neck. "Well, Arnold," I said, "maybe it's best if you do stick with me until I can teach you to eat the kinds of food you'll have to exist on in nature. It really wouldn't be fair to send you away to starve to death." I wasn't convinced it was time for him to leave my nest anyway—not yet. I knew I had to do something, though.

It was Hanna's bright idea that restored my freedom and made Arnold happier than he'd ever been. "Mumma, this is nonsense!" she had said the second time I told them to "go along without me" for an outing. "I want to spend time with you, but not all of it cooped up inside the house. You have to do something about that bird. He's ruining your life!"

"What can I do?" I asked miserably. I'd had the same thoughts over and over again and come up with no solution. "It breaks my heart to see him so miserable

42

in that cage, but I can't turn him loose yet. On the other hand, I'm a nervous wreck when I leave the house because I'm afraid something will happen to him while I'm gone. He is a problem, but I just don't know what to do about it."

Hanna's eyes twinkled. Though amused at my impracticality, she understood very well how I felt about animals. "The problem seems to be that particular cage. Who can blame him? It's so small for a bird like him. He needs more space, and something to perch on. Then he'll be happy. Other people keep aquariums in their homes. Why can't you have an aviary? Space for him, freedom for you. Think about it. You're clever enough to come up with a design."

She and the group went off to see a tractor pull, in which behemoth pieces of farm equipment compete at various tasks in an enormous mud bowl, and I was left pondering the Arnold situation for the umpteenth time. An aviary? Of course! Why not? I'd learned that all building projects are little more than basic jigsaw puzzles. An aviary would be simple.

The leftover lumber pile provided most of my building materials, so I only had to make a few minor purchases at the hardware store. When finished, the cage was two feet deep by two feet wide and almost eight feet tall. Filled with a ladder of perches, it had a Plexiglas back wall with screened sides and front door. Once upright, it became a unique room divider. Standing back, I surveyed it smugly. As a piece of furniture, it met with my approval, but my approval wasn't what counted. Arnold had to like it as much as I did.

Having supervised the entire operation, with a great deal of help from the cats, perhaps he would take something of a proprietary attitude toward it. Crossing my fingers, I reached for him so I could put him inside for a trial run. As usual, he read my mind and fled. This time, however, he flew right into his new house and hopped up the ladder of perches to the topmost one.

Leaping into midair, he turned around to face me, fluttering his wings in pleasure. He stared at me with what I knew must be a grin of appreciation and settled down. Then, tucking his head right into his wing, he promptly went to sleep.

He loved it! From that very first moment, Arnold loved the aviary and considered it to be his. He seemed to know it was custom-built just for him. I didn't have to chase him anymore. Now, he came out by invitation for feedings, companionship, and entertainment, but genuinely preferred his private quarters. His contentment and safety were assured, and my freedom restored! We both enjoyed the benefits of the aviary so much I couldn't believe I hadn't thought to build it sooner.

"Oh! What now?" I was brought rudely out of my reverie by Bundy, nipping at the back of my leg again. I would have to save my reminiscing for another time. Right now, he wanted a second helping of breakfast. I noticed that my coffee had finished dripping and realized I hadn't even brushed my teeth yet. I'd better get busy.

"Arnold," said Arnold.

I smiled at him, remembering how unpromising he'd looked sitting among the daisies that day. It still amazed me that he'd survived. I had planned to set him free all along. I'd sheltered and nourished him with that goal in mind. Taught him to fly. Taught him to perch. Taught him to love, I think. And now, it seemed, taught him to talk. I imagined him flying from branch to branch, seeking the companionship of his own kind, calling after them, "Arnold, Arnold, Arnold." He'd be a freak, a certain misfit now. Some wild bird he'd turned out to be. Wild birds simply did not talk.

"Arnold, Arnold, Arnold, Arnold, Arnold, Arnold," he sang happily.

"Mitzi, you're the wise one," I said. "You heard

him, didn't you? What am I to do with him now?"

She stopped washing her face and stared at me. Her whiskers twitched, and her expression registered exasperation at my ignorance of the obvious. How could there be a question in my mind? There was none in hers. What to do about Arnold, after I'd taken in the two stray cats she so disliked? Mitzi liked Arnold! She hated the other two orphans I'd foisted upon her. As far as she was concerned, I could turn them out any day. They were mere commoners. Arnold, on the other hand, had quality. He was her equal, a real class act. Mitzi's face expressed her opinion clearly. *What to do about Arnold? What a stupid question! Only a human would think to ask it. Humans can be such dumb animals sometimes!*

Sammie and Bundy nodded. I swear they must communicate by telepathy, and they were certainly in agreement on this matter. They all liked Arnold. They're in league against me, I decided. All four of them are presenting a united family front to the evil stepmother. I felt myself caving in.

Arnold had woven himself into my little family until he'd become part of the fabric of our daily lives. I should have realized that when the cats began to ignore him; they only ignored what they accepted as belonging among us. Trusting cats and humans as he did, he'd never survive in the wild. Besides, I had fallen in love with him. Despite all my resolve.

I shrugged with resignation. "I guess I've always known, way down deep, what I was going to wind up doing about you, Arnie." I could call him Arnie now, the softer name of endearment instead of the formal Arnold to which I had held so firmly in the belief that it would help me to maintain emotional detachment. I could allow myself the softening now. My mind was made up.

"You win," I said, addressing all of the animals. "I give up. You all win. He stays with us."

"Arnold," he said softly, approvingly, understandingly.

Yes, Arnie would stay with us.

He was family.

vi "Arnie, say Travie."
"Arnie, say Kyle."

The two boys were sprawled on the floor next to the aviary, their heads side by side, their noses pressed against the screening. Obligingly, Arnie sat on the perch that was level with their faces. Hugging the side of the cage nearest to them, he watched them intently. Bundy sat at Travie's knee as my grandson absently stroked him with one hand.

"Arnie, say Travie."
"Arnie, say Kyle."

They were determined to teach him. Though pleased to hear Arnie had begun speaking his name while they were on the trip, the boys had not been surprised. They had assumed all along that he would get around to talking someday. If he could say one word, they reasoned, he could learn others.

Oh well, it was a game we could enjoy together; but who ever heard of a wild bird really learning to talk? Surely, if that were possible, it would be common knowledge, and Arnie's kind would be in pet stores throughout the country. Secretly, I thought it was a fluke that he'd learned to say his name. I suspected he would forget the word as soon as maturity jogged instinctive birdsong. Meanwhile, it wouldn't hurt to humor the children at their game.

"Boys, you must remember, when you teach any bird to talk, it's important that you repeat over and over again what you want him to say; but *only* what you want him to say. You're going about it the right way, basically, but you're using too many words. If you say 'say' to him, he'll wind up saying 'say' right back to you. Then it'll sound like he's the one trying to teach you to say your own name."

"Huh?"

"Listen to the words you're using. If he repeats any of them, chances are he'll repeat all of them. Do you want him to look at you one day and speak the words, 'Arnie, say Travie' and 'Arnie, say Kyle'? I think you would prefer that he simply say 'Travie' and 'Kyle.' So, keep it simple."

Listening to my own words, I wasn't sure *I* got it. It had been years since I'd had Hanna around to keep my teaching skills honed. I was rusty at the art. But the boys got the point anyway and resumed Arnie's lessons.

"Travie."

"Kyle."

As far as I was concerned, their fascination with

Arnie was saving the summer. I worried chronically that they would be bored.

Their mothers had had to cut short their own vacations and return to Florida a few days after completing the Texas excursion. But I had had little difficulty convincing them to leave their sons with me for the rest of the summer.

While their mothers carefully itemized what they must and must not do, the boys listened solemnly, nodding their heads in agreement. Only I saw the winks and elbow nudges they exchanged afterward. Instinctively, they seemed to know what pushovers grandparents can be when it comes to bending everyday rules.

"I know what you're all thinking," Hanna whispered to me as we hugged at her departure. "I had Grandma and Grandpa, remember? We had our little secrets, too. Just remember that Travis gets cranky if he doesn't get enough sleep."

An hour after their normal bedtime that night, the boys and I were making vacation plans during television commercials. I heard them whispering and giggling for another hour after I'd tucked them into bed, but pretended not to. I was as excited as they about the things we'd do together.

Mother Nature double-crossed us, however. Wishy-washy as ever about the weather, she canceled the bright, sunny days with which summer had begun. Hanna and Joanne had driven off into a rainfall that didn't cease for days. Baked to a rock-hard clay after weeks of drought, the earth was having difficulty absorbing the badly needed water, so now we were coping with a minor flood. In the brief periods between downpours, the sun sucked moisture back into the air, turning the outdoors into one gigantic sauna. The humidity hovered at 100 percent, the temperature at 95 degrees.

Not exactly ideal vacation weather, I fretted. My

concerns were needless, however. Those two young men with their wonderful gifts of imagination could probably have entertained themselves under any circumstances. They seemed perfectly satisfied being cooped up inside the house. "It's fun playing with Arnie and the kitties, Margarete," Travis assured me when I asked if they were bored. "I don't get to see them at all when I'm home, you know."

When it wasn't raining, my guests played outside. To them, wading and tumbling in ankle-deep water was fun. With four acres of lawn and field in which to romp, with trees more than a hundred years old to climb and swing upon, the boys had room to expand their games far beyond the horizons of their customary small city lots. Cuttings from my stand of bamboo became lances and bows, airplane parts and tent poles. Forts and castles were created from scrap lumber, fallen tree branches, and chunks of broken concrete intended for driveway fill. My grandson and his friend were cavemen slaying dinosaurs in the morning, astronauts on the way to Mars in the afternoon. But half an hour of play at a time seemed all the boys could tolerate before, sweating and flushed, they would return to air-conditioned comfort, declaring, "All our energy's gone, Margarete. Can we play inside now?"

Inside play invariably included the cats, but Arnie was the star attraction. His education had become the boys' most important project. The novelty of being teachers themselves added special spice to their experience. The precise nature of each lesson was the subject of much heated debate. Since he would not say their names, they tried other words. Obstinately, he stuck to "Arnold."

Arnie and the cats weren't enough diversion for two boys on summer vacation, however; at least not as far as I was concerned. I wanted to give them a memorable visit, so I took them every place I could imagine.

Crabbing had become a favorite activity, probably

because they could do so much else while waiting for the creatures to find the dangled bait. Between watching sailboats and feeding wheeling sea gulls, they built docks and ships from flotsam in a tidal pool behind the sea wall. Each kept a long-handled net handy, ready to take his turn at snaring a crab when I called out that a line had gone taut.

For diversity I also took them fishing, swimming, and to movies, model-airplane exhibitions, and the junior rodeo. Grandmother was having a wonderful, though exhausting, vacation. The boys, however, invariably prodded me homeward quickly after each activity. "Gee, I'll bet Arnie really does miss us when we're gone. And Bundy, too. And Mip-Mip and Sammie. Are we finished? Can we go home now, Margarete?" I began to feel that they were politely humoring what they perceived as my desire to go places to have fun. When I overheard them whispering one morning that they hoped it would rain so I'd have to cancel our plans for the day, I knew my feelings were correct.

Arnie positively mesmerized them. Whenever I would allow him out of the aviary, he was their constant companion. He perched on their shoulders, often eliciting laughter with a darting beak-probe into an ear, and he sat so frequently on top of their heads that they began to call him "Arnie the hat." Determined to be the center of attention at all times, he and Bundy conspired to disrupt every activity with which the boys became preoccupied. They teased their human friends unmercifully, and the boys made certain I knew about it.

"Margarete, Arnie's stealing the Lego pieces." Giggle, giggle. "He's hiding them under the bed. Maybe he's building his own spaceship." Giggle.

"Bundy, I can't draw if you're sitting in the middle of the paper! Arnie, quit tearing off the corners! Arnold!!" Tee-hee-hee. "Now he's taking my pencil. Margarete! Help!" Tee-hee, tee-hee-hee.

"Arnie's playing with my toes!" Heh-heh-hee-hee-hee.

"Bundy's licking my feet!" Titter, titter.

Invariably, laughter belied the wails with which the boys protested the interference. When I scolded Bundy and tried to put Arnie back into his cage, Travie and Kyle immediately leapt to their defense, begging me to allow them to continue playing. All four of them loved every moment of the companionship, though I kept expecting the boys to run out of patience. Mitzi and Sammie looked in on them occasionally, but seemed to understand that this was an all-male club.

Through it all, the boys worked on Arnie's lessons, taking it for granted that he would learn when he was ready. They never entered or exited a door without a greeting or farewell. "Hi." "See you later, alligator." "Bye-bye." "See you soon, baboon." Giggle.

To my complete amazement, Arnie began cooperating!

He mimicked the shouted, strained "Arnold!" we used on occasions when he misbehaved or became too mischievous. He repeated the "Arnie" we called him during normal conversation and the silly "Arnie-ly" I used as a lovey-dovey expression. Though his tone was that of a bird, his enunciations and inflections were ours.

He began to initiate the greetings and farewells before the boys could get the words out of their mouths. At times, he even seemed to link the words properly to the occasion. He said, "See you, bye," when they gathered toys for outdoor play, and "See you soon," when they went only to the bathroom or bedroom. When he heard their first steps at the bottom of the stairs, he knew they were on their way in from the yard and frantically began yelling, "Hi! Hi! Hi!" For a three-month-old infant, his vocabulary increased rapidly, though his words were sometimes nonsensical. "Two-two" came from the boys' laughing imitation of a television commercial that featured a sing-song recital of a telephone number involving five two's. That gradually evolved into "He's a two-two." "He's a..." came from the one phrase I feel every talking bird should learn: "He's a pretty boy." Which he honestly wasn't. He'd finally become cute, but not pretty by any stretch of the imagination. In heart and personality, however, he was positively beautiful, so I thought "He's a pretty boy" was justified.

As though knowing I lied when I said it, Arnie didn't say "He's a pretty boy" very distinctly, though he tried it out a few times. Then, following his instincts, he turned it into birdsong, instead. He drew out the "pretty" until it became "pretty, pretty, pretty, preeeetttttyyyyyyy, pret-ty-ty-ty-ty." Once he hit his stride, he was shrieking obnoxiously. It was a terrible noise, not designed for peaceful coexistence and certainly not for friendly harmony.

"Pretty, pretty, preeettttyyy, pret-ty-ty-ty-ty," rapidly became his favorite expression and the bane of our days. It was music to his ears, I suppose, but certainly not to ours. Everyone else in the household covered their ears to block the sound when he began hitting "pretty" in repetitious song. The cats ran under the beds, into closets, anywhere to escape from that piercing sound. It was impossible to think through it or to hold a conversation. Shouts of "Arnold" only made him sing with renewed vigor, however, and he'd continue for hours on end.

Trying to ignore "pret-ty-ty-ty," I remembered an advertisement I had once read in a San Diego newspaper: "Free to good home, small parrot. Must give away to patient person. He barks like my dog. Constantly." I had laughed when I'd read it and felt sorry for the unappreciated bird. Now I understood. If Arnold couldn't be stopped, he'd soon be shrieking "pretty-ty-ty-ty" from the treetops.

"We must break him of that bad habit," I told the

boys, when the nerve-wracking noise had become Arnie's only form of speech.

With their hands over their ears almost constantly, it was impossible for the boys to play or hear television. They were hasty to agree with me. "Please do, Margarete! How? Can we help?"

"I don't know. He probably thinks we're enjoying the serenade."

"We could throw things at him every time he starts, Margarete," Travie suggested. "It would scare him without hurting."

My grandson is a genius.

We readied ourselves with private stockpiles of ammunition—rolled socks, soft slippers, fishing bobs, stuffed animals—and lay in wait for the next onslaught of sound. Arnie watched with great interest as we prepared for war.

Once we'd settled, his serenade was resumed.

Wham! Thunk! Ka-thud! Three objects struck his aviary with varying degrees of accuracy. The bombardment had startling effects on its inhabitant. Arnold—he was being entirely too obnoxious for me to think of him as Arnie at the moment—jumped into midair, shrieking and squawking in his most scolding tones. He fluttered his wings with such vigor that he careened into the ceiling of his house. Dazed, he settled onto the top perch and, with a mingling of question and accusation, stared from one to the other of us. Quietly.

The boys grinned and slapped palms in congratulations.

Shaking feathers in his equivalent of a shrug, Arnie hopped down three perches, flexed his throat muscles, and began anew.

We hurled our missiles again, and again and again and again and again, until our shoulders were sore with the effort; until we were doing it by reflex at the first utterance of any sound from Arnold; until I caught myself doing it in my sleep at night. We continued for almost a week, until Arnie began catching himself in midnote at the mere raise of a hand. Finally, quiet was restored to the household.

Unfortunately, it was too quiet. Arnie was silent again. It dawned on me that we might have traumatized him into muteness.

"He's a bird. He wants to sing," I concluded. "We must teach him a song more pleasant to our ears, boys."

Predictably, their suggestions included various pop tunes. Though it would be fun to have a bird singing rock-and-roll as I danced my way through household chores, that kind of music was quite beyond my ability to whistle; and neither of the boys yet possessed pucker power.

We settled on "Mary Had a Little Lamb." I threw in what I could remember of Beethoven's Fifth Symphony for a touch of class and a bit of variety. Arnie loved both. He snatched up the airs as though he had composed them himself and added them permanently to his repertoire. His flat notes and omissions were the result of the teacher's failings, not his; unfortunately, he mimicked perfectly. Both of his new songs were certainly more pleasing to us than his original "pretty-ty" composition had been, of course.

Arnie settled back into his charming ways. He usually caught himself after two or three notes of "pretty-ty-ty-ty," and when he forgot, an uplifted hand served as a reminder. We felt it was safe to resume his lessons.

As we sat at the breakfast bar mixing up a batch of chocolate chip cookies one day, the boys began discussing the topic that intrigues observers of talking birds and is a topic of debate among scientists. "Margarete, do you think Arnie knows what the words mean when he talks?" Kyle asked as he emptied an egg into the bowl.

Travie turned off the mixer and looked thoughtful. "Sometimes he does."

I pondered the question a moment myself, then shook my head. "No, I really don't think he does. He calls us all Arnie, you know. I think he just substitutes words for notes of a song."

The boys resumed measuring and mixing, the expressions on their faces indicating deep thought. Travie paused again, faced me, and stated adamantly, "But, he always says 'Hi' when we come in the door!"

"And he always says 'See you, bye,' when we leave the house," Kyle said.

"Or, 'See you soon, baboon,' when we go into another room."

They were right. Although he used the words of greeting and farewell randomly in song during the day, Arnie did use them correctly upon the proper occasions as well. His vocabulary was small, but when he launched into it, he often continued a running monologue for an hour at a time. Such lengthy sessions, of course, required that he use repetitiously every word and phrase and sound he'd learned to utter. Still, he did use certain expressions as properly as a human would.

"You may be right, boys," I said. "Most scientists would disagree with us, but I've believed for a long time that birds who learn to talk can attach meaning to their words if the people teaching them take the time to help them learn what the words mean. I had a small parrot once, a half-moon conure named Bimpy, who definitely seemed to know what many of his words meant. Arnie's just a wild bird, though, so I have no idea how smart he is."

"Could I talk when I was three months old, Margarete?" Travie asked.

"No, I'm afraid not, darling. You were still a very young baby when you were three months old. No one can talk when they're that young."

"Then Arnie must be really, really smart. He's only three months old, and he can talk already!" Travie plopped a spoonful of batter onto the cookie sheet with a flourish. Arnie whistled a few bars from Beethoven's Fifth Symphony.

I tousled my grandson's hair. "You're not so dumb yourself, kid. You're right. Whatever else he is, Arnie's turned out to be one pretty smart bird."

"He's a pretty boy," Arnie said, stopping short of the screeching song.

"Yes, Arnie, you are a pretty boy," I agreed. "And a pretty smart boy, besides."

vii "He's a starling."
I hadn't known. Arnie was still nondescript. His feathers were a brownish-grayish color with no distinguishing markings. His sweet face, cocky personality, and overall charm had endeared him to me, but even I had to admit he was no beauty. I'd been too preoccupied to have more than a mild curiosity about his precise identification, and his plain appearance gave no obvious clues. Never more than a casual observer of wild birds, I only knew that he didn't look like any of the ones that frequented my yard.

Travis and Kyle had stared out the windows for hours on end, watching the other birds, trying to spot one like Arnie—to no avail. Their attempts to link him to a family outdoors were as fruitless as mine.

I'd thought to check the nest of his origin, of course, but had delayed doing so until too late. The only birdly comings and goings in the vicinity of the nest were those of a sparrow family. Though his coloring seemed right, Arnie was already far too large to be a sparrow. His family must have used the nest only until the babies were big enough to fly, then departed.

"I hope he's a cardinal," Travie told me often.

"Or maybe a blue jay," Kyle wished.

It's obvious what feature in nature appeals most to the young. As with cars, clothing, toys, movies, and cereals, they choose according to the package's visual appeal, with no regard for the contents. That's natural, of course. Deeper values require exposure to differences, sophistication, maturity. Personally, I'd hoped he was a Baltimore oriole.

A starling? The young man who delivered the pronouncement had just deposited a new television set to replace the one that had died in the middle of "Battlestar Galactica" the week before. He and his helper walked over to Arnie's aviary to peer through the screen. Arnie scooted to the opposite end of his perch and cowered. Though he wasn't normally so unfriendly, he objected to their hats—a cowboy hat on the one, a baseball cap on the other. Arnie hated hats, no matter who was under them. The two men ignored his consternation and continued to inspect him.

"Yeah, it's a starling, all right," agreed the second, shifting a toothpick from one corner of his mouth to the other.

"Sure is," the first reiterated. "I oughta know. I stuffed one for some guy last week. A young one— just like this one. Musta been for a joke. Don't know what anyone would want with a stuffed starling, but I don't ask questions long as they pay me. Nice sideline, taxidermy. Someday I can quit this job and make all my money at home stuffing birds and fish."

"Nickel apiece."

"Huh?"

"Nickel apiece. That's what the rice farmers pay anyone can bring in a bagful of dead starlings from their fields. Good practice for duck season. They can fly almost fifty miles an hour, you know. Tough little targets. They're only twenty-two game, though. Use a shotgun, and there won't be enough left to 'em to prove they're starlings, you know. Gotta leave enough to tell what they are. Farmers don't pay for no other bird. I don't mind much. A twenty-two's good enough to keep the aim and reflexes sharp, you know. Kinda fun shootin' 'em."

My blood ran cold. I resisted, but barely, the temptation to put my hands over the ears of the young boys in my charge, to protect them from hearing further horror. Their eyes had widened to saucers at the conversation. Shoot and stuff an Arnie? Despite their great interest in guns, military uniforms, and weapons of war, Travie and Kyle might shoot a dinosaur or a space invader, but certainly no real creature.

"He's no ordinary bird. He talks," I said defensively. I began babbling about Arnie's accomplishments.

"No joke? He really talks? Imagine that! Guess he's worth more than a nickel, then." Skeptical, the men looked closer. "Say something, bird." One of them tapped on the screening.

Arnie flew frantically about the cage, rebounding against the sides and ceiling with great agitation. Squatting on the top perch, he glared at them with all the ferocity of an eagle. I suspected he wished he were a fierce bird of prey at that moment, but one way or the other, he was ready to defend himself if necessary. He wouldn't stand alone, either. Samantha jumped onto the countertop and stood near the perch he'd just vacated. Mitzi sauntered over and posted herself at the door of the aviary. Bundy crouched in the corner, hunched in ready-to-spring position, his tail whipping with warning. Travie and Kyle stood with fists clenched at their sides and stern looks on their faces. If I wouldn't protect Arnie, all of them would.

The young men intended no harm, of course. They were merely curious. A talking wild bird would give them an interesting tale to tell when they got back to the shop. They asked questions, wanting details with which to embellish their story. Their skepticism changed to amusement when Arnie said, "See you, bye." Though his words were clear, his suggestion was unheeded. The men lingered, hoping to hear more. Chatting with me, they didn't notice the glares directed their way by the cats, the boys, and the now-silent Arnie. Well behind schedule, they departed reluctantly when it seemed evident Arnie would not perform for them again. As they went out the door, however, he repeated, "See you, bye," and whistled "Mary Had a Little Lamb."

"Wow, lady, that's some bird all right," the hunter said. "You oughta write to 'Those Amazing Animals' or 'That's Incredible' about him, you know. Get him on TV. I bet a lot of people would like to know about him. Bye-bye, bird."

Maybe, I hoped, he would think twice before shooting another starling. Just maybe.

"That's a great idea, Margarete. Arnie is better than any of the amazing animals I've seen," said Travis, after the two men left.

"Yeah, he's a super bird! You should write to them, Margarete," agreed Kyle.

"You two are prejudiced," I laughed. "You're only saying that because you love him."

"Uh-uh. No way! We're not prejudiced. Arnie really is Superbird!"

"*We* know that's true," I replied, "but so far we're

62

the only ones Arnie has let in on his secret identity. To most other people, he's just an ordinary bird. He's not ready to show anyone else how well he talks. He's still a baby, you know. Maybe he'll learn more words and be more willing to talk for other poeople when he gets older. Just between us, I think it's his secret mission in life to let people know all birds are special creatures. That they're too precious to be shot just for the fun of it."

"Yeah! He's only Superbabybird now. He needs a secret identity until he grows up. That'll give him time to learn how to talk really, really well."

"We'll teach him more words, won't we, Travie?" Kyle's voice held the conviction of a missionary.

"Yeah!" They scrambled to the aviary, eager to resume the lesson. "Arnie's a Superbird. Arnie's a Superbird."

"He's a two-two," Arnie responded.

"What's a starling, Margarete?" Travie asked.

"I'm not sure." I didn't want to mention the newspaper articles I'd read about starlings. They'd all dealt grimly with man's attempts to get rid of Arnie's relatives. "We'll have to see what we can find out about them."

We went to the library, then curled up together on the couch with our borrowed collection of bird books, intent on tracing Arnie's roots. His likeness was nicely protrayed in Roger Tory Peterson's esteemed book, *A Field Guide to the Birds East of the Rockies*. "How different the juvenile starlings look from the adults," I commented to the boys. "No wonder we had trouble deciding what kind of bird he is."

"Yeah, he's shaped like them, but his coloring sure makes him look like a completely different kind of bird," Kyle said.

"The grown-up starlings are in your yard all the time, Margarete," said Travie. "They're the black ones with the speckles that are always pecking around on the ground. I've never seen any of the young ones like Arnie, though."

"Me neither," Kyle agreed.

"Maybe they're in school all day, like kids," Travie speculated.

"The book says starlings are gregarious and garrulous." Kyle stumbled over the pronunciations but managed to say the words properly. "What does that mean? Is Arnie like that?"

"I would certainly say he is," I laughed. "Gregarious means he likes to socialize with others, and we know how much he likes being with all of us, including the cats. For a bird, that's really gregarious. As for garrulous, well, that's a word used for someone who talks on and on and on without saying anything interesting. I guess that describes Arnie fairly well."

"I think Arnie's interesting," Travie defended his friend.

"He wouldn't be if he was a person, Trav," said Kyle objectively. "He always says the same things, you know."

"Well, what do you expect of a baby bird? He hasn't learned how to say anything interesting yet. Give him time!"

"Isn't this interesting?" I said. "Arnie's ancestors are from Europe, just like ours. There are one hundred and three different kinds of starlings in the world, but Arnie's species is the only one of them to make it to the United States."

"That makes him something special then, doesn't it, Margarete?" Travie said. "I'll bet kings and knights used to have Arnies, just like they had hawks and peacocks. He's probably a royal bird. Let's see what the rest of the books say."

Unfortunately, most of our references didn't support my grandson's high regard for our friend and his family. I suspected a certain prejudice against Arnie's kin the moment I read their official Latin name—*Stur-*

nus vulgaris. Vulgaris? That looked suspiciously like the root word for vulgar, which Arnie certainly was not. And vulgaris was only the beginning. Every tome of birdlore through which we pored unleashed a stream of defamatory adjectives about the poor, unloved little starling: "trash" bird; "junk" bird; "most quarrelsome and aggressive" bird; a "major pest," regarded as the "bane of songbirds" and a "plague to farmers" throughout the country. Even the venerated National Audubon Society, friend and champion protector of almost every bird in existence, refers to the starling as "a naturalized American citizen of questionable character."

Actually, the story of the American starling began with William Shakespeare. The tale he tells made me suspect that the bard must have met, at one time, a starling as talented as Arnie. In Shakespeare's play *King Henry the Fourth, Part I*, Henry holds a grudge against Edmund Mortimer, the Earl of March, whom he considers to be a traitor. Henry Percy, known as Hotspur, counts Mortimer as a great friend and patriot, however, so he risks the ire of the king by pleading Mortimer's cause. Hotspur makes such a nuisance of himself with constant references to Mortimer that Henry thunders a kingly decree—forbidding Hotspur to so much as say the name Mortimer in his presence again. But Hotspur proposes to his uncle, Sir Thomas Percy, a sly way to continue bedeviling Henry: "I'll have a starling shall be taught to speak nothing but 'Mortimer,' and give it him to keep his anger still in motion."

Just then, Arnie wound up and almost forgot himself. "Pretty, pretty, pret-ty-ty-ty..."

"Hotspur must have met Arnie's great-grandfather to think of that idea!" Travie giggled.

"Can you imagine," said Kyle, "how mad King Henry would have been if an Arnie chased him around the castle singing 'Mortimer, Mortimer, Mor-ti-ti-ti-mer-mer-mer-mer' like Arnie says pretty?"

"If we ever have space invaders, I bet Arnie could

drive them back to their own planet just by flying around and screaming 'pretty, pretty' into their antennas!" Travie said.

"But how did Arnie's relatives get over here, Margarete? Isn't that a long way for them to fly, all the way from Europe?"

"I was coming to that," I answered Kyle, and resumed the story.

It was Hotspur's proposal that led to the branching-off of the starling family tree to America. Eugene Schieffelin, a wealthy New York drug manufacturer who loved both Shakespeare and birds, decided to introduce to the United States all birds mentioned in the bard's plays. On two occasions, in 1890 and 1891, Mr. Schieffelin released eighty pairs of Arnie's ancestors into New York's Central Park, thus guaranteeing himself a page in American bird books forevermore.

Like the Pilgrims, the starlings had a rough time at first, and not all of them survived in their new homeland; but those who did soon began claiming the countryside for themselves. Following the paths of the pioneers, the starlings crossed the mountains, plains, and deserts of North America and became established all the way to the Pacific Coast within sixty years. By that time, they had multiplied greatly and had acquired the dubious distinction common to so many newcomers to the United States—they were a despised minority group. They had taken over the role formerly held by the house sparrow, that of "most unwelcome immigrant to the United States." In their success, the starlings had made enemies.

"Why would anyone hate an Arnie, Margarete?" the boys asked in unison. "He's friendly and fun to be with. He'd never hurt anyone."

I had to agree with them on the basis of my own observations. Although the books I read stated that starlings are deplorably aggressive toward other birds, I had never seen the flock in my yard to do anything worse than ignore the robins, mockingbirds, blue jays, sparrows, quails, and others who fed among them. Of course, if food had been scarce, I realized that the peaceful gathering I saw every day might well have changed into a rabble fighting for survival. Since the starlings always stayed together in groups, it was easy to imagine which bird would prevail; it was easy to imagine how they had managed to survive when they'd been thrust into a new country. Like most Americans of European origin, they must certainly have displaced many of the natives while making themselves at home in the new country. And I doubted if they'd done that by being meek and mild.

The more I researched, the more I came to realize that Arnie's kin deserve a great deal of praise. Starlings are staunch allies in one of humanity's oldest battles. Though these birds are accused of destroying agricultural crops, scientific studies have shown that most of their food consists of harmful insects. In Europe, farmers concede that the starlings' help with pest control abundantly pays for what little fruit and crops they may eat. In fact, Arnie's ancestors are solely credited with having saved the magnificent forests of Bavaria during the Great Spruce Moth Invasion a century ago. I was happy to learn that starlings are among the best bird predators of the greedy and destructive gypsy moth and Japanese beetle, too.

I had to ponder hard to explain to the boys why some books claim that the starling is "disliked by almost everybody" and is "rated a major pest." Resisting the temptation to glorify starlings because of my attachment to Arnie, I tried to present the other side of the coin. "We know that the starlings almost always travel in flocks," I said, "because they work cooperatively to make a good life for the whole group. Unfortunately, that's exactly what creates some problems. Where there's one starling, you see, there are usually too many starlings to suit people. Just imagine how noisy it must be to have a couple of dozen birds sitting together, all chattering away. A lot of people would call that noise pollution and find it very annoying. Besides, where there are birds, there are always bird droppings, you know; and where there are a lot of birds flocked together, that gets pretty messy. It's unhealthy, too, especially in cities and towns."

"They should stay in the country, where there are lots of fields," said Kyle. "Then they wouldn't annoy anyone."

"The farmers wouldn't like that," I explained. "Remember, to the farmer, those fields are his way of earning a living. Since most farmers now use pesticides to control insects, I guess the starling does more harm than good in the fields."

"Then why don't they just stay in the wilderness, where they won't bother anyone?"

"That's silly, Kyle," said Travie. "Even I know the wilderness is shrinking. There's not even room for really wild animals anymore, like wolves and mountain lions and condors. It's a good thing Arnie found Margarete, that's all I can say."

I hugged him. "I'm glad, too, Travie. He's really become something special to us, hasn't he? To me, Arnie's a darling starling."

After I'd tucked them into bed that night, I sat with Arnie perched companionably on my shoulder. He serenaded me quietly as I reflected on the conversation I'd had with the boys earlier that day.

The story of the starlings in America seems a good example of the prevailing attitude we humans have about life on earth. Far too many of us regard the planet as humanity's exclusive possession, to do with as we will. Thank goodness there are people who feel the earth and its creatures are in our sacred trust. Because there are different viewpoints, the matter of starlings has actually been debated in Congress as well as in town meetings across the country: Should they be protected? Should they be destroyed? What should we do about starlings?

We have enacted laws to protect almost every species of bird within our borders. But no law protects the starling. Thus it is legal to kill them for the fun of it; legal for the farmer to pay a nickel apiece as bounty on their dead carcasses; legal for the U.S. Army to spray them with deadly chemicals in order to kill flocks en masse for the crime of getting in the way of maneuvers.

Starlings are criminals, of course. As a species, they are guilty of the one great crime that humans find unforgivable in all but our own species. They survive. Despite everything man does to make that feat almost impossible, despite our manipulations of the environment, which make it so difficult for any living thing to survive, starlings do.

The trouble is, it's not just starlings that humans tend to regard as pests. It's all wildlife. Animals are fine as long as they stay in their own habitats. Yet *we* have a long history of expanding our territories with little thought for aything but our own needs. Quite routinely, we turn wildlife habitats into people habitats. And, of course, man has long had difficulty with the idea of sharing any ecosystem with any other living creature. When animals won't cooperate with our desires, they are regarded as pests, nuisances, to be disposed of summarily. The starling is one of many such animals, for he sometimes interferes with our convenience simply by being.

I know I'm prejudiced because of Arnie, but I think starlings have admirable character traits. They are persistent, tenacious, intelligent, courageous, tough under adversity, loyal to their own, generally tolerant of others, and adaptable to new circumstances. Where the individual may be weak, the species thrives because of a tightly knit cooperative society that ensures virtually equal opportunity for all. And they are capable of feeling great depth of emotion—notably, they're capable of loving. I happen to know that for a fact, because I've come to know one starling very intimately.

I believe I have the perfect way to eliminate the bird's nuisance value. Since we never consider as nuisance those creatures with which we choose to share our lives, my solution would be known as Adopt a Starling. After all, we drag parrots out of faraway jungles and put them into cages to share life with us for one primary reason—parrots can speak to us in the human tongue. So can Arnie. Presumably, so can other starlings. Rather than try to eliminate Arnie's cousins, we could fill the bird-loving households of the nation with starlings that "shall be taught to speak nothing but 'Mortimer.'" Or "Arnie."

viii "Hi! Hi! Hi! Hi!" Holding on to his perch with tightly clenched talons, Arnie flapped his wings in time to his excited words of greeting. With his beak pointed forward and his neck stretched to its limit, he resembled a sandhill crane in flight. As usual, he was telling me the boys were coming long before I heard them.

These days, I really appreciated the warning. Undoubtedly, their feet would be wet and splotched with mud. Although they had strict instructions to rinse their feet in the bucket of water at the foot of the stairs, they were always in a hurry and seldom did the job thoroughly. Quickly I grabbed two old towels from the linen closet and ran to meet them at the door.

Noah's forty days and nights of rain couldn't have been much worse than the deluge that was still pounding southeast Texas late that summer. Schools and other civic buildings were being used as shelters for families flooded out of their homes. Fortunately, I lived on a high piece of ground. The only problem the boys and I had to contend with was boredom. Although we could hear the mighty motors straining round the clock at the nearest pumping station, the efforts to drain off all that excess water seemed futile. That year, I finally understood the necessity for the elaborate system of earthen levees and enormous drainage ditches that cobwebbed the area.

Once the ground had begun to absorb some of the moisture, the clay soil had acquired the consistency of thick stew. Gumbo, the natives called it, bringing me to the unpleasant realization that it must be rather a normal condition to have earned its own name. Walking about my lawn, I sometimes sank to my knees in gumbo. If not for the thick grass, my house would have been an island in the middle of a quagmire. Though I was feeling restlessly housebound, I wasn't dissatisfied enough to venture many strolls in the yard. Children have a great affinity for mud, however, and Travis and Kyle looked for any excuse to squish through the gumbo during respites between rain showers. Suddenly, both seemed cursed with extraordinary clumsiness. How else to explain the number of "accidental" falls they had?

Today, as usual, I met them at the door and toweled them vigorously. The boys bore the treatment without words. An incredible variety of grimaces contorted their faces, however, speaking eloquently of the martyrdom to which they felt subjected. Sympathetic, Arnie whistled a bit of Beethoven, then swung into "Mary

Had a Little Lamb" to cheer them up.

"How did the hunt go today?" I asked.

It was beginning to be a sore subject with them. So far, they had struck out three days in a row. Veteran bug catchers from way back, they had not succeeded in capturing a single specimen. Catching insects to feed to Arnie had been my idea, they insisted. And they had promised me they would do it. "A promise is a promise," Travie said solemnly.

"Sorry, Margarete," they apologized each day, looking woebegone. Failure doesn't sit well on young shoulders. When I asked the ritual question this time, however, their faces brightened.

"The hunt went great today!" Travie said.

"We told you we could do it!" Kyle rejoiced. "See?" With a flourish, he thrust toward my face one of the pickle jars I'd given them for the insects.

Glaring balefully from the glass prison was a hairy, black-and-yellow banded spider. Banana spider, the locals called it, because of the bright color combination. Even with its legs tightly drawn up to its body, it was as large as my hand. From terrifying experience, I knew it was capable of spinning twenty-foot webs— big enough to stretch from one of my pecan trees to another. Having become entangled too often in those tough silken webs while doing yard work, I had developed a loathing for the creatures that spun them. Though banana spiders are reputed to be harmless, they resemble tarantulas too much for my comfort, and no one can convince me that anything so repulsive isn't deadly.

"Are you two crazy?" I croaked. "How do you expect Arnie to eat that thing? It's bigger than he is!"

"No it's not," Kyle protested. "Here, Margarete, look at it closer." He tried to give me the jar. "See how pretty it is."

I stepped back, holding my hands protectively in front of me. "No, I don't want to see it closer. Get it away! Please get it away. That's one of the ugliest things I've ever seen in my life!"

My beloved, respectful grandson giggled. "Don't you like spiders, Margarete? I think they're the neatest bugs of all."

"No, I do not like spiders. I hate spiders."

"Let's put him in the cage and see what Arnie will do," Travie said.

"Don't you dare turn that beast loose in this house! You two march right back outside and put him back where you found him."

"Aw, Margarete."

"Can we at least keep him for a pet?" Travie pleaded.

Vagabond ambled up, stood on his hind legs, braced one front paw against Kyle, and stretched the other toward the jar. Arnie fluttered in his cage. "Hi! Hi! Hi!" he said. "Arnie-ly. Hi! C'mere." Boys and bugs! I wondered why these boys had to have such stereotypical interests. I was glad I'd had a girl and that she'd never had a particular interest in entomology.

"No, you may not keep him for a pet." Seeing their disappointment, I calmed myself and tried to be reasonable. "He'd starve to death if you kept him, and that would be cruel. Spiders feed on insects, you know. After the past few days, do you honestly think you'd be able to provide him with food?"

"He could eat steak, like Arnie," Travie said brightly.

"No way. Some creatures are not meant to be pets. Specifically, spiders are not meant to be pets."

"I saw a man on television with pet tarantulas one time," Kyle said. "They're spiders."

Their arguments were too logical. I was forced to revert to adult dominance. "Out! This household may resemble a zoo at times, but this is where I draw the line. No pet bugs! Out. Out! Out!! Just open the jar and leave it on the ground. He'll crawl out on his own."

"Gee, Trav, I thought you said Margarete liked all

animals," I overheard Kyle say as they walked back down the stairs.

"Aw, you know what sissies girls are," my grandson explained.

"Hi? C'mere. See you, bye?" Arnie didn't understand why they'd left the house again without taking a few minutes to talk to him. "They'll be right back, Arnie," I assured him. He lapsed into disappointed silence. Vagabond stretched out, his head on his paws, resigned to another wait. I stood by with the towels, prepared to go through the cleaning all over again. When they didn't return after several minutes, I decided I'd have to go after them. They were probably playing with the spider, and it would take the voice of authority to make them come in this time. As I went down the steps, Arnie screeched, "See you, bye!" in a tone sounding like, "You, too?"

The boys were standing beside the shallow drainage ditch that bisected the property behind the mulberry tree. Each had a long, bamboo pole in hand and was poking at something in the slowly draining water.

"Margarete, come here. Come see!" Travis yelled.

"No, you may not have a pet crawfish, either," I shouted back, assuming they were tormenting one of the lobster's tiny cousins. "It's time for you two to come inside before the mosquitoes start swarming all over you. C'mon, give a tired old grandmother a break."

"Please, Margarete, come see first, then we'll go in. This isn't a crawfish. You have to see this. Really!"

"Hurry! Hurry! Hurry, Margarete," the boys shouted. "He's getting away. Hurry!"

He's getting away? He? Oh, no. An unfortunately vivid picture flashed through my mind. The newspapers had reported alligators turning up in the most unlikely places lately, including residential yards. Our floodwaters, after all, were being pumped into their marshland habitat. With their dry ground rapidly disappearing, the alligators were seeking refuge from their inundated homes. "Travis! Kyle! Leave them alone. Get away from him this minute, do you hear me? Just back away. Now!"

I ran to the ditch and froze in horror. Just completing a languid 180-degree turn was one of the largest snakes I'd ever seen. Its color blending almost perfectly with the muddy water, it would have been difficult to spot if not for the wake created by its head. Cold, hooded eyes were fixed with malignant gleam on a target dead ahead. Undulating through the water, it swam with quiet, menacing determination and incredible speed— straight toward my grandson's feet!

"Water moccasin! Run, boys, run!" Reflexes taking over, I grasped Travis under the armpits, yanked him off his feet and set him down behind me. "Run! You, too, Kyle. Go!" For once, they did as they were told without hesitation. Grabbing the bamboo pole Travie had dropped, I lifted it high and swung downward with all my might, clouting the snake soundly on top of the head. Not waiting to see if it was willing to do battle, I joined the boys' retreat.

"That's it," I gasped once we were safely inside the house. "No more insect hunts, no more outside play, no more scaring Margarete to death. I can't take that much excitement. You two will just have to entertain yourselves inside the house until everything dries up outside."

"Aw, Margarete, there was nothing to be scared of. We had our lances," Kyle said.

"We wouldn't have let him get close enough to bite," Travie added. "Snakes are pretty dumb, you know."

"Little boys who don't know the difference between foolishness and bravery are pretty dumb, too," I scolded.

"Can't we hunt bugs for Arnie if we stay close to the house?"

"Absolutely not! Arnie's perfectly happy with his

steak and corn. We'll leave it that way." Little did I know Arnie was going to make that statement sound like a lie.

Though he would spit out everything else I offered him for food, Arnie did eat enough corn and steak to stay healthy. He still ate only what I placed directly into his gaping little beak, however. Hoping he would someday realize it was supposed to be eaten, not played with, I made it a practice to leave a small dish of corn in the bottom of his cage during the day, adding a few pieces of minced steak in the afternoon—all to no avail. Arnie continued to play with the food but would not eat on his own.

Suddenly, that situation changed drastically. The day after I ordered the boys to abandon their insect hunt, Arnie decided he was fully capable of eating on his own. Nonchalantly, he picked a kernel of corn out of the dish with his beak, flipped it toward his throat with a toss of his head, and swallowed it expertly. I was jubilant over his achievement! But Arnie was disdainfully indifferent, acting as though he'd been doing it all along. Bratty bird! He became scornfully independent of help with his feedings. When I offered him food with my fingers, he either rejected the offer outright or snatched the tidbit and ran to the back of his cage as though he'd stolen it. Darn if he was going to open his beak wide enough for me to insert anything. He'd decided he was a big boy, not a baby anymore. That was great progress, of course, but simultaneously he quit eating steak.

Each evening, I fretted a bit more as I removed the dish of meat, untouched, from his cage. After all, the books had indicated that starlings are primarily protein-eaters. He consumed more and more corn, sometimes eating voraciously, as though he could not get enough sustenance into his system. He'd always had a way of prodding and probing curiously at everything with his beak, but now he seemed to do so with an urgency. He paced the floor of his cage, looking at it searchingly, pecking incessantly. He would work at the newspaper I placed in it each day, poking at it with the tip of his beak until he'd made an opening, then insert his mandibles and scissor them open to enlarge the hole. Surely he was searching for something; and there was little doubt in my mind what he wanted: proper nourishment.

"We'll find bugs this time, Margarete," Travie said seriously. "We just didn't try very hard before."

"Yeah," Kyle agreed. "Arnie didn't really need them then. Now he does."

Watching Arnie, I was tempted to put them to work again. I remembered the snake too vividly, however, and the alligator stories continued to make the news. "No, boys. It's nice of you to offer, but I don't think that's the solution for Arnie. If we start him on bugs now, who's going to catch them for him after you've gone home? I know I wouldn't be able to do it."

"Will Arnie starve to death?" Travie asked.

"No, we certainly won't let that happen. We'll just have to put our minds to work and think of something logical."

The boys sat on the floor and watched Arnie's frantic search in thoughtful silence for several minutes. Abruptly, Travie's face brightened. "I've got it! I know what we can do!" he said. "You can buy him some worms like Dad gets for fishing, Margarete."

Fishing worms? Why not? Robins eat worms. Maybe starlings do, too, I thought. Maybe Arnie could be persuaded to eat them, anyway. If he did take to them, at least he would be getting his protein in a form I could provide. We drove to a nearby hunting and fishing store and bought a carton of worms. It cost $2.25 and contained sixteen of the squirmy creatures, none of any great substance. I'd read articles proposing that worms be used as protein for the impoverished people of the world. At that price, it would be less expensive by far to feed them filet mignon.

When we returned with the worms, Arnie was pacing the floor of his house, prodding and probing with his beak in what had become an everlasting search. I crossed my fingers that the worms would fulfill his needs. Opening the small door at the bottom of the aviary, the boys placed one worm inside, then squatted back to see if their friend would accept the offering. "C'mon, Arnie, eat," they said, encouraging him.

Pausing in the act of ripping the newspaper at the back of his cage, he eyed them suspiciously. He eyed the worm even more warily, cocking his head back at an angle. It was his first exposure to food that moved, but he trusted his human friends. Jutting his beak forward like John Wayne advancing to do battle for right and good, he swaggered over to give the worm a closer inspection. Frozen momentarily, paralyzed by fear no doubt, the worm lay still, not twitching a muscle.

Arnie cocked his head to the side again, peering at the object with one eye as though conducting a microscopic examination. Satisfied that it was benign, he stretched his beak toward it.

The worm, deciding it was better to beat a retreat than to cower in fear, began to move away.

Arnie squawked and leapt backward half the length of his floor. Fluttering his wings in agitation, he began to screech vehemently, raucously. He flew to his top perch, then catapulted from one side of his house to the other, front to back, over and over again, using his screening like a trampoline, protesting at the top of his lungs.

I sighed. "I don't think he likes worms, boys."

"I think you're right," Travie agreed seriously.

"I think he's afraid of them," Kyle giggled.

Holding his mouth to suppress his own laughter, Travis removed the worm from the cage. "Don't let

him see you laughing at him, Kyle," he said. "It might hurt his feelings."

The boys ran into the bedroom they were sharing. I could hear the bedsprings creak as they rolled and tumbled, overcome by merriment.

"Imagine, a bird afraid of worms!" one of them shrieked, setting off a renewed peal of giggles.

I smiled and shook my head. "I don't know what I'm going to do about you, Arnie."

He'd calmed down considerably, though he remained on his top perch, scrutinizing the floor of his dwelling with utmost suspicion. At the sound of my voice, he turned to glare at me. *Don't ever do that again*, he seemed to be saying.

"C'mon out," I invited, opening the door of his cage. "You can help me prepare lunch."

He hesitated a minute, fluffing and shaking his feathers, then launched into the air, heading for the boys' bedroom. "Hi, Arnie," I heard them say. "We're sorry we scared you, Arnie." Apparently satisfied with their apology, he flew back into the living room, made a couple of quick turns through the air, then landed on my shoulder.

As I peeled and cut boiled eggs for tuna salad, he hopped down to sit on the rim of the bowl. Critically, he watched each piece of egg as it left my hands and plopped into the container. Abruptly, he opened his beak wide over a bit of yellow yolk, then snatched it up. He flipped it around in his mouth a few times, tasting, then swallowed it and reached for another. "Well, Arnie," I said, "it looks like you've found your own form of protein. It's not as good for you as meat, but eggs are better than nothing."

Arnie acquired such a liking for egg yolks that they became a regular part of his diet. Seemingly satisfied, he ceased his frantic searching at the bottom of his cage. In the beginning, I was able to serve him eggs in whatever form I happened to prepare them for human consumption, but Arnie was not content to let me off that easily. No matter how I fixed it, he would never taste the white part of the egg. He quickly established a decided preference for his egg yolks fried to a very exact degree midway between soft and hard and, having established the preference, he refused to eat them any other way. In his own manner, Arnie was becoming a gourmet.

Breakfast became the most demanding meal of the day. From the moment I awoke, it seemed I was serving food to specification for a small army. Mitzi insisted on having her special tuna, for no other flavor of cat food would do. Vagabond alternated, demanding something different each day. Samantha had to have her crunchy dry food. Kyle, allergic to milk, liked cereal floating on orange juice. Travie favored blueberry pancakes. Arnie and I shared the egg. Everyone ate at a different time, of course. But whatever grumbles I might have made were stilled by the knowledge that the situation was only temporary, at least as far as the boys were concerned.

The days of tranquil enjoyment disappeared one by one until there were no days remaining of their summer vacation. Despite a great deal of assistance from Arnie and the cats, Travie, Kyle, and I managed to pack their things. We did so in deep, gloomy silence. Youngsters don't yet understand the inevitability of endings. They're not without regret for grandmothers, either.

"Can we come back next year, Margarete?" Kyle asked.

"Of course we can, dummy," Travie snapped. "We have to. Arnie needs us to teach him what we learn after a year in school."

The boys thought of every excuse to delay our departure for the airport, but finally we had to go. They paused at the door, their eyes glistening, tears threatening to brim.

"Don't forget us, Arnie. We'll be back."

"Bye. See you. Bye. See you soon!" Arnie's tone begged them to stay.

He wouldn't forget them.

ix Grandparents everywhere know what it feels like to have grandchildren come and go. It's something special, that "grand" relationship. The awesome responsibility of having to care for, to teach, to mold new human beings over two decades until they're capable of facing life's hazards on their own—it's wonderfully absent with grandchildren. The fear of failure no matter what you do, the helpless sensation of foundering so often, doesn't exist. Instilling discipline is, thank goodness, the parents' responsibility.

Perhaps grandchildren are, ultimately, the reason

we have children in the first place. Grandchildren are fun. One can relax and enjoy them to the fullest. Treasure their foibles. Become privy to special pieces of their lives. Spoil them without shame. For brief periods of time. Very brief periods. Then they're gone. And life returns to normal.

It's a good feeling. A relief. You kick off your shoes, shed your apron, pick up the overlooked pieces of Lego, relax with a good book you haven't had a chance to read. And listen to the echoing silence. It's the empty-nest syndrome all over again.

I wasn't the only one in the household who had to get used to life without the boys again, either. The animals moped, refusing to eat.

Vagabond stationed himself at the window from which he'd always watched the boys play outdoors, patiently awaiting their return. His eyes constantly scanned the lawn, hoping for them to appear. Travie had become his playmate when Bundy was a kittenish two-month-old clown. Now that he was a stern-faced tom, he had used Travie's visit as an excuse to behave like a kitten again. The excuse was gone now.

Mitzi sat disconsolately on top of the television set with her head drawn into her shoulders. She growled grumpily if anyone even glanced in her direction. On the occasion of Travis's birth, Mitzi had been stuffed into a specially designed cat travel bag. Protesting all the way from her place under my seat, she had flown with me on an airplane for our first meeting with my grandson. Their friendship went back a long way, indeed.

Samantha curled up on the pillow where Travie's head had rested the night before. Her paw was draped over the big black rubber spider he'd left as a final prank. Her expression was undeniably sad. From Travie, she had learned how tender can be the touch of a gentle child's hand, how delightful the game of chase.

Arnie was silent as he'd not been since the morning

he'd said his first "Arnold" to me. He squatted on his security perch, his feathers fluffed in misery.

Animals don't feel emotion. I had read that. The opinion was written by an expert on animal behavior. Perhaps the animals he'd studied had chosen not to display their emotion to him; maybe because he'd shown no emotion to them. Certainly if he'd studied these four animals he would have changed his attitude.

A glass of wine before dinner would be good medicine, I decided. Soothe away that annoying lump in my throat. Help sleep to come easily, so I could overlook the fact that there'd be no one to tuck in before seeking my own bed.

I poured the wine and opened the door of Arnie's aviary on the way to my easy chair. This was his favorite time of day for togetherness. Normally, he would have flown out with a happy chirp, made several circling passes around the room, then landed on a curtain rod or a lampshade to think over what to do next.

Today, he just sat there, glaring at the gaping doorway as though he found it offensive.

"C'mere, Arnie. C'mon. You come outside. Have a drink of wine with me." I tinkled the ice cubes invitingly. He was always happy when I decided to have a glass of wine before dinner. At the proper time of day it was undoubtedly his favorite beverage.

Today, however, with the boys gone, he had to think twice whether he wanted to bother leaving his house, even for the temptation of wine. I tinkled the ice cubes again. Without particular enthusiasm, he launched into a slow, gliding swoop and landed lightly on my shoulder.

"Arnie?" he inquired softly.

"Hi, Arnie. You realize they're gone, don't you? And I think you're going to miss them as much as I will."

"See you later. Bye-bye," he said mournfully. It was the first time he'd used the full expression. Too bad

86

the boys weren't there to hear it.

Soothing as it would have been to stroke one of the cats, Arnie was more comforting just then. The cats never talked to me, at least not with words. Sometimes we humans simply need the sound of another voice, no matter how inane the things that are said. This is undoubtedly the reason for our fascination with talking birds of all types. They are the only animals we've found capable of speaking to us in our own words.

"Arnie. Arnie-ly. See you. See you soon, baboon? Arnie-ly. Bye-bye, see you later."

Despite his limited vocabulary, he made perfect sense to me. "You are truly amazing, Arnie," I told him. He whistled four bars of "Mary Had a Little Lamb," then fell silent. I didn't know if he understood my words, but he certainly picked up on my moods with uncanny empathy. "Yes, they're gone. They'll be back, of course, but it's going to seem like a very long time before they are. I know you could use a pick-me-up right now. C'mon, don't you want a drink today?"

Obliging, he hopped down, waddled slowly along my arm and dipped his beak into the glass. Tilting his head back, he allowed the drops to slide down his throat. After several sips, he raised one wing slightly away from his shoulder, dipped into the glass for a few drops, and used his beak to dab wine on the feathers under his wing. He repeated the act on the other side of his body. When he'd finished the perfuming ritual, he pecked at the ice cubes, looking for a flake small enough to take into his beak. Finding none of the proper size, he dipped into the wine, taking another few drops to swallow.

"Take it easy," I cautioned. "You don't want to overdo it."

He hadn't gotten drunk since that night when the boys and their mothers arrived. After that one frightening experience, he'd always known to stop drinking before he reached his limits. That's better sense than many humans possess. He truly enjoyed his wine, though. The odd ritual of dabbing it under his wings reminded me of a human applying underarm deodorant. Wine was the only thing he used in that manner, but it seemed to be one of his great pleasures in life. Given a choice between his two favorite beverages, he stuck to orange juice during the day, but preferred his nips of wine in the evening, for dabbing and for drinking.

Despite my warning and his normal reserve, this evening he seemed to be throwing caution to the winds and was drinking far more than he usually did. I wondered if he somehow understood the concept of drowning sorrows, but I would not allow him to make that mistake. "Arnold! You've had enough now. Stop it!"

He paused in mid-sip, looked at me guiltily, then placed the beakful of wine in careful dabs under each wing. For an animal with so little ability to convey emotion with facial expression, he managed to communicate an amazing range of feelings with his eyes, the tilt of his head, the angle of his body, and the set of his feathers. Anyone who knew him could clearly see how sad he was. He fluffed his feathers, shook his body, and walked up my blouse to perch on my shoulder again. Softly, he began to whistle "Mary Had a Little Lamb" into my ear.

I sighed. "Honestly, Arnie, they'll be back. And we'll go visit them. Our world isn't ending, you know."

Bundy jumped onto my lap, put his nose against mine, and looked inquiringly into my eyes. "So you've decided to give up your vigil, have you?" I said. "You're just going to have to resign yourself to a long wait, boy. You might as well join us. Make yourself comfortable." He rubbed his whiskers against my cheek once, then stretched out full length on my legs. Absently, I began to stroke him, but stopped to make room for Sammie to join us. Sprawled out, Bundy covered every inch of my lap, but Sammie wasn't going to let that stop her. Carefully, she eased herself down alongside her son, wiggling and squirming until she'd managed to fit in quite snugly.

Fortunately, Mitzi has never been a lap kitty. It's quite beneath her dignity to admit a need for so much closeness, I believe. Judging by the expression on her face as she stared at us from her throne upon the TV set, however, she might have made an exception to her rule upon this occasion if there had been room. It was the saddest I had ever seen her look.

The companionship of my four little friends was a great comfort at the moment.

The degree to which animals are capable of sharing life with their human friends is a constant source of amazement to me. In my family, animals have always been close and vital members with their own niches in the household. When my daughter was growing up, we were primarily a dog family, with a decided preference for German shepherds. Two of them, Rex and Prinz, grew up with us. Only dogs could have touched us in quite the ways they did.

Rex had a nose that would have made any bloodhound drool with envy. When my husband returned from the Korean War on a troop ship, Hanna, Rex, and I went together to greet him. Thousands of men poured off the ships that day, and countless families were there waiting for them. The returning soldiers were one vast, khaki-colored sea topped by bobbing infantry caps. "We'll never find him," I said to Hanna. "Yes, we will," she replied. "Rex, find Daddy. Find Daddy and bring him here, Rexie." The dog was off like a shot before I could say anything. "Hanna, he was less than a year old when your father left for Korea," I reminded her gently. "That was two years ago. He'll never find Frank." "Yes he will, Mumma," she stated adamantly. Less than ten minutes later Rex raced up to us, his tail wagging mightily, his paws dancing, his teeth clenched firmly about an infantry cap. And before I knew what was happening, I was locked in the embrace of my grinning, hatless husband. "I see Rex hasn't forgotten any of his old tricks," Frank said. "He always welcomed me home by stealing my hat."

Rex died with a .22 bullet in his heart. It was the first bullet fired from the barrel of a rifle our twelve-year-old paper boy had received for his birthday. The boy had loved Rex, but no one had bothered to teach him enough about guns before turning him loose with one. Our family was devastated by the loss. We filled the gap with Prinz.

When Frank received orders to report to an army post in Germany, I was overjoyed. I loved America but, suddenly, I was afflicted with homesickness. I hadn't seen the land of my birth in almost twenty years. Naturally, Prinz went with us. It was only fitting, while we were there, that he receive a proper European education. Prinz was a shepherd, after all, a breed often referred to, with some justification, as German police dog. The only proper education for a shepherd in Germany is through the guard dog academies reserved for that breed. Prinz, who'd always been a sweet, lovable, gentle clown, spent weeks being trained intensively in the shepherdly arts of defending, tracking, and attacking. *Schützung I, II, III* is the honored notation such training earns for a shepherd's pedigree. Taking top honors in all classes, Prinz emerged a trained killer canine. He was highly regarded as such in dog circles, anyway; to us, he remained a gentle friend.

After we returned to America, Hanna started dating, and our highly trained guard dog went along as her chaperone. Prinz, Hanna, and her date would all sit in the front seat of the car at a drive-in movie, watching the film, munching popcorn, enjoying themselves. It was a cozy arrangement—until the young man's arm began to steal along the back of the seat and across Hanna's shoulders. At that point, Prinz drew back his lips, bared glistening teeth, and began a soft, singing growl deep in his throat. If the young man's hand continued to advance, it invariably wound up gently, but firmly, grasped in Prinz's mouth. The teeth and growl were always sufficient to persuade Hanna's dates that holding hands was enough intimacy. It was a fine arrangement all the way around.

Prinz was run over by a recklessly driven car one bright afternoon while taking a walk with my parents. My mother had her first heart attack when she realized he was dead. Much as I love dogs, I couldn't bring myself to get another after that. Animals are necessary to my life, however, so I switched to cats and rats and birds. They're easier to keep under watchful eye.

Many people really don't understand the deep friendship that is possible between animals and people. Some who profess to love animals keep dogs or cats during transient periods, when convenient, then abandon them as though they were outgrown toys. On the other hand, there are people who treasure animals for their many useful purposes, but who would no more think of loving one than they would a tool. Human closeness with animals is often mocked, laughed at as an odd eccentricity, or thought to be a substitution for children.

To my mind, an animal can no more take the place of a child than a child can take the place of a family pet. Their roles are totally distinct and different. My animal friends have never been substitutes for my daughter, and they weren't substitutes now for my grandson. It certainly was soothing to have them near at that moment, however, to keep me company while I adjusted to the absence of Travie.

The cats purred in my lap as I stroked them. Arnie walked from my shoulder, down my shirtfront, and clung there, looking up at me with his head cocked. Lost in reverie, I had been silent too long for his liking. He stuck his beak into my mouth, prying my lips open with insistent mandibles.

"Peek-a-boo," he said. "Kiss Arnie. Hello. Hi. Hi there. Kiss Arnie."

I laughed. How foolish I was being! Before my grandson's visit, I had worried about having to rearrange my schedule to find time for him. Now that he was gone, I was concerned about how to fill my hours without him. Nonsense!

"Hi. Hi! How are you?" Arnie said. Not waiting for my reply, he launched into Beethoven's Fifth.

"I'm going to be just fine, Arnie." I laughed again, feeling immensely better. "I think it's a good time to resume your lessons. We'll make you the greatest genius bird of all time. Whenever the two of us have a few moments to spare for the process, that is. I have a great deal of catching up to do with my normal activities, you know. Somehow, though, we're going to squeeze in your lessons. It's obvious you're an eager student."

"Arnie-ly," he said. "Hi. How are you? Arnie. He's a two-two."

And I had thought at one time that it was impossible for him to learn how to talk. I hadn't given him the benefit of the doubt because I had preconceived notions of the capacities of a wild bird. I had no idea how much Arnie was capable of learning, but I intended to give him the opportunity to expand his vocabulary as much as he could. I had a feeling he would learn as much as I was willing to teach.

For starters, I decided to introduce him to the most important words in human vocabulary. They were words I thought he needed to express his feelings, those feelings he's not supposed to have. I was certain he would learn to say them.

"I love you," I said. "I love you."

X The day started normally enough. As usual, I opened the curtains to admit dawn's feeble light. Then, two steps past the last window, I did an abrupt about-face and returned to stare through the glass in astonishment. The entire back quarter of my lawn looked as though it were covered with dozens of bed sheets, casually strewn by the wind or the hands of a prankster. For a moment, I thought a newspaper had been separated and scattered by the breeze, but the objects were pure white and too large for newspaper pages. The rays of the rising sun bounced dazzlingly off them.

Curious to know what had grabbed my attention, Samantha sprang gracefully up and sat erect on the sill. After one look outside, she dropped into a crouch, flattening her ears against her head. Her tail swished with slow, jerking thumps against the frame as she peeped over the bottom edge of the window.

"Whatever that is out there looks as strange to you as it does to me, doesn't it?" I said. "This calls for a better view than we have at this distance. I'll see if I can find the binoculars."

On the way to the closet, I opened the door to Arnie's cage so he could have his first outing of the day. Flying to my shoulder, he said, "Good morning." "Good morning," I responded absently, already digging through the contents of the closet. I was certain the binoculars were in there somewhere. Arnie fluttered over to perch on the edge of a coffee can filled with nails and began rummaging through them with his beak. As I searched, he meandered from one object to another on the shelf, probing at everything.

"I give up," I said several minutes later. "I guess the binoculars aren't in here after all. C'mon, Arnie. Come out so I can close the door." Without dropping the leather strap he was tugging at, he glanced backward and replied with a sound remarkably like a Bronx cheer.

"Arnold!" I scolded.

"See you soon, baboon," he said and continued to tug.

"You are disrespectful, Arnold. What's that you're playing with?" I reached for the strap. Arnie surrendered his toy and flew out of the closet, sounding another Bronx cheer as he went. Curious, I followed the strap to the back of the shelf and pulled out a black leather case with a familiar shape. Intentionally or not, Arnie had found the binoculars.

I closed the closet door and walked back to the window. Sammie had kept the vigil without moving

and Mitzi was behind her. Bundy would have made it a threesome on the windowsill, but a growled warning from Mitzi sent him trotting off to another vantage point. Not to be left out, Arnie flew over and sat on Mitzi's head. Her fur rippled visibly at the touch of his talons, but it was her only reaction to him. The five of us looked out over the lawn with the rapt attention of a theater audience.

Putting the binoculars to my eyes, I adjusted the focus. My "bed sheets" proved to be a sizable flock of large, white birds, scattered loosely around the lawn. I'd never seen such a sight before and had no idea what kind they were. What were they doing in my yard? They just lay there, unmoving, their wings fanned widely to both sides of their bodies. The birds' postures made me wonder if they were alive.

"What am I going to do if they're all dead?" I said. The cats looked at me, but offered no answers. Arnie flew back to the breakfast bar to resume his tug of war with the binocular case. I heard a thump as Vagabond left his window. Mitzi yawned, stretched, and jumped down also. Sammie sat up, looked at me, glanced out at the lawn again, then followed the others. Things that do nothing don't hold their interest for long. Even my attention span was lagging. The birds hadn't twitched a muscle.

As I lowered the binoculars, one of the birds moved. Ponderously, it folded first one wing and then the other against its body and stood. Slowly, the others followed suit. "Cowbirds!" I uttered the local name for the cattle egret, which I'd seen often in the fields, sitting atop cows and wandering through grazing herds. The cattle egret was a fairly common sight here, but I'd never seen them so close up. They'd be fun to watch. Seeing that Arnie was back in his cage, I closed his door on my way into the kitchen to pour a cup of coffee. When I got back to the window, though, the flock of egrets was gone.

Closer to the house, the yard was alive with other birds. The cardinals and mockingbirds and blue jays flitted through the leaves of the mulberry tree in flashes of red, white, and blue. For the second time that year, the tree was filled with berries, which always drew the birds. Even the shy bobwhite quail was drawn out of the fields by the tree's bountiful droppings. Three of them pecked about in the grass among the sparrows and blackbirds and a flock of starlings. Robins hopped jauntily nearby and—starlings! For the first time, I had the binoculars handy while they were about. Now I could get a really close look at Arnie's cousins.

With magnification, the starlings were much more attractive than the description "speckled blackbird" had led me to believe. When the sun hit their feathers, the glossy blackness was transformed into iridescent hues of purple and blue and green. The speckles that tipped each feather were light brown on their backs, but white on the throat, chest, and stomach. The brilliant yellow beaks of summer were beginning to darken for winter, and smudges of black had begun spreading toward the tips of their mandibles. Their legs were bright fuchsia, an unusual color I've seen only on starlings in that part of the country.

Though Arnie had not yet achieved the adult appearance of a starling, I saw now that he certainly behaved like one. Unlike the robins and jays, who hopped erectly, the starlings strolled, usually with their heads down and eyes riveted to the ground. Like Arnie, they waddled when not bent over. Their beaks were in constant motion, scissoring apart blades of grass, pecking and probing at the ground, hovering with widely parted mandibles above each spot, prying apart the dirt, then snatching up morsels of food. There wasn't another bird in the yard that used its beak the way the starling did. Arnie's method of scissoring open his mandibles had looked peculiar to me, but now I saw that the wild starlings used the same action to hunt for their food. They seemed capable of detecting their prey beneath the dirt as they lingered with open beaks above each spot of ground. I had often suspected that Arnie smelled and tasted things that way—through the roof of his mouth, with the help of a set of sensing organs that resembled tiny, fleshy shark's teeth. Of course, Arnie had cultivated the rudimentary sense until his was as discriminating as a gourmet's palate—severely limited, but discriminating.

The adult starlings didn't have Arnie's sweet face, but their fierce expressions were belied by clownish behavior. Watching them, I was reminded of children playing. Teasing, they stole tidbits from each other, ran a short distance, then stood with defiant posture until a game of chase had been provoked. Leapfrog seemed to be another favorite game. One minute, two starlings stood side by side, busily poking through the grass. Suddenly, one hopped into the air with a great flutter of wings, propelled himself sideways, and leapt over the back of his fellow, landing on his opposite side. The leaper would then calmly resume prodding the grass. Frequently, I would see one jump into the air, flutter his wings a bit, then parachute lightly down as if dancing in sheer exuberance at life.

Captivated with watching the starlings that day, I lost all track of time. As though awakening from a dream, I was startled to realize the sun was going down. Forcing myself to lay aside the binoculars, I stretched to work the stiffness from my body and blinked my eyes to revive normal vision.

Only then did I notice the great blobs of white in the Chinese tallow trees at the back of the yard. The cattle egrets were back, this time roosting in the trees. Looking through the binoculars again, I saw that the egrets sat with their heads drawn into their shoulders. Motionless, they looked like vultures waiting for their next meal to present itself. Compared to the starlings, they were boring. After fifteen minutes or so, I decided they weren't going to do anything interesting so I might as well go ahead and make dinner. The last time I looked out the window that evening, there were still soft shimmers of white within the darkly silhouetted trees. The egrets were still roosting. The next morning, they were once again strewn about the lawn, their wings splayed, recreating the illusion of bed sheets. The entire scenario of that first day was repeated every day, for almost a week, before the egrets departed for good. Although I was left to wonder why they had come at all, I was grateful they had; otherwise, the binoculars might have remained in the closet for the next year, and I would not have begun watching the birds.

The more I looked at the other starlings, the less healthy my little Arnie appeared. Although I'd not seen another juvenile for comparison, I was certain his legs shouldn't be such a pale, sickly, yellowish-white when his cousins' legs were that bright fuchsia. Where their coats were glossy, his was dull. They were in perpetual motion, while he seemed to tire easily and rested a great deal. Inside his mouth, the flesh was white, anemic-looking. Maybe I was overly concerned, but I felt that I must be neglecting something that was important to his health. A sickly bird simply would not do in my household. Now that he was family, I intended him to have a full, happy, long starling life.

I decided I must do something to improve Arnie's health. I couldn't do much about his limited food preferences, but I could take him outside for the fresh air and sunshine that are so vital to good health. It was the nicest time of year as far as I was concerned. Monsoon season had ended. Now it was almost fall. The ground had dried sufficiently to be worked after two weeks of sunshine, and a cool preview of winter had sopped the steam from the air. I looked forward to the opportunity to push my too-sedentary body a bit with some yard work.

I had somehow convinced myself that I would create

an estate upon acreage that had lain fallow for years. I had already planted thousands of hedges and flowering shrubs and trees, and now I was ready to concentrate on flower beds. I missed the tulips and crocuses and daffodils that are the harbingers of spring in the North. It would be worth the trouble of digging up and replanting them each year for the cheering effect they would bring. I would plan and dig and prepare the beds in advance so that when the bulbs arrived it would be a simple matter to plunk them into the ground. Then I could look forward to the welcome splashes of vivid color in the midst of dreary January.

Arnie would be welcome company as I gardened. I should have thought to give him outings before. I was certain the fresh air and sunshine would provide him with something his system was missing.

I borrowed a parakeet cage from a friend. I thought it would be a perfect cabana for Arnie's airings. But when I put him into it, he quickly mastered the trick of shoving out the food tray, which created a nice Arnie-sized opening. Promptly, he climbed to freedom and flew back into his aviary. He clucked in amused triumph all the way. "Smart boy," I complimented him as I secured the trays with masking tape.

When I put him back inside, he went immediately to one tray, then the other, straining to repeat his performance. Realizing escape was impossible, he began squawking with agitation, scolding me. "You'll get used to it, Arnie," I said. He switched tactics and tried cajoling me with sweet talk. "Arnie. Arnie-ly. Hi. How are you? Peek-a-boo. Kiss Arnie. He's a pretty boy. Arnie-ly. C'mere. Kiss Arnie. Kiss Arnie!" When I picked up the cage and began walking, he resumed the scolding, fluttering about within his confines.

"Give it a chance, Arnie," I urged. "You're going to enjoy this, you'll see." I carried him outside, confident I was speaking the truth. I set the cage high up in an enfolding arm of the mulberry tree. He'd be safe from harm there and the sunlight would be tempered by the fanning leaves. He'd be able to see me as I went about my chores. I would take frequent breaks so I could visit with him. I talked soothingly, trying to calm him before walking away.

He huddled miserably on the bottom of the cage, his eyes jerking nervously in every direction. The soft caress of the breeze through his feathers terrified him. He started constantly at the gentle rustling of the leaves, panting through widely open beak, his heart racing a mile a minute. Maybe he'd forgotten his previous experience with the outdoors, and all the newness frightened him. Perhaps he thought I would throw him into the air again, bidding him to fly, discarding him from his adopted home, sending him back to the wild. Whatever the reason, he was clearly frightened.

I sighed and reached for the cage, then withdrew my hand. I must be firm. He would get over these momentary qualms. I was being too protective. He needed fresh air and sunshine. He was a creature of the wild; it was inconceivable that he would be uncomfortable for long in his natural surroundings. He would become accustomed to the outdoors and realize he was in no danger. In time, he would learn to love these excursions, to look forward to them.

My presence would give him confidence, I thought. I would stay with him until his fears were soothed. I talked softly, urging him to relax and look at the wonderful world around him. He cowered on the bottom of the cage the entire time, seeming not to realize that I was there to protect him if need be. Every feather on his body quivered as though he were freezing. My insides clenched in sympathy. This was terrible, cruel. Poor Arnie. I carried him back into the house and gave him a double shot of orange juice.

Still convinced I was doing the right thing, I tried again the next day. All he needed was time to adjust, I told myself. In no time he'd be begging me to let him fly about through the treetops. Not today, though. His reactions were more severe than they'd been the day before. I couldn't watch for more than ten minutes before I took pity and carried him back inside. "Kiiisss Arnie," he said pathetically once he was safely on the top perch of his aviary, making me feel like a wretch.

It rained the next day, forestalling another attempt. Arnie didn't want to stay in his cage at all. Instead, he attached himself to me with the tenacity of a tick, talking and singing nonstop. With the fervor of a recruiting sergeant, I extolled the merits of outdoor sojourns. I cajoled Samantha, so wise in wilderness lore, to tell him how wonderful communion with nature could be. Her look would have dehydrated a watermelon. Sammie's experience outdoors had been one long nightmare. When she had awakened in my home after her operation, she must have thought that she'd died and gone to heaven. She had eight lives yet to live and intended none of them to include a breath of nature. She was Arnie's ally in this matter, certainly not mine.

I was determined to try one last time before admitting that he simply did not want to go outside. My third attempt began with Arnie's refusal to enter the parakeet cage. He flew all over the house to avoid capture, but I chased him until my superior size prevailed over his speed and agility. "I'm doing this for your own good, Arnie," I said.

He huddled dejectedly in the cage, silent, not reacting to my voice in the least. The three cats glared at me. I ignored all of them and carried the cage outdoors.

I had decided on a new approach. I would stay away from the cage today. Without me as a crutch, Arnie would have to stand on his own. Perhaps it was his dependence on me that was making him a sissy of a bird. I had to cut the apron strings. I forced myself to walk away.

He was safe in the arms of the mulberry tree, protected within the enclosure of his cage. Besides, I would be only a few feet away. I gathered my tools and began digging. As I worked, I glanced constantly over my shoulder at him cowering in the cage, pathetic and miserable. I was so distracted that I dug an area twice as large as I had intended for the new flower bed. Arnie hadn't moved a muscle, nor uttered a sound the entire time. He looked more like the product of a taxidermist's art than a living, breathing bird. "Okay, I give up," I said as I looked in on him. "I guess you'll never be a nature lover, Arnie."

Just then, my evening newspaper was hurled into my driveway. "I'll be back in one minute, Arnie," I said. "Then we'll go inside." He just stared at me. I walked to the roadside to pick up the paper.

A helicopter flew overhead, ferrying workers to an ocean-bed oil rig. It was an everyday sight and sound. The Gulf of Mexico was being made into a sieve in search of black gold. The helicopters beat the air overhead with the regularity of scheduled airline service. This one was even lower and noisier than usual, though, skimming just above my trees. The top branches swayed as though bowing before a storm. "If they keep that up, someday they won't clear those trees," I muttered as I walked back to get Arnie.

"Okay, little boy," I said as I rounded the tree. "I'll take you home now. This is the last time I'll put you through this ordeal. That's a promise."

The cage was tilted at an angle, probably dislodged by the onslaught of the helicopter's downdraft. A piece of tape flapped in the breeze. One of the food trays lay upon the ground.

Arnie was nowhere in sight.

XI A bird can fly far in a short while—especially a frightened bird. I had been gone only a couple of minutes, but Arnie could fly very quickly when he set his mind to it. I hoped he hadn't gone far enough already to confuse his sense of direction.

"Arnie," I called, cupping hands to mouth. I felt so helpless. My heart sank to the vicinity of my solar plexus, making its location known with leaden heaviness. "Arnie, come. C'mere, Arnie. Arnold, you come here! Please, Arnie, come." If he was lost, surely he could home in on my voice. "Arnie. Arnie-ly. Come home, Arnie."

He should have come immediately. I had always represented the ultimate safe haven to him. How he must have panicked at losing sight of me! He could not have seen me around the trunk of the tree; and there had been the helicopter. An everyday sight and sound to me, it would have seemed a terrifying bird of prey to Arnie. The piece of tape on the cage flapped like a tattered flag. It had required prodigious effort for Arnie to dislodge that food tray—the strength of desperate fear, the reaction of a cornered animal.

"Arnie, come back, please. Arnold, you come back here where you belong! Arnie!" I tried to whistle "Mary Had a Little Lamb," which usually drew him like a magnet, but my lips were too dry to whistle. "Arnold, you come here!" I cried with command in one breath, pleading in the next. "Arnie, please come here. Arnie, c'mere. Arnie. Arnie-ly. Arnie, come! Please come home, Arnie."

I moved into the middle of the yard, fearing he might not see me beneath the tree. I paused, listening for the sound of his voice. Turning in slow circles, I looked about with growing dismay. If he chose not to respond to my call, finding him would be an almost impossible task, I realized. The trees were too tall and full to distinguish a small bird body amid their leaves.

There were so many places he could be. Even if I saw him, I'd never be able to reach him; I would have to persuade him to come to me. There were snakes in the hedgerow—cottonmouth moccasins and rattlers among them, I was certain! What if one of them bit Arnie? Suddenly, my familiar surroundings were filled with menace.

"Arnold, come here!"

Arnold did not respond.

I began to panic. Maybe he had run away from home, protesting the way I'd dominated him the last few days.

Perhaps with a taste of freedom, he would find it to his liking. After all, he was a wild bird. How could he do that to me, though? Darn him, he'd had his chance at freedom before! At a time when I had not permitted myself to open too large a place in my heart for him, when the emotional stakes were relatively small, I had tried to set him free. He'd blown it! Darn if I was just going to shrug my shoulders and walk away now without trying to recover that piece of my heart. I wanted Arnie back! "Arnold, if you don't come home right now, I'll cut off your orange juice for a week!"

I stood beneath every tree on the front two acres, peering upward into the branches, calling his name, cajoling, pleading, commanding, crying out forlornly. Birds of every description flew into the air when I drew near; none of them was Arnie. There wasn't a single juvenile among the starling flock I stampeded from their feeding ground on the lawn. Despite my fear of snakes, I plunged into the bamboo, then into the hedgerow. Vines grabbed at me; thorny things ripped my bare legs; whiplike little branches lashed my face and body. Like a maniac, I ran headlong about the neighborhood, calling into every tree and bush, looking everywhere, not realizing, not caring what an insane apparition I must appear to passers-by and neighbors. Tears streaming down my face, I sat on the grass near the hedgerow, listening for the sound of his voice. I imagined I could feel his presence nearby, that his little beady eyes were watching me. Why didn't he come to me? Or at least answer my call so I'd know he was all right?

I enlisted the assistance of the friendly young couple across the street, who tried in vain to make a bloodhound of their German shepherd. Like a search party, we fanned out, calling Arnie by name and whistling "Mary Had a Little Lamb."

Suddenly, I thought I heard him screaming "Arnie!"

in a tone fraught with wretchedness. I stopped dead in my tracks, called to the others, then rushed in the direction from which the sound seemed to have come. "There it is again," I said to my fellow searchers. "Now it's coming from over there. Listen!" They did, then shook their heads sadly. The sound wasn't repeated. "Maybe I imagined it," I said, but continued to listen with strained intensity for the sound of "Arnie" or "Hi. Hi. Hi!" or "Good morning" or "Mary Had a Little Lamb"—anything. I was certain I heard him from time to time, but the music of his voice came only in muted uncertainty, muffled under environmental noises and our own harried calling.

I realized eventually that we were competing with thunder rolling in off the Gulf. It was accompanied by flashes of lightning and gusts of bough-bending wind.

"Arnie will never survive a storm," I said when the others suggested we give up. "He doesn't even know to take shelter from the weather." We redoubled our efforts, calling into the same trees and bushes for the dozenth time, desperation driving us.

Darkness and swarming mosquitoes finally forced us to call off the search. We couldn't even see where we were walking, let alone spot a tiny bird in the brush. Arnie was on his own for the night. Reluctantly, we went indoors.

The three cats were lined up near the door, waiting with inquiring stares. Their eyes searched each of us as we came through the door. It was obvious they knew something was going on; and they had a good idea what that something was. They had watched us from the windows, heard us calling for Arnie. Distress etched frowns upon their faces. Their gloomy expressions were too much. Tears popped into my eyes again.

"Arnie's lost," I explained, feeling I must. "I did a dumb thing—left him alone, and a helicopter passed over, so he flew away. It's too dark to look for him anymore tonight, so we have to wait until tomorrow. We can only hope he has enough sense to find shelter for the night."

I went to the kitchen to feed them, but Vagabond was the only one who took me up on the offer. He thinks better on a full stomach. Mitzi and Samantha looked disgusted that anyone could even consider food at such a time; it was insensitive, to say the least. They took up sentry posts at different windows, letting me know they weren't going to give up on Arnie even if I had. Vagabond conducted a close scrutiny of the aviary on the off chance some big mistake had been made, that Arnie might actually be hiding somewhere inside. Then he took up his own watching post at a window.

How frightened Arnie must be out there in the hostile, unfamiliar night, I worried. Predator cats hunted at night, as Samantha once had. As did owls. And a storm was rolling in across the marshes. Arnie could not have chosen a worse time to disappear.

Politely, the young couple baby-sat with me for a while. "Don't worry, Margarete, he'll turn up tomorrow," they consoled. "A lot of animals run away from home, but they almost always come back." Their words barely registered with me; carrying on conversation was a major effort. I was glad when they left, promising to help resume the search the next day if he hadn't come back by then.

I needed to be alone. I needed solitude so I could turn my energies to willing away the storm, as though I could somehow hold it at bay with the power of thought. Foolishness, of course. Mother Nature goes about her business with indifference for the affairs or feelings of mere mortal beings, intending us neither deliberate harm nor benefit. Thunder crashed and rolled outside. The air thrummed, alive with the electricity of gathering power. Tree branches thrashed in protest against the rising wind.

Was Arnie sitting on one of those limbs, being whipped mercilessly to and fro? Had he learned his perching lessons well enough to cling to a foothold under such conditions? Was he brave enough to survive such a frightening experience?

I ran downstairs and flipped on the floodlights. Framed within the doorway, clearly visible, I called him. Gusts of wind flung my voice back at me; rumbling thunder overpowered my hoarse cries. Even if Arnie was nearby, he couldn't have heard me. I gave up and trudged back up the stairs.

Deep in unconstructive thought, I began biting my fingernails—a thing I hadn't done in years. I stared at the empty aviary with its gaping door. Missing the amusement Arnie always provided, I feared he would never again perch on my shoulder, whistle his tunes in my ears, help me make coffee in the morning, rasp his version of the words he had learned from us, or soothe my minor worries with his unconcern for the irrelevant.

Mitzi jumped onto my lap, a thing she never does, and stretched her neck to peer closely into my troubled eyes. She was feeling as distraught as I. She lay down with her head between my knees. Large comfort in a small furry package. I stroked her back absently, saving my nails from further gnawing.

Raindrops began to splash against the windows, upon the roof, into the ground. They plopped with obese heaviness, sparsely at first, then building in crescendo. The storm began with unabated brutality. Ravaging poor Arnie, I knew.

The night was endless. Unable to sleep, I paced the floor restlessly. I'd sit in my easy chair when tired, then rise for renewed, aimless meandering about the room when I could tolerate inactivity no longer. I resisted the irrational urge to dash into the night to rescue Arnie, my darling little feathered friend. I would have braved any hazard if I'd had any idea where he was.

I flipped the floodlights on and off, calling from the door into the darkness. My voice was lost in the storm.

Arnie was out there, caught up in that fury. It was an immensely hostile storm in which he was experiencing his first night of unsheltered existence. One minute the sky was pitch black, the next, brighter than day with lightning's dreadful illumination. The house shuddered as bolt after bolt hit the ground with awesome crashes. The wind attacked first from one direction, then, deceivingly, from another. Tree branches snapped with loud, jarring cracks, breaking jaggedly and tumbling in defeat. It wasn't a tornado, but the storm wreaked destruction like one. If the trees couldn't withstand it, how could a frail, frightened, inexperienced little bird? Birds have been known to have heart attacks and die in moments of extreme fright. There was little reason to think Arnie could survive the night.

By morning, I knew I had to face the facts. In all probability, Arnie was dead already. As the storm continued, my distress was transformed to cold fury. I raged at the fates. Why did there have to be a storm now? Why couldn't that helicopter have waited five minutes before flying over my trees? Why, why, why?! Darn it, I wanted Arnie back, desperately! What I wanted didn't matter, though. There was little hope I'd ever see him again.

The storm continued unabated well into the next afternoon, daylight distinguishing itself only by a lessening of the darkness. Two of the oaks, one of the pecans, and several persimmon trees leaned at precarious angles, tipped by the unrelenting wind, holding balance with tenacious toes imbedded deeply into the soil. The entire landscape was a vivid reminder of the complete helplessness of humanity in the face of one natural power we've not yet learned to tame.

Sporadically, I roamed the neighborhood for the next few days, calling to Arnie. My heavy spirits told me I might as well give up the fruitless search. The passage of time rendered it ever more unlikely I would see him again.

The storm had brought clear skies and the gift of fullfledged autumn. The crisp air smelled good enough to be bottled. Soft breezes seemed to be apologizing for the destruction caused by their bullying big brother, the storm wind. The sun cast benevolent warmth by midday instead of summer's furnace blast. It was a fine time to be alive. Poor Arnie. I mourned.

Forcing myself, I began the task of cleaning up the storm damage. My grief turned to anger, easier to purge from the soul through hard physical labor. Heaving and yanking and pulling and sawing and pounding at the fallen branches, I scolded myself for allowing such a deep attachment to develop in the first place. For a wild bird! How foolish I had been. But, I could not bring myself to put away the aviary. Not yet.

A strange stillness settled about the house. I didn't remember—had it really been that quiet before Arnie joined the family? Though they respected my feelings, Mitzi and Samantha and Vagabond went about their business as usual. Cats are quite practical in such matters, knowing that grief accomplishes naught, that life continues regardless of individual small tragedies. Humans cling overlong to emotional attachments.

A painful eternity later, I was on my way to the mailbox when I heard the flutter of wings, sensed a hovering at my back, felt a touch on my shoulder as tiny talons settled and clung to my blouse. It was an ordinary day, just like any other day, when a very special music returned to my life. It was delivered in a rasping little voice that spoke intimately into my ear. "Arnie-ly. Peek-a-boo. Hi! How are you? Kiiiisss Arnie. I love you!" Then he began to whistle "Mary Had a Little Lamb."

It's such a silly song. Appropriately, it's the favorite song of a silly, lovable, heartbreaking, joy-giving little bird. He was alive! Arnie was alive, and he'd come back to me! I wanted to grab him, to hug him, to never let him go again. "I love you, too, Arnie-ly," I said instead.

It occurred to me suddenly that what I wanted was to possess him, and that wasn't right. He'd been gone for days; perhaps he'd already made a new life for himself. He'd come back to me, letting me know he was alive, but perhaps I was already nothing more to him than a fond memory revisited. If I truly loved him, I had to grant him freedom if it was what he wanted. It had to be his choice.

With "Mary Had a Little Lamb" echoing in my ear, I turned and walked toward the house, speaking softly to him. Opening the door, I left it ajar behind me so he could decide. When he showed no inclination to leave my shoulder, I walked up the stairs and into the living room. He flew immediately to the aviary and clung to the screen, squawking until I opened the door so he could fly inside. He ate the corn I poured into his dish until he couldn't swallow another kernel. Then, I persuaded him to perch on my finger and walked back to the open door, intent on allowing him to fly away.

He took one look at the wide open spaces through the door, squawked loudly, and flew from my finger directly to the top perch of his aviary. Clinging tightly, he glared at me with his head cocked. "Kiss Arnie!" he said. "I *love* you!"

As I closed the door, he began to whistle "Mary Had a Little Lamb" again. Silly song. The most beautiful song I knew.

XII I'll never know where Arnie went, what he did, how he survived during that absence. I've often wondered, of course, filling my mind with fantasies of his exciting adventures. What an incredible learning experience it must have been for him to return to the world of his birth, a world he had never really known. It must have been overwhelming.

Though I liked to believe his return was prompted by love and affection, I would not question his motives. I gave him the option of freedom several times afterward, but from then on he shied away from all exits leading outdoors. He wouldn't even go near a window any longer. He made it very clear he had no liking for the world outside the walls of his home. That suited me just fine. I was not inclined to tempt the fates any longer. Arnie had come home to stay.

He seemed healthy, very normal in every way, though he was ravenously hungry for days. Like a child given the run of a candy store, he couldn't seem to get enough of his favorite foods. Doting, I indulged him in his every wish. Snugly indoors, no longer exposed to the elements, nor vulnerable to predators, well fed, cared for in every way, Arnie would give me no further cause for worry, I thought with relief.

One evening less than a week later, I had visitors who stayed a bit late. As usual, Arnie was happy to have company. Although he usually allowed his sleep periods to be dictated by the comings and goings of the sun, he wasn't about to miss out on anything when I entertained. He loved parties: the more people, the louder the talk and music, the better. Of course, he enjoyed quiet gatherings, too, like the one I had that night. I pulled his blanket down, darkening the top part of his cage in case he wanted to go to sleep, but he sat on a lower perch where he could keep an eye on us and be a part of the group. He listened with great interest as we became involved in a lengthy conversation, and didn't even look toward his bedtime perch until I closed the door behind our departing guests. Then he hopped up, waited for me to walk past the cage on my way to bed, and whistled a few quiet bars of "Mary Had a Little Lamb."

He wasn't very perky the next morning, but that was to be expected. Arnie was definitely no night owl, and he always paid for it when he stayed up later than usual. The poor cats couldn't do anything right that day; cranky Arnie hissed at them constantly. When I looked closely, I could see deeply creased little bags etched under his eyes. Before the afternoon was over, he was really dragging, sneaking his beak into his wing for a quick nap whenever he thought no one was looking. Well before sundown, he hopped to his top perch, drew one leg up into his underbelly and tucked his face into his wing feathers without a word to me. It'll do him good to go to sleep early, I thought. I pulled down his blanket and tiptoed around until my own bedtime. There seemed no reason for concern.

The next morning, however, he didn't even greet me when I walked out of my bedroom. Staying on his top perch, he kept his head tucked into his wing, not even seeming to notice the day had begun. I thought surely he would wake up and hop down his ladder a few minutes after I began to move about, but he still hadn't budged when I finished brushing my teeth. It appeared he wasn't even going to supervise my early morning chores.

"Good morning, Arnie," I said, measuring the grounds and pouring water into the coffee maker. No answer. "Aren't you going to get up today, lazy-bones?" I asked as I opened cans and fed the cats. "Arnie? Time to wake up, Arnie."

"'Brrrraaaddddttttt,'" he replied quietly. He shook his body slightly and tucked his head even further into his wing.

I shrugged. He's really, really tired, I thought, removing the dish of leftover corn from his cage and replacing it with fresh. He could not have had much rest during his nights in the wild, and he had stayed up quite late the night before last. Poor baby. It had all caught up with him.

When I opened his door to offer orange juice and he still didn't respond, however, I began to suspect things were not at all as they should be. Orange juice was Arnie's morning eye opener, the spark to ignite daytime activity. Without his morning orange juice, he wasn't good for a thing all day, and he knew it. Arnie would never, never spurn his orange juice.

As I sipped my coffee, I kept a careful eye on him. A memory I had filed away as inconsequential emerged from the back of my mind—Arnie had sneezed several times the day before, hadn't he? I had dismissed the sneezes at the time, scarcely registering them. Of course, he'd been listless, too, though I'd thought there was a simple reason for that. Maybe he was coming down with something. Suddenly, I was sick with worry.

While he was gone, Arnie must have been exposed to many things. Birds have little resistance to disease and they seldom survive more than a couple of days when sick, so any sign of illness in one is to be taken very seriously. Arnie's little sneezes, his failure to begin morning routine as usual, added up to a definite reason to worry.

Eventually, he hopped down from his sleeping perch to eat breakfast. He played with the food, though, picking up one kernel of corn to swallow, another to drop onto his floor. He dipped his beak into his juice glass for no more than a drop or two, though he usually drank greedily. Then he hopped back to his top perch and went to sleep again.

"Best to nip this thing in the bud," I muttered. Leafing through the phone book, I found the number of the nearest animal hospital and dialed it. "I have a wild bird that's sick," I told the receptionist. "Would one of your doctors know how to treat him?"

She giggled. "A wild bird? Why ever would you want to go to all that trouble for a common ole wild bird?"

I didn't bother trying to explain. A person with that attitude would never understand. I didn't have much confidence in a veterinarian who would have such an insensitive receptionist working for him, either. Besides, the fright of an automobile trip and the strange surroundings of a vet's office might be more than Arnie could bear. Birds don't always know who their friends are and have been known to die of fright at the touch of a stranger. I couldn't bear for anything like that to happen to Arnie. I would just have to take care of him the best way I could.

I devoted the entire day to him. Watching, waiting for signs of change, I urged him to drink more orange juice, to eat more corn. I enticed him with tidbits. He didn't even show much interest in any of his favorite treats. "Please, Arnie," I begged over and over again, holding out pieces of grapes and garlic and apples. "Please eat for me." I bit my lip to control the quiver in my voice. "Please be well for me, little boy."

He watched me through glazed eyes, sitting on his top perch instead of bouncing around the aviary as usual. His feathers were so fluffed he resembled a fuzzy, fat tennis ball. He didn't clean himself, either, and that was something he normally did many times a day. Silent, except for an occasional "razzberry" to indicate annoyance, he picked at my food and drink offerings with no interest. I remembered a small bottle of liquid vitamins I had bought for him just before his disappearance. It was late to be thinking of it, but maybe vitamins would help a little. I mixed a few drops with orange juice in Arnie's glass and coaxed him to drink. To please me, he did, but not much. I hovered over him, disturbing his rest until he learned to ignore me when I checked on him. He didn't get any better as the day progressed, but he didn't get any worse, either.

That evening, I went to bed quite early, praying for his improvement by morning. Maybe another good night's rest was all he needed. The cats elected to sleep in the living room instead of my bedroom as they usually did. They were going to keep their own vigil. If love alone can cure, surely he will get well quickly, I thought hopefully.

But loving concern wasn't enough. If anything, Arnie was even sicker the next morning. He hissed his irritation at the disturbance caused by my normal morning rituals. Peering accusingly at me through one eye, he kept the other tightly shut. He clung to his perch with both feet, apparently too weak to stand on one leg as birds usually do when resting. His head was tucked tightly into his shoulders, and his beak was pointed into the air instead of snuggled into one wing. With feathers fluffed even more than before, he appeared three times his normal size. And no amount of coaxing would persuade him to eat a crumb, to drink a drop.

Arnie was dying. I was certain of it. His will power, our love and devotion, nature's healing, were not enough to make him well. It was time for desperate, heroic measures. I wondered what heroic measures I could take that would not cause more harm than good. I ruled out a veterinarian entirely now. The stress of riding in a car for the first time and then being handled by a stranger would certainly kill him in his worsened condition. There was a limit to what I could do, but common sense dictated most of it.

Above all, Arnie had to have nourishment to keep up his strength and fluids to prevent him from dehydrating. Birds, with their incredibly fast metabolism, will deteriorate much, much faster than most creatures. It's possible for them to starve to death literally in a matter of hours. Arnie could not afford for me to wait any longer. If he would not take nourishment on his own, then I would have to force-feed him.

I arranged his food on the breakfast bar, mixed vitamins into the orange juice, and dug through the kitchen drawers until I found the eyedropper. Finally, I gathered up Arnie with both of my hands. Much as he hated being handled, he didn't even struggle to protest. His tiny body trembled, radiating the heat of fever. Yet he seemed to possess all the strength Travie would have attributed to Superbird, every bit of it concentrated on the task of holding his beak firmly closed. No matter how I tried, I could not persuade him to open his mandibles so I could get food into his mouth. His eyes begged me to leave him alone. It seemed that Arnie had decided to give up on life, that he had ceased eating in order to hasten an end to his misery.

How dare he?! I would not let Arnie surrender life. Not after all we had struggled through together. He would not be allowed to give up so easily. He would not! The thought was intolerable.

With renewed resolve, I used the tip of my small fingernail like a miniature crowbar, wedging it between Arnie's mandibles and prying them apart. Quickly, I slipped the eyedropper beyond his tongue and doled out the orange juice mixture drop by drop to avoid choking him. As I had done in his infancy, I shoved kernels of corn and bits of hamburger far down his throat, then held his beak shut until he'd swallowed them. He glared at me and tried to spit it all out, protesting the undignified treatment every step of the way. He was making it as hard as possible to save his life. I was determined to out-stubborn him, though, to force him to live if force was necessary.

He felt so frail, so fragile, that I felt like an absolute brute. There were times when I worried that I might break his neck or crush him by accident since he was causing me to resort to force. Beneath his fluffy feathers, there was little of substance to Arnie; he only weighed three ounces.

Despite all I could do, though, Arnie's fever continued to rage. Steadily, he lost vitality in seeming proportion to the amount of food I managed to get into him. "What he really needs is antibiotics," I muttered to Mitzi, who had not left Arnie's side all morning. "Tetracycline. That's the only antibiotic I know of that's safe for a bird."

Sammie jumped up and rubbed her head against my arm, looking inquiringly into my eyes. "Tetracycline ...tetracycline! Of course. That's what I gave you when you had the infection after your hysterectomy, Sammie, wasn't it? And there are still a few tablets left in the bathroom, aren't there?"

I put Arnie back into the cage and rummaged around in the bathroom until I found the jar I was looking for. Thank goodness I was right; the tablets were tetracycline. I crushed a small piece of one of them to a fine powder and dissolved it in orange juice. Conscious of his small size, I didn't want to give him too much; an overdose might cause as large a problem as I was trying to cure. Once the powder was thoroughly dissolved in the orange juice, I added it to the larger portion containing the vitamins. Praying as I worked, I felt very much the witch doctor mixing up a potion in which the incantation might be more potent than the herb.

I force-fed Arnie the mixture every six hours that day, continuing well into the night. Between doses of medication, of course, I continued with food, as much as I could get down him. He was more passive with each feeding, seeming not to care what was done to him. Somehow, I liked it better when he was fighting me. Eventually, he didn't even open his eyes to see what was going on. I sat with him nestled in my hands all day. Gradually, his fevered body cooled. It seemed a good sign until it swung to the other extreme. He grew so cold, so unmoving, he was almost stiff. His heartbeat weakened.

After a final dose of the antibiotic mixture that night, I swathed him in soft rags for warmth and comfort and laid him on the floor of his aviary. He had fallen into such a deep, motionless slumber toward the end of day that, in my mind, I likened it to a coma. Much as I was tempted to keep him near me, he would sleep most comfortably within the security of his own home, surrounded by his own familiar smells—or die there more peacefully. With leaden feet, I walked to my own room.

The next morning, I dreaded getting out of bed. There was little doubt about what I would find in the aviary. I didn't want to face the fact that Arnie was gone forever. He had touched my life with so much delight. As I lay there, I made plans to plant something, perhaps a tree, perhaps a rose bush, with him in the ground. The roots would embrace him, the branches would reach toward the sky above, and Arnie would again be a part of nature. He would like that. But, oh, how it hurt to think about it!

I blew my nose and wiped my eyes. Much as I dreaded the thought of seeing his little body with all signs of life gone from it, I could not put it off forever. The longer I put off the moment, the worse it would be. Tears continued to pop out of the corners of my eyes, no matter how I squeezed them shut. I forced myself to get out of bed.

With great trepidation, I peered around the corner into his cage. The little bundle of rags in which I had wrapped him was exactly as I had placed it the night before. There were no signs of movement within it. I sighed in despair.

"Arnie. Goomoring," his voice startled me.

Arnie was sitting on his top perch, looking down at me as he'd done every morning since I built the aviary. He didn't even look as if he'd been sick. Sliding down three perches, he scooted to the opposite side of the aviary and stared at me. "Goomoring," he repeated. *It's time for you to make coffee. You can see I'm waiting for you. C'mon now, get busy*—that's what he meant. The signal was quite familiar to me.

"You really do have to work to get your 'good morning' back into shape, Arnie," I said. I looked at the cats, wanting to share the moment of celebration. The three stood practically shoulder to shoulder at the foot of his aviary, united in a rare moment of togetherness.

"He's a pretty boy," Arnie said. I couldn't have expressed it better myself.

XIII Click. Click, click. Click, click, click-click. Arnie's talons beat a rhythmic tattoo as he tap-danced on the enamel finish of the kitchen sink. He enjoyed the sound created when he walked on hard surfaces, and invariably did a jig every few steps. Ka-ting, ting, ting, his beak tapped at the metal faucet. I waited, listening for the signal I knew to expect next. There were a few more dancing clicks, followed by a vigorous splashing of water from a pot soaking in the sink. His playtime finished, Arnie was ready for his bath. Of course, he fully expected me to run a proper one for him.

"Arnie want a bath?" I asked, hoping as always that he would become exasperated at my delay and speak his wishes and words. Water droplets began to spout upward from the sink, splattering wall, cabinets and floor in an ever-widening pattern. If I wouldn't set him up with fresh water in his own bowl, he would be content to wash himself in the dirty water. When Arnie wanted a bath, he wanted it right away, immediately, and I had to hop to it or I'd wind up mopping water splattered from kitchen countertop to dining table and all points in between. Already, he'd worked up enough momentum to pelt the stove and refrigerator, and he wasn't even warmed up yet. "I'm coming, Arnie, just wait one minute, will you, please!" I knew better, of course, than to think he would wait. Although he avoided soapy water, he always knew when I'd left something to soak in the sink. He also knew I'd respond quickly, before he got too carried away.

I ran to the sink and whisked a hand under Arnie, lifting him up. Grabbing the pot by its handle, I dumped the dirty water down the drain. "You'll get your bath, Arnie, but let's do it right." He glared at me, glanced at the sink, then put his beak against his chest, looking at his body. The customary gesture always made me think he was smelling himself for body odor and telling me, "Look, see how dirty I am." Even without speaking, he made his points well understood. As I reached into the cabinet for his bath bowl, there was a knock at the door. "Come on in," I called out. "The door's unlocked." The knob turned and the door began to inch open. Barely glancing up, I continued to prepare Arnie's bath. "Eep!" he shrieked abruptly, flying from my finger. With a quiet thud, the door closed.

"Freeze, lady. Don't make a sound," a deep voice warned. "I have a loaded gun, and I'll waste you in a minute. Where's your money?"

My heart pounded and my knees went weak, but I

managed to spin around. "Lenny, don't do that! You scared me to death!"

"Hi, Arnie. How's the bird?" he said in his normal voice to the mass of wet feathers clinging to his sweat shirt. "Lady, I keep telling you, you're gonna be in big trouble someday if you don't learn to keep your door locked."

"It's the middle of the day!" I said.

"Doesn't matter. That's a mean world out there. Fulla rapists and robbers and murderers and muggers just prowlin' around lookin' for ladies like you, alone at home with an open door."

A darkly handsome young man, Lenny hunched to minimize his six-and-a-half-foot height. His long, straight hair was slicked back from his forehead and behind his ears. A bushy mustache hid most of the scar that disfigured his upper lip; it also minimized the rigid set of his mouth, which seldom smiled. The jogging shoes he wore were as dirty and ragged as his nondescript sweat suit, which was his cool-weather uniform. He changed to shorts when summer heat set in, but always wore long sleeves to hide his track-marked arms. His big hands gripped either end of a newspaper-wrapped bundle, which all three cats were straining up his legs to smell. He leaned down with it so they could get a good whiff. "See what I brought you, kitties?"

"Fish?" I asked. "One of these days they'll follow you home and never come back, Lenny. Since you've started spoiling them, they think I'm feeding them garbage when I dish out canned food."

"It is garbage. Looks like the stuff they feed us in the joint. Even kitties gotta go for the gusto when they can get it. Right, big dude?" He reached down and ruffled the fur on Bundy's head. "This here's a gar I just pulled outta the bayou. Ever see one, lady? Gotta snout fulla teeth on him just like a gator. Mean dude, but good eatin' this small. I'll clean him downstairs at the faucet, okay?"

"Sure, that'll be fine. Put it on the stairs for now and clean it later, though. You're just in time for Arnie's bath."

"Outta sight. Go on, little dude. Don't wanna take a chance on you flyin' out the door when I open it." Gently, he shoved Arnie with one hand, sending him flying back to me, and reached for the doorknob. By the time he arrived back at the sink, Arnie was engrossed in his bath preparations. Propping his elbows on the sink rim, Lenny leaned over and rested his chin on his hands, intent on getting as close a view as possible.

Arnie sat on the dish drainer, shaking his body and fluffing his feathers as he watched the water flow into the plastic margarine tub. He turned his head to the side, inspected one wing and then the other, turned a critical eye to his chest, and preened a few feathers with his beak. "Arnie, take a bath," I said, rippling the water with my fingers. He hopped onto the edge of the bowl, dipped his beak into the water for a few drops to drink, then quickly immersed his entire head several times, shaking it vigorously back and forth. Clinging momentarily to the rim of the bowl with one foot, he jumped into his bathtub like a swimmer plunging into cold water and waddled hastily to the opposite side. After several wades across the tub, he began his bath in earnest.

I held up a towel as a shower curtain and turned my head to the side to avoid the flying deluge. Fanning his wings rapidly, Arnie scooped up water, tossing it over his back and high into the air. The spray splattered everything within five feet. Lenny watched without flinching as Arnie treated him, too, to a shower. "Next time I go to the joint, I'm gonna be like the Birdman of Alcatraz," he mumbled.

"Don't talk that way. You're not going back," I snapped. He cocked an eyebrow but didn't reply. He'd already encapsulized his feelings on a previous occasion with the comment, "Once a bird, always a bird. Too bad I ain't got wings."

Arnie fluttered back to the dish drainer, gave his drenched body a quick inspection, and labored on wet wings to the top perch of his aviary. He began combing individual feathers with his beak, and Lenny closed the door of the cage. "Go to it, little dude. I'm gonna clean the fish now, lady."

Lenny often brought gifts when he came to visit. The fish was always as much for the cats as for me. There'd been other things, too, over the months: a six-pack of German beer, which we shared; bottles of wine, when he learned Arnie liked it; a bouquet of roses, cut from his mother's garden, I think; a clutch of wild-flowers. Our relationship wasn't exactly a friendship, but Lenny and I went back a long way.

Because of his height, he had stood out from the other adolescents who hung out at the all-night grocery on the corner across the street from my property. Though the individuals changed from year to year, the group was a permanent fixture. They whiled away the hours smoking marijuana and drinking beer and wine they'd stolen or persuaded someone to buy for them. "Hanging out" was "something to do," as they put it, until they were old enough to drive. To the despair of nearby property owners, the group also regarded vandalism as "something to do." The policemen who occasionally came by disregarded the gathering as a relatively harmless evil about which they could do little.

A stranger to the community, I hadn't known until too late that the corner that was so serene by day belonged to Lenny and his friends at night. The evening I moved into the building, I seethed for almost an hour as they shouted obscenities at passing cars, broke bottles in the street, and threw rocks at whatever target was handy. How dare a gang of children disturb my peace that way when I was so exhausted! I marched across the street and into their midst. The tall one stood out as a prime target. Standing with hands on hips, I yelled at him until I was hoarse. I don't even know what I said. When I finished, you could have heard a pin drop. By twos and threes, the group dispersed until there was only Lenny and I.

"Hey, lady, why pick on me?" he asked. "You don't even know me."

"And you don't know me, but you've certainly made yourself an obnoxious part of my life tonight. You're too old to be hanging around on street corners throwing rocks like a little kid having a temper tantrum. Why do you do it?"

He shrugged. "It's somethin' to do. Daddy won't let me have the car. Gotta do somethin' with my energy."

"Then take up tennis or jogging or something that'll really use up your energy. You're almost a man. You should be ashamed, acting like a child—a stupid child at that." I turned on my heel and marched away from him.

The group didn't quit hanging out on the corner, but they were usually quieter after that. When I opened the sandwich shop downstairs, I decided to add an arcade to give the boys something to do and to fill the space where I hoped to build booths someday. Lenny always greeted me with the words, "Hi, lady. Peace. See, I ain't doin' nothin' wrong." He and the others I'd encountered that night established first an uneasy truce, then a similarly uneasy rapport with me. When Lenny disappeared from the group, his friends told me he was in jail. Later, I learned that he'd been sent to the state penitentiary on drug charges.

It was years before I saw Lenny again. When I did, I was carrying the garbage out to the road for collection and he was jogging. "Hi, lady," he said. "Peace. See, I ain't doin' nothin' wrong." Stopping beside me, he took the heavy can from my straining arms and walked the few feet necessary to put it in place. "Got another? I'll carry it out for you." His shoulders had broadened and the mustache was new to me, as was the scarred lip, but I knew him instantly. He'd popped occasionally into my thoughts over the years. Something about him had always haunted me. "It's good to see you again, Lenny," I said. "No, there's no more garbage. Thank you."

"Okay. See you around." He jogged away without another word.

I saw him often after that, always under similar circumstances. He jogged past my house twice a day. Sometimes we talked, sometimes we simply exchanged greetings. No matter how often I told him my name, he always called me "lady." Even as a casual observer, I sensed that a keen-edged sword of restrained violence walked sheathed in Lenny's being. He lived in such a state of perpetual tension that I thought him the epitome of "uptight." To him, of course, I was the one who was uptight, simply because I was older.

Somehow, though, Lenny was drawn to me. I have no idea why. Casually, he dropped pieces of his history and bits of his soul into our roadside chats. He had been a child of institutions since the age of nine: juvenile detention homes, reform schools, city and county jails, mental institutions, penitentiaries—he was a veteran of them all. He told me he came from a good family, that his only regret about his history was the embarrassment they had to endure. His crimes had always been petty, but there were a lot of them. "That's 'cause I get caught every time I even think crooked," he explained matter-of-factly. I had known young people who used drugs before, even a few who were addicted; but no one like Lenny. There was nothing he wouldn't ingest or inject or sniff or smoke or in some manner take into his body. Nothing. He played Russian roulette with capsules and tablets and powders and all the assorted chemical bullets, in every conceivable combination.

I never pretended to understand him and had ceased questioning his motivations once I realized he didn't understand them himself. Gradually, it had dawned on me that there was considerable intelligence and ability lying fallow within Lenny. He disturbed me deeply, for I often felt unfathomable anger that this young man should choose to throw away his life like so much garbage. I truly liked him but could think of no way to help him.

Once I'd found Arnie among the daisies, the bird had become a primary topic in our conversations. Mutual interest in a bird was safe, comfortable ground for us to meet on. For the first time, Lenny had begun hinting for me to invite him into the house so he could meet Arnie. "He won't talk for you," I'd told him. "I can't persuade him to talk for anyone he doesn't know well. He won't even talk for friends who visit me regularly." To my dismay, that had been a statement of truth. It had also been a good excuse. It's a hazardous world we live in. Talking to an ex-convict drug addict in plain sight on a busy street is one thing; inviting him into one's home is quite another. As fascinating as I found him, Lenny frightened me.

Then, in one of my weak moments, he had quit hinting and asked outright if he could come in for just a moment to catch a glimpse of Arnie. Without thinking, I'd said yes.

"Hey, lady, you got good vibes in here," he'd said once we were inside the house. Nervously, I invited him to sit in the living room and offered him a beverage. Absently, he requested water and walked to Arnie's cage as though in a trance. Arnie hopped down to eye-level, and the two of them began an intense inspection of each other.

Mitzi pranced over to sniff at his sweat pants. He

leaned over and scratched her head. "Hey, kitty, how are you?" he inquired of her. "Hey, I didn't know you had cats, lady. I'm a real cat man." He reached to pick her up, but that sniff had been the limits of Mitzi's tolerance for this stranger. She pranced away, her head held high with disdain. Still, from her, the Palm Beach snob, that sniff had been a major compliment.

Again I invited him to sit. Reluctantly, he backed to the chair nearest to Arnie's cage, captivated by my birdly marvel. Samantha promptly seated herself on Lenny's cap, curling into a ball, purring as though she had discovered a long-lost love. Vagabond plopped on top of Lenny's jogging shoes and sprawled.

I couldn't believe my eyes. Lenny had been embraced immediately by the cats as though he were a cherished member of the family! None of them had ever been so friendly with a stranger before.

Arnie began to fly against the front of his aviary, bouncing from perch to screen, trrrppping for attention, his signal that he wanted to come outside. Lenny stared in silent fascination.

"Hey, he's some bird, all right. I bet he'll talk for me, lady."

"I really wish he would, but I doubt it. I've tried so often to get him to talk for my friends that I'm embarrassed to mention he talks anymore. He always makes it seem I'm lying."

"Hi! Arnie. Hi. Hi! Good-morning, Peek-a-boo. Coo-coo, coo-coo. Hi. C'mere. Gimme kiss, smack-smack-smack. Hi there. Hello. Come see Arnie."

I sighed. Unpredictable bird! He was making a liar of me again. Seated uneasily on the edge of my chair, I realized Arnie was doing exactly as I'd been wanting him to do for months, talking in the presence of someone to whom I'd bragged about him. Recovering from a moment of stunned astonishment, Lenny began to laugh, a very wholesome, happy-sounding, normal sort of young man's laugh. I'd never seen Lenny smile before, let alone heard him laugh.

"Hey, he really does talk, don't he? I thought you were puttin' me on, lady. No jive. That little fella really does talk. Son of a . . . gun. Can he come out?"

I sensed the four-letter expletives Lenny was accustomed to using, reluctantly withheld by respect for me. He slipped every now and then, but had watched his language around me for some time. I had to admire his restraint under the circumstances, seeing the obvious wonder on his face.

"Certainly he can come out," I said.

I opened the door of the aviary. Arnie flew straight to the top of Lenny's head, perched there comfortably, and began belting out every word and song he knew. Lenny tried so hard to see Arnie that I feared his eyes might roll up into his head.

On impulse, I grabbed my Polaroid camera and snapped a photograph of the two of them, handing it to Lenny when it had finished developing. His entire demeanor softened when he looked at it. Smiling, he stared for a long while before offering to hand the picture back to me.

"You keep it," I said. "I can take photos of Arnie anytime."

"Yeah? I can have it? Really? Hey, thanks." He reached into the zippered pocket of his sweat shirt, pulled out a wallet, and carefully placed the photo inside, giving it all the tender consideration he might accord a memento of his girlfriend.

My household made an indelible impression on Lenny. From that time on, I was never surprised to find him at my door. I relaxed enough to enjoy his visits, though I suspected it was the animals he really came to see. He would sit silently for long stretches of time, stroking the cats, listening to Arnie talk, and watching him simply being a bird. His parting words were always an echo of Arnie's "Bye-bye, see you." And he usually entered with the offering of a gift— like the alligator gar.

That particular day, after he'd cleaned the fish, he sat with a freshly bathed and dried Arnie perched companionably on his arm. He opened his mouth to speak several times, but no words came out. Then, in a hesitant, shy voice, Lenny said, "You know, you're right, lady. I ain't goin' back to the joint. Guess I can't be like the Birdman after all. Decided I'm goin' straight. Gonna clean up my act, lay off the drugs. Got myself a good job on one of the oil rigs in the Gulf. Think I might even go back to school. Y'all are gonna see a new Lenny from now on. Bet you'd like that, huh, bird?"

"C'mere. Gimme kiss," Arnie replied.

That was the last time we saw Lenny. A few days later, I heard from some of his friends that he'd moved away from home after a fight with his father. Then I heard he'd been busted for cocaine and was on his way back to prison. He never answered the one letter I wrote to him. Perhaps he was ashamed at having failed. Lenny had never lied to me, nor said anything he didn't mean. I believe he really did try to keep his resolution, and that he could have made it. I like to think his friendship with Arnie had something to do with him even bothering to try. He'd never cared enough to make the effort before. Lenny was the first outsider to whom Arnie spoke without inhibition. The cats liked Lenny, too. I believe animals sense qualities of human character that are not always obvious to us. Somewhere at his core, there was a precious ingredient of good in Lenny.

I like to think he still has the picture of Arnie in his wallet. Judging from its worn appearance the last time I saw it, he must have taken it out often to show to friends, or perhaps just to look at by himself. I hope he still glances at it from time to time, reminding himself that life can be sweet and thinking of new beginnings for when he rejoins society's mainstream.

Somehow they reminded me of each other, the bird and the boy. I think this big, beautiful, complicated world of ours frightened them both so much they only felt completely secure within a cage. I had hoped Arnie would never change his mind on that matter—and I'd prayed that Lenny would.

I wondered if he fed the birds in the prison yard, as a Birdman would.

xiv "You can save him, Margarete. I know you can. Like you did Arnie." Chris's cherubic face puckered with sincerity as he stared up at me, his eyes soft with compassion. Clutched carefully in his chubby hands was a tiny, wiggling bundle of brown feathers.

"I don't think there's too much wrong with him," said Sammy Lee, his emerging man's voice changing pitch in midsentence. He was as dark as Chris was fair, but otherwise they looked so much alike anyone could tell they were brothers.

"Please help him." Chris extended his cupped hands toward me.

"Let me see what I can do," I said. I knew better than to make promises about helping any wild bird; I still thought it was almost a miracle that Arnie had lived. Looking closely, I decided that Chris's foundling was a sparrow and told the boys so. Judging by the soft fluffiness of the feathers, he was a baby, but older than Arnie had been when he fell from the nest. There was nothing conspicuously wrong with him. "He seems okay," I said. "I think the best thing is for you to put him back into the nest, Chris. He probably just fell out. His parents know how to take care of him much better than we do, you know."

"Uh-uh. He didn't fall out of his nest, Margarete. He had an accident."

"Oh? What happened?"

"He flew into Sidney's truck," Sammy said. "He must have knocked himself silly. Maybe he has a concussion." Sidney was their older brother.

"Sid thought he flew away again," Chris elaborated, "but I found him on the ground. He can't fly. Will you fix him up so I can have a pet like Arnie? Please, Margarete?"

"You know, most wild birds don't make good pets," I cautioned. "They're usually very unhappy in captivity, Chris."

"Arnie's happy."

"Arnie's different. I never intended to keep him for a pet. I tried to return him to the wild. He made up his own mind to stay, but that's not something you can usually expect from wild animals."

"This bird must not be wild. He doesn't even try to get away from us."

"Chances are, your little bird is stunned by his accident, Chris. He'll probably be ready to fly away again today. You wouldn't want to keep him if he'd be unhappy, would you? If I make him well, will you let him decide if he wants to stay with you or rejoin his own family?"

Chris's face clouded with disappointment, and he stared at the floor in unhappy concentration. Clearly, my proposal had never entered his mind. As with many children, to him all animals were potential pets.

"You wouldn't want him to be unhappy, would you, Chris?" Sammy coaxed, maturity winning out over his own boyish inclination to have a new pet.

"He won't be unhappy. He likes us."

"You like me, too," Sammy said. "But how would you feel if I locked you up in your room forever? Would you be happy then?"

"No," he answered, still looking at the floor, tears muffling his voice.

"That's a big, brave boy," I encouraged. "It's a wonderful thing to help an injured animal so he can go back to a normal life with his own family, you know. I'll bet his mother and father are worried sick about him right now, just like your parents would be if you were missing."

"Do I get to turn him loose again when he's well?" he asked, his mood brightening a bit.

"Certainly you can. You're the one who rescued him. Let's see how badly he's hurt."

The sparrow had no obvious injuries, I determined after close scrutiny. He had no detectable broken bones, no bleeding, nothing to give a clue to precisely what was ailing him. Perhaps Sammy had been right and the bird had suffered a concussion. There was something strange about him, though, a strangeness that nagged at the back of my mind, yet I was unable to put my finger on it.

"I'll bet Sidney feels terrible about running into him," I said.

"Oh, Sid didn't run into him," Sammy said. "The truck was parked in the driveway, and the bird flew into the window like he didn't see where he was going. Dumb bird."

"That's strange. Maybe he's ready to fly if we give him the chance." I placed the sparrow on the breakfast bar, wanting to see how well he maneuvered on his own. Promptly, he sat upon his rear end, his legs jutting straight forward, his tail feathers splayed backwards, his wings extended to the sides and resting on the slick surface as though for balance. It was a very strange posture for a bird. He looked bewildered and frightened and pathetic. He stared at me as though asking me to explain his plight to him. Slowly at first, then faster and faster, he began to spin—round and round and round. Propelling himself with wing tips and legs, he looked for all the world like a child's wind-up toy.

The boys giggled. The bird kept chirping and spinning.

"Listen to what he's saying: 'Chip, chip, chip.' I'll call him Chipper," Chris said. "He must be feeling better already. Look how he's playing."

"Looks to me like his legs are paralyzed," Sammy observed. "Maybe they're broken."

"Looks to me like he's hungry," I said, picking him up again. It was breaking my heart to watch him. I cuddled him, making soothing sounds to calm him. That's when it all clicked into place. I sniffed at his feathers. He had a familiar, penetrating, musky sweet odor: the smell of modern chemistry. "Pesticide!"

"Huh?" The boys looked puzzled.

"He's been poisoned. Here, you can smell it up close. He's covered with pesticide. That's what's wrong with him." I wondered what to do about it.

"Why don't you give him a bath?" Sammy suggested.

"Good idea," I said. "I'll wash off as much as possible. The trouble is, we don't know how much he inhaled already, how much soaked into his skin, or just how it's working on his body. All we can do is try, and hope we're in time to help him."

"If he's poisoned, maybe you could pump his stomach and make him throw up, Margarete," Chris suggested brightly. His chin propped between his hands at the bathroom sink, he was watching the bathing operation with great interest. The little bird submitted to the bath without protest.

"I wish it were that simple, Chris, but it's not. This poison is all over his body. If we can wash it off, that'll prevent him from getting any more into his system, but it won't take out what's already inside of him."

"He's not going to die, is he?" Chris asked with alarm.

"Maybe, just maybe, he'll get well, but I can't promise you he will. You're a big boy, and I want you to understand that he might die no matter what we do. Even if he lives, he may be crippled for life. Poisons can be weird."

"If he gets well, I'll help him find his home, Margarete. And if he's crippled, I'll always take care of him. Just don't let him die, okay?"

"I'll do everything that's humanly possible," I promised.

"You saved Arnie. I know you can save Chipper, too."

"I'll try my best to help him," I told Chris. He and his brother left, trusting me to work a miracle. The bird looked at me with eyes reflecting the same faith I'd seen in Chris's.

I dragged the rat cage out of the closet again and turned it into a hospital unit. Right away, I gave the little bird a dose of vitamins and antibiotics. He took readily to the same basic diet I'd settled on for Arnie. Loudly demanding food when he was hungry, he eagerly opened his beak and tilted his head back to receive it. I dared to entertain hope at that; at least he had a strong will to live. He accepted me immediately as a substitute mother, never once seeming afraid.

The cats, each in turn, sniffed curiously at the sparrow, then walked away. I'd seen them exhibit more interest in a bit of lint on the rug. Their reactions surprised me because he was new, and he was extremely active with his spinning motions. It was just as well that they ignored him, though, because he was afraid of them. Where Arnie had actively reached toward the cats in curiosity, Chipper became terribly agitated if they so much as looked at him.

All the time I tended to Chipper, I watched Arnie for signs of jealousy. This was the first time I'd brought another bird into the house, and I wasn't sure how he'd react. Knowing how hard he could peck, I was reluctant in the beginning to allow him near the smaller bird. I wanted to assure him that he was the only birdly love of my life, so I invited him out of his aviary more often than usual and devoted extra time to him, but I made certain Chipper was securely locked up in the rat cage when Arnie was out.

As he usually did with strangers in the house, however, Arnie reserved judgment on Chipper until he had an opportunity to get to know him. He wouldn't go near the despised rat cage at first, but he craned curiously toward it from a safe distance, obviously inspecting the little stranger inside. He flew from my shoulder to the breakfast bar to the bookcase to the couch, reconnoitering the situation from every direction. Then, he gathered his courage, fluttered to the floor, and walked hesitantly around and around the cage, poking gently with his beak at the screening. Chipper quit spinning, settled into his odd, splayed posture, and watched Arnie intently, turning his head as necessary to keep his observer in view. Bold now, Arnie flew to the top of the cage and began to pace. His eyes never left Chipper's upturned face. He had little interest in me or anything else that day. With a pang, I realized he might have been lonely for his own kind all along and was glad to see another bird, even one from a different family.

As a precaution, I kept them apart for several days. Each time Arnie was out of his aviary, he went through the same routine, gaining a little more confidence with each visit to the cage. Chipper began to cheep to him, seemingly trying to carry on a conversation, but Arnie simply looked at him without responding. Instead of following the usual active pattern of his outings. Arnie spent almost every moment on top of the sparrow's cage, as though keeping him company.

Since they seemed so friendly, I finally decided there was no sense in keeping them separated by the bars of a cage. So, I let Arnie out one day while Chipper was still cupped in my hands. As usual, after I opened the door to the aviary, I turned and walked away, leaving it up to Arnie where he would choose to investigate in the first minutes of his outing. He quickly followed me and settled on top of my head. I could feel his talons slide toward my forehead as he stretched downward, obviously wanting a close look at the bird in my hands. "Hi! How are you?" he said. "Come see Arnie. Gimme kiss." When I sat down, he skidded down my biceps and did a little hop-walk across my forearm, cocking his head to peer with one eye at the little brown guest.

They were only a neck-stretch apart, so I tensed alertly in case Arnie decided to lunge with his beak. Chipper lay quietly in my hands, looking at Arnie with curiosity. Slowly, ever so gently, Arnie stretched forward, touching his beak to Chipper's wing and parting the feathers with his mandibles. He looked the sparrow over closely, cocking his head to one side and then the other, occasionally opening his beak over the little bird with that gesture I had come to regard as a taste-smell. Then he settled back upon my wrist, said "I love you," and launched into his entire happy repertoire. Chipper listened intently.

Afterward, I allowed them together routinely. Whenever the sparrow was with me or in his cage, Arnie usually stayed near him, sometimes serenading him, sometimes simply watching him. Often, when Arnie was talking and whistling, Chipper would cheep along with him, the two of them making a terribly discordant duo. I believe they thought they were making beautiful music together, however. Each seemed content with the nearness of the other. Chipper watched Arnie so intently that I often wondered what thoughts were going through his mind. Did he admire Arnie, regard him as family, or, perhaps, envy him?

My telephone rang a great deal more than usual during that time. Sandy, Chris's sister, would dial my number at least once a day, get me on the line, then hand the telephone receiver to her little brother for his inevitable questions: "How is my bird doing? Is Chipper any better? Is he getting well?" Sammy Lee and Sidney in turn would call with the same questions or drop by the house with Chris to see for themselves. Their cousins, Brian and Kelly, would call to ask, "How is Chris's bird doing? You're going to make him well, aren't you, Margarete?" They were all such loving children, I really did want Chipper to get well for them.

Sadly, he was not getting well. The poison had done permanent damage before we washed it off. It appeared that Chipper would always be a cripple, condemned to spend his life as a little spinning top, with his legs stretched out helplessly in front of him, his tail feathers splayed behind, his wing tips propping him up. He slept on his side, or stretched out on his tummy and chin with his beak pointed uncomfortably straight ahead. When he was awake, he would spin constantly, trying to regain proper posture, until exhaustion would overcome him. Then he would lie panting until he was rested and could start all over again.

After three weeks, he just gave up. Abruptly, he quit eating. Nothing I could do would persuade him to take food any longer. Arnie inspected him a few times at that stage, probing gently at him, urging him to quit lying there, to keep trying. Then Arnie, too, gave up. He walked away from Chipper one day and would not go near him or the cage again. When I had the little bird in my hands, Arnie would not even come near me.

Afraid he would linger, suffering needlessly, I asked seventeen-year-old Sidney if he felt capable of executing a coup de grâce, a quick twisting neck-wrench that would have ended the pain quickly. I could not bring myself to do it, no matter how much I thought it would be the right thing. Sidney looked at me with horror and swallowed mightily. He cleared his throat and blinked away the tears that he had welled into his eyes. He had been raised to believe there are some things a man must do, however, no matter what the personal price. He nodded. "I'll take Chris home and then come back," he said.

"Wait until tomorrow," I said gently. "Maybe it won't be necessary. I just want to do something if he seems to be suffering too much. You understand." He did, but I could see in his eyes that I had asked too much from a gentle, tender-hearted young man.

Chipper cheeped constantly until he was exhausted that night. His eyes watched me intently from the cradle of my hands until he could keep them open no longer. He struggled until the last to stave off sleep, as if wanting to savor every waking moment. Arnie kept a strangely still, quiet vigil upon my wrist, staring alternately from my face to the little bird's. I think we all felt the need for communion in those hours. When Chipper closed his eyes that night, it was for the last time.

We buried him in my back yard and planted a mulberry tree seedling to mark the spot. "He'll like that," I announced cheerfully to the mournful gathering. "A mulberry's such a friendly tree for birds. Now he'll always be a part of every bird family that plays and lives in this tree."

Some people would say we were being silly, of course, that the world hadn't lost much with the passing of one tiny sparrow. As I put away the shovel, though, a haiku popped into mind that pretty much summed up my sentiments. I wished I'd thought to use it as a eulogy for Chipper.

> *So one sparrow fell*
> *But suppose they all were gone*
> *Along with their song*

XV Slowly, methodically, she moved toward me. Her course was a bobbing zigzag as she moved from the roadside, down the slope, into the drainage ditch, and back up again, dragging a black plastic bag behind her. A rope belt about her waist tentatively held in place a faded chambray shirt and jeans that were several sizes too large. A red baseball cap was the only spot of color in her otherwise drab attire. Upright, she stood barely five feet tall, but then I seldom saw her upright.

Suzanne must have bent and stooped at least a thousand times every day, picking up and depositing into her plastic bag the aluminum cans and pop bottles that seemed to sprout like mushrooms overnight along the sides of the roads, in the ditches, in the middle of neatly manicured lawns. I had seen her in so many scattered parts of the community, I often wondered how many miles a day she trudged. The recycling chore she took so seriously supplemented her household's meager income and helped keep the neighborhood clean. Unfortunately, her efforts were little appreciated. As she walked, she endured the glares of people who wished she would go back where she had come from; and as she stooped, she ignored shouted insults form passing adolescents.

As I later found out, dirty looks and jeers were insignificant compared to what Suzanne had already endured. A Vietnamese refugee, she had lived her entire life under siege: the siege of a war so old few seemed to know or care what it was all about; the siege of striving to survive under brutal conditions; the siege of mass bigotry within her own country, where her half-French bloodline made her an object of scorn. Born to pain, Suzanne was blessed with stoicism.

She'd cleaned my ditch daily for weeks before we met. Walking in different directions one morning, we'd found ourselves on a collision course. She ducked her head and swerved to one side just as I sidestepped in the same direction. Her head snapped up, her cap fell off, and her long hair fell to her waist. She was very pretty. Her hair had always been tucked up inside the hat, and until that moment, I had thought her a boy. When our eyes met, she quickly looked down and tucked her chin against her collarbone. Her face was blandly expressionless.

"Hello. How are you?" I said.

She looked at me then. Her mouth opened and closed again without a sound. She mumbled something incomprehensible in Vietnamese.

"Oh, you don't speak English, do you?" I said and smiled.

She hesitated a moment, then smiled back, her eyes crinkling at the corners with the gesture. Her features were suddenly transformed from merely pretty to stunningly beautiful. "No," she said simply and shrugged. I sighed. She clucked her tongue loudly as she tucked her hair back under the retrieved baseball cap. Strangers without a common language, we couldn't very well converse. With another shrug and a parting smile, she stepped around me and continued on her way.

After that, we exchanged waves and smiles whenever she came by and I was out in the yard. Her greeting was always quick, as though she dared not tarry at her task.

One day, I carried a sackful of aluminum cans out to the road when I saw her rounding the corner. (The children for whom I'd been collecting them had lost interest in recycling for spending money.) She kept her hands at her sides as I held the sack out to her. "For you," I said and opened the bag to show her the contents. Her hand reached out, then withdrew again as she shook her head no. "For you," I said again. I grabbed her wrist and thrust the sack into her hand.

"Parlez-vous français?" she asked hopefully.

"No," I said regretfully. *"Sprechen Sie Deutsch?"*

She shook her head no. I sighed and she clucked her tongue. Simultaneously, we shrugged, smiled, and went our separate ways again. The next day, I found a bagful of cucumbers at the foot of my stairs, the treasures from her garden declaring that she was grateful for the cans but unwilling to accept them as charity.

My heart went out to her. We were sisters in many ways. I, too, had spent childhood years in a homeland wracked by war. I, too, had come to America speaking no English and possessing little more than a determination to find peace. Even now, we were both outsiders within a small, insular community. We were different

146

in one important way, though: I had found some close friends here, and I didn't think she had. It's difficult to achieve friendship without a common language. I was certain she was lonely, but she invariably declined when I invited her into my home.

We would have continued that way, our entire acquaintanceship comprised of distant greetings and frustrated shrugs, sighs, and clucks, but I thought I knew of a way to persuade her to come into the house, where we might have a better opportunity to get to know one another. She loved birds, I had discovered, or at least I had observed that the one thing that could distract her from her tedious task was a bird: a mockingbird dive-bombing a passing cat; purple martins gliding high in the sky; cardinals flitting through the treetops; a flock of geese, honking on their way to a morning feeding at a nearby rice field; starlings pecking about in the grass. Any flurry of feathers would bring her to a halt. She would stand transfixed, a sparkle of wonder in her eyes, a wistful smile upon her lips as she watched the birds. She had to meet Arnie!

With that resolution in mind, I had watched for her this particular morning. When she rounded the corner, I walked out to the end of my driveway to wait for her. It was distressing to watch her working so hard for so little reward. One, two...twelve...twenty ...mentally, I found myself counting the number of times she bent over for her treasured trash. I suppose she had reason to be grateful for litterbugs. Unexpectedly, rain began falling from the one dark cloud in the blue spring sky. Drops spattered in the dust at the edge of the road. Suzanne looked up, squinting her eyes against the sun, and smiled at me. Then she dug into her bag and pulled out a rain poncho. She slipped it over her head, then continued her bobbing zigzag until she drew abreast of me. By that time, the rain was pouring, creating a thousand shimmering rainbows in reflection of undaunted sunshine.

"Good morning," I said to her.

"Good...mor-ning," she struggled, then grinned. She'd recently begun attending night school to learn English, but it was an effort for her to speak it.

"Come inside," I said, tugging at her arm and pointing toward the house. "I want to show you something."

She stepped back, her eyes widening, and looked up and down the street. She had reasons for her fear, I knew. Two crosses had been burned upon nearby lawns within the past year; one to greet the first black family to move into the neighborhood; the other in the yard of the rented house where Suzanne lived with twenty assorted relatives. She shook her head no, made circles with her thumbs and forefingers, put them in front of her eyes like glasses and looked quickly from side to side, then pointed at me. She was afraid someone might be watching, worried that it would cause trouble for me if she accepted my hospitality. A drop of water rolled down her cheek, maybe rain, maybe a tear.

"Please come inside," I insisted. "I want you to see my bird." I flapped my arms, pantomiming, and pointed to the house again. "Please. A favor for me."

She wavered, looked worriedly about, then nodded. "For you, a favor, yes." When I turned, she put her hand between my shoulder blades and shoved to hurry me along. As we ran, her bag of cans and bottles clanked at her side. At the foot of the stairs, she set the bag down and began to strip off her dripping outer garments. "Hi. Hi. Hi! C'mere," Arnie screeched from behind the closed door upstairs. Her face brightened with astonishment as she dropped baseball cap and poncho to the floor. Eagerly, she climbed the stairs behind me and stood near the door, looking at the aviary with a smile.

I grabbed towels from the linen closet. Drying my hair with one, I tossed the other to her. She caressed the thick, plush towel as one would the hair of a loved one, rubbing it against her face with pleasure.

"Nice home," she complimented, looking around. She hugged herself. "Feel good. Nice home."

It reminded me of what Lenny had often said, that my home had "good vibes." I like that expression and consider it particularly appropriate when applied to a home. It's "good vibes" that make one feel immediately comfortable and warm within strange surroundings. I was pleased with her reaction.

"Thank you, Suzanne," I said. "I think so, too. Come here. This is what I wanted to show you." I led her to Arnie's aviary. He hopped down to eye-level, craning forward to peer at her with curiosity. "Hi there. How are you?" he inquired courteously.

Suzanne put her hand to her mouth and giggled. "He talk." She tittered from behind splayed fingers.

Putting water on the stove for tea, I smiled and signaled for her to sit. She shook her head no, indicating her wet clothes. Firmly, I took her by the arms, guided her to the couch, and gently pushed her down. Arnie began rebounding against his screening, trrrppping in annoyance that I had deprived him of this new attention. I went to his door and opened it a crack. "Okay if he comes outside?" I asked Suzanne.

She clapped her hands together, her face brightening. "Oooohh, yes, please!"

Arnie flew straight to the top of her head, where he began parting her hair with his beak. Then he slid down the back to catch the end of one long black strand and climbed with it back to the center of her crown. She giggled again. When he had tired of playing with her hair, he settled on her shoulder and launched into his version of "Mary Had a Little Lamb," followed by his entire repertoire of words and sounds and whistles.

Suzanne sat frozen, not wanting to move enough to disturb him, her tea cooling in its cup. She faced straight ahead, smiling broadly, only her eyes moving to the side in a vain attempt to view him. Clearly enchanted with Arnie, she stayed a long time that day, politely trying to converse with me. Somewhere in the middle of the conversation, she made the statement, "I love birds. They so free, go where want, be happy all time. No birds in Vietnam. Arnie like miracle. He smart. Speak English better than me." Struggling to understand her pronunciations, I assured her that her English was good already and that it would get better with time.

As she donned her clammy outer garments at the foot of the stairs, she thanked me, hesitated a moment, then said a few words as though unsure if it was all right to say them. "Okay I come back?"

"Certainly," I said. "Yes, very okay you come back. Please do come back." I squeezed her hand with friendly assurance.

She doubled over and ran across the clearing, then sidled away up the hedgerow beneath the pecan trees. I wondered if she had always moved so furtively, if she would ever learn that it was no longer necessary to do so now that she lived in a land untouched by war, blessed with peace and justice and the American Way. Then I remembered that the reality of the American Way occasionally includes the burnings of crosses upon well-manicured lawns in tranquil neighborhoods. There are rotten apples in every nation's barrel, unfortunately.

I was glad I'd been able to persuade her to come into my house, to begin a tentative friendship. Reflecting on our visit and the way she had delighted in Arnie, I realized I'd really enjoyed having her as a guest. We had managed to struggle through conversation with a combination of hand signs, facial contortions, body language, and acting-out to fill in the gaps between the limited vocabulary we shared. What a nice mutual interest we had—a love for birds. How sad that she'd had no . . . ?! "No birds in Vietnam"?!

Her words hit me now with cold horror. Had we really done that? Had Agent Orange and fire bombs and the steamroller of violence really eradicated the birds from Vietnam? How strange it must be, to live in a world without birds, in landscapes rendered barren by defoliation, where people walked in joyless furtiveness. The more civilized we become, the more barbaric our wars are. I had heard birds singing even after the last bomb fell on Munich during World War II. No birds? Of course, Suzanne had spoken only of her own experience, and she was just one small individual. Wasn't she? Perhaps I had taken her too literally. Or maybe I had heard her wrong. With a shudder, I forced my thoughts back to everyday reality in time to hear a melodious "Bobwhite" ring across the field next door. I went back upstairs and let Arnie out of his aviary for an extra outing.

Suzanne came back after that, always creeping stealthily to and from my door, seeming afraid to walk in the open. Apparently, the caution was ingrained into her psyche as necessary to survival. She always arrived with an attitude of barely suppressed excitement, however, her face beaming like that of a small child on the way to the circus. Nevertheless, she spaced her visits well apart, as though seeing Arnie was a special pleasure she reserved until the yearning was almost unendurable.

She was enraptured at seeing him close up; enthralled with his ability to speak; overcome with amusement that he would walk all over her, intimately probing and prodding with busy beak at her person, her clothing, her hair. She talked to him more than she did to me. It was an idiosyncrasy I understood well. Talking to an animal, she didn't have to struggle and fumble for her words. I had the feeling she was telling him her highest hopes, her darkest fears, and her deepest hurts, and that she was feeling better with the sharing. I was not privy to much of her personal life or private feelings. These intimacies she reserved for Arnie, confiding with whispered words of her native language. With me, she was polite, appreciative, but never overly revealing.

I knew of her gentleman friend only in that I knew she had one; but she never told me enough about him to make him any more real than a phantom. I knew about her children, about her hopes for them, and about her beaming pride in them. While America was not quite heaven for Suzanne, it would be for her two sons. She was pleased that their Oriental blood was diluted by her half-French genes and the American genes of their father. In this new country she thought the mixed ancestry would be an advantage for them.

As we spoke our farewells at the foot of the stairs one day, she hesitated, then spoke with pleading eyes. "Okay I bring kids? See Arnie?"

"Of course! Yes, okay you bring kids." I was delighted. I imagined them to be as sweet of disposition as she, round-faced, smiling toddlers.

I was shocked to find her at my door one day with two teenagers. Both boys were tall and muscular with dark hair and eyes, golden complexions, and finely chiseled Western features. Hauntingly handsome, they would have stood out in any crowd. Their splendor was marred, however, by stern frowns and the tight look of anger about their lips and eyes.

Suzanne's hands fluttered to her mouth, then back down again. She, too, wore a frown. "These my boys," she said. "Okay see Arnie?"

"Of course. Please come in," I said. "Hi. I'm Margarete." I held out my right hand to shake theirs, but dropped it when they ignored the gesture and stared down at their shuffling feet instead of looking at me.

Suzanne snapped a quick spate of words in Vietnamese. Puzzled, I led the way up the stairs as they followed with heavy footsteps. When they entered the door, all three cats ran for hiding places. Instead of sitting when I invited them to do so, the boys stood rigidly near the door, their thumbs hooked into the pockets of their jeans. They looked around my living room, barely moving their downcast heads, until their baleful glares came to rest on Arnie's cage.

Suzanne's face brightened as she walked over to talk to Arnie, beckoning the boys to follow her. When they didn't do so immediately, she spoke in Vietnamese again, softly this time, a hint of pleading in her tone. They moved to join her at the aviary, dragging their feet as though headed for a dentist's chair. When they drew near, Arnie hopped to his top perch and crouched. The boys gave him only a perfunctory glance. Suzanne's face fell.

The entire visit went that way. The boys moved like marionettes, reacting only to Suzanne's Vietnamese pleas and commands. When I asked her if they spoke English, one of the boys said tonelessly and without accent, "Yes, we speak English very well." It was the only thing either of them said the entire time. I offered them something to drink, but they refused with headshakes, never once looking at me. I felt as though I had stumbled into the middle of a family quarrel that would resume as soon as they were in private again.

My own family wasn't exactly at its best, either. The cats wouldn't come out of hiding to greet our guests. Even Vagabond, who'd taken a particular liking to Suzanne during previous visits, didn't so much as peep around the corner. Though I left the door of his aviary open, Arnie refused to come out. Aside from an occasional Bronx cheer, he didn't make a sound.

Undoubtedly, Suzanne had praised Arnie mightily to the boys, and I think she'd planned proudly to show her sons off to me. How disappointing the occasion must have been for her. I felt great compassion as we said good-bye at the foot of the stairs. The boys walked away while she and I talked. I noted that where she always crept furtively under cover of landscape, they swaggered boldly across open spaces to the road. A frown creased her face as she watched their retreating backs. Today, for the first time since I'd known her, she looked old enough to be the mother of adolescents. "I so sorry," she apologized. "They not polite."

"They are teenagers," I said lamely. "Teens are hard years for kids."

She clucked her tongue, momentarily at a loss for words. "They not bad boys. Everything so hard for them. So much new to learn. Americans not like them, they not like Americans." As though a dam had burst, she began to pour out her troubled heart, which was filled with trepidations about her children. Their new home had not proved to be the haven she had expected.

"Two, three times in week, all time my boys have fight," Suzanne said. "No one want be friends. Sometimes they say war better, maybe better we go back Vietnam. They very *misérable* here." She paused, seeming to have run out of words.

"Do they hate all Americans?" I asked.

She clucked her tongue, nodded. "Even my boyfriend. He so good to them. They not trust. I think meet you, see Arnie, they know all Americans not full of hate. They laugh at stories I tell of Arnie. Say only special person have bird like him. I call you friend, they think you Vietnamese." Again, she expressed herself with the tongue-cluck, a shrug, the spreading of hands in frustration. Then she began to cry.

"Oh, Suzanne, all Americans do not hate. Most of us are good people, loving people, peaceful people. But..." How could I ease for her the fact that she hadn't left all the world's ugliness behind in Vietnam? How could I explain that, even in America, all the goodness and love and peace in the world still have not overcome bigotry and hatred and violence? In the face of her experiences, how could I make her believe that, despite it all, she must continue to believe in the possibility of a better life for herself and her two sons? "Suzanne, I wish..." I fumbled.

"I know," she said softly. "I know how is. I live

long time, learn much. My boys young, must learn, too. I not know how help."

I grabbed her by the shoulders and shoved her back up the stairs where we could sit comfortably until she had it all off her chest. She had to talk to someone sometime; and maybe Arnie would serve as a minor anesthetic for a while. Regaining composure over a cup of tea, neither of us knew what to say at that point. I couldn't come up with a single comforting thought, and I think she was ashamed of having let her feelings show as much as she had. She kept her head bowed, avoiding my eyes.

I opened the door of the aviary, allowing Arnie to join us, hoping he would amuse her as always. This time, true to habit, he flew immediately to Suzanne's head and began to play with her hair. Her mournful expression disappeared as she succumbed to the charm of her little feathered friend. "How are you?" Arnie said. "Hi there. C'mere. Gimme kiss. Peek-a-boo. I love you." Suzanne giggled. "I love you, too, Arnie," she said.

"Every place in America is not like here, Suzanne," I said, shattering the camaraderie of the moment, but feeling I must speak. "This is such a big country, filled with so many different kinds of people, that there's room for everyone to find happiness somewhere. Don't give up, Suzanne. We all have to search for happiness until we find it. We have to keep a dream in our hearts and keep believing the dream is possible."

"I know. I dream. I think boys, me, be happy here. How can be happy? So many people want us not here. Is hard. Is very hard."

"Yes, I understand. Your people have been welcomed in some places in America more than they have been here, though. Maybe someday you can go someplace else, someplace where you can find your dream."

"That what he say. My boyfriend. He want marry. Take boys to Colorado." She paused, then added in a wistful tone, "He say there mountains in Colorado. I homesick for mountains."

"Oh, how wonderful! Colorado is beautiful. Everything is different there. I think you and the boys will all be very happy there."

She didn't reply, concentrating her attention on Arnie. The mournful expression was back on her face.

"You are going to do it, aren't you? You are going to marry your boyfriend and go to Colorado? Aren't you?!" I felt like shaking her, like screaming at her until she realized it was the only sensible thing to do. "Suzanne, you must!" I commanded indignantly.

Without looking at me, she shook her head firmly in the negative, clucked her tongue in agitation. She spoke to Arnie in Vietnamese.

"Why not?" I demanded to know, ashamed to find myself acting as though I had the right to control her life, yet wanting so badly to persuade her to reach for happiness. "Don't you love your boyfriend?"

Tears in her eyes again, she said, "I love him, yes. Very much. Can not go to Colorado. Too hard start over again. All places same thing. Better same thing I know than new same thing. Too hard."

The soul-weariness in her voice stilled my tongue. I couldn't guarantee she would find happiness anywhere. Certainly, though, she would have a better chance in Colorado, married to a man she loved. It seemed to me a door had been opened to a promising new future for her and her sons, yet she was going to slam it shut rather than risk being disappointed again. I was convinced she was making the wrong decision. Staying here would continue to be heartbreakingly difficult for her. Given the choices, this place was as wrong for Suzanne and her sons as...as...I had a flash of inspiration.

"Suzanne, all places are *not* the same! I want to show you something."

For once I was glad of my basic laziness. The things

156

I needed for my little demonstration were still in the closet instead of the attic where they belonged. Digging them out, I set the stage on the breakfast bar. Now, if only Arnie would cooperate, just this once, and do what I expected of him.

"You think Arnie is happy, yes?" I asked.

She looked puzzled, but nodded her head emphatically.

"Arnie is happy because now he lives in a place he likes." I pointed to the aviary. "That place is the right place for Arnie. But he has not always been happy. Here, I will show you what a difference a place can make to happiness."

Arnie, curiously checking out what I was up to, never suspected a thing. I grabbed him. He squirmed and squawked loudly. "It's for a good cause, Arnie," I murmured. Hastily, I put him into the rat cage and closed the door.

"This was Arnie's first home," I explained to Suzanne's wide-eyed astonishment. "To him, this cage was like Vietnam was to you. It was not the right for him."

Nicely cooperative, Arnie fluttered with great agitation about the small cage, banging into the sides, clinging upside down from the top, screeching loud protests.

Opening the door just wide enough to admit my hand, I grabbed his tiny body again and transferred him to the parakeet cage. Obligingly, he repeated his reaction to the rat cage. "Because the other cage wasn't right for him," I explained hastily to Suzanne, "I put Arnie in here for his second home. He didn't like it any more than the first cage, you can see. To Arnie, this cage was like Texas is to you now." On cue, at that moment Arnie remembered his old trick with the food dishes. He shoved one of them out onto the countertop and hopped to freedom through the opening. Scolding me every wingbeat of the way, he flew directly to the top perch of his aviary. I closed the door. He launched promptly into "Mary Had a Little Lamb."

"See," I indicated to Suzanne, so proud my little drama had gone exactly the way I had hoped it would. "Different place. Right place for Arnie. He's very happy in that home. All places are not the same, Suzanne. You are not happy in this place, like Arnie was not happy in his first two places. The change made him happy. Maybe a change will make you happy. I think Colorado would make a big difference in life for you. And for your boys."

"I go now," she announced absently. She didn't comment at all on my demonstration, didn't even say good-bye to Arnie. She was so preoccupied that she forgot herself and walked directly across the lawn instead of hugging the shrubbery as usual.

Weeks went by and I didn't see Suzanne, but she was on my mind frequently. Perhaps she came by the house when I wasn't home, I thought, for I was very much on the go during that period. Even so, I began to worry that I had offended her by trying to tell her what to do with her life. It really was none of my business, was it? But then, I wasn't able to allow a stray cat to go hungry, or a newly hatched bird to lie helpless among the daisies. How could I stand by and do nothing while a friend threw away her best chance for a promising new beginning, for the possibility of happiness?

"I guess I blew it, Arnie," I confided gloomily. "I really have to learn to keep out of other people's business someday. I think I've lost us a good friend."

"I love you," he comforted. "Gimme kiss." Little darling, he was oblivious of my faults.

I continued to be troubled over Suzanne. Then the postcard arrived in the mail. The photograph was of breathtakingly beautiful snow-capped mountains—the Rocky Mountains of Colorado. The postmark was illegible and there was no return address, but the message was clear.

"Hi to Arnie. I happy. Boys happy. Thank you. Suzanne."

XVI Monsters of every description lay in ambush over each hilltop and around every bend. Crouching behind billboards, sprawling across the interstate highway, lurking atop overpasses, were giant spiders, fire-breathing dragons, loathsome blobs of slime, vile-smelling skunk-apes and, of course, alien invaders. It was a dangerous drive we were making from southern Florida back to southern Texas. We had picked up Travie and Kyle in Boca Raton for another summer interlude, and they were busy protecting us.

"Ka-pow! Ka-pow-pow-pow! Pow! Pow! Kaa-pow! Ka-pow!"

"Ack! Ack! Ack! Ah-ah-ah-ah-ah-ah-ah! Rat-tat-ta-ta-ta-ta-ta-ta-ta-ta!"

I gritted my teeth, tried to close my ears, and focused my thoughts on the road ahead as a good driver should do in the face of such danger and so much noise. The reverberations of their gunshot sound effects echoing within the car were jarring. With luck, nature grants nerves of steel to parents and deafness to grandparents for such times. Blessed with neither at the moment, I resorted to deviousness. "Boys, this is the space age; aren't your guns outdated? I'll bet you could kill the monsters better with lasers." *Heh-heh-heh*, this clever grandmother smirked to herself; *lasers are quieter than machine guns*. Nature compensates us with some degree of wisdom after we've run the gamut of experience.

"Hey, she's right, Kyle. Change guns, hurry! There's another giant spider up there. Va-rooooom! Va-room! Va-rooooooooom! Got him! Oh-oh, there's another one! Va-rooom!"

"I'll get him. Ka-shoooom! Ka-shoom! Wow, I got him with only two shots, Trav. You better work on your aim. Here come two more! Shoot, Travie, shoot!"

Arnie had inspired this game with which the boys whiled away the tedious hours of driving. Perched within a travel cage that was a miniature replica of his aviary, he had proved to be a happy traveler—except when we had to drive under overpasses. They terrified him. The shadow that enveloped the car for those brief moments triggered an instinctive reaction in Arnie, causing him to duck and crouch in obvious fear. Though he probably thought the shadow was that of a bird of prey, the boys fabricated their imaginary monsters as the danger from which he must be protected. The game kept them entertained, but did little to reassure Arnie.

Aside from those occasional shadows, however, he

thought life on the road was a marvelous experience. He enjoyed every new thing he encountered with the curious delight of any inquisitive, intelligent creature, and he serenaded us constantly during the hours of riding in the car. From his observation post in the back seat, he watched the scenery with great interest as we whizzed through four states.

Though Arnie probably would have ridden forever, enjoying every moment of the adventure, we humans were unanimously overjoyed to pull into my driveway in Texas. It had been a brutally tiring trip. The boys had been scheduled to fly to me that year, but two friends and I had decided to take a whirlwind sightseeing vacation and go pick them up. By the time we arrived back home, an old belief of mine had been confirmed; the typical American vacation is designed to test the limits of human endurance.

I had taken Arnie along because I would not risk the possibility that he might quit eating and die of loneliness while I was gone. Birds have been known to do that. The cats, however, absolutely would not fit into the car in which we'd decided to go. Reluctantly, I had left them at home under the watchful eye of a friend. Back in Texas, I was anxious to see how they had fared without me.

As the boys and I struggled through the door with our luggage, I expected a grand welcome. Instead of running to greet us, however, the three felines waited side-by-side like Supreme Court justices convened to render an unfavorable verdict. Their eyes, fixed upon me, held all the depthless malevolence that has earned cats a bad reputation since the beginning of time. I knew immediately I was in serious trouble with them.

I countered their condemnation with cheerfulness: "Hi, kitties! We're home! Aren't you glad to see us? Come, Mip-Mip. Come, Sammie. Come, Bundy. Say hello to the boys."

Vagabond wavered for a moment, and then started

toward us, but Samantha cuffed him back into line. Mitzi pointed her nose high, sniffed and pranced with regal disdain toward the bedroom. With a plebian imitation of the snob's practiced snub, Samantha trotted to a window, hopped up and stared out at the yard with great concentration. Vagabond looked uncertainly from his mother to us and back again, then decided to sell out. He ambled over to his food dish and glared to let me know the price of his good will—Bundy can be bought as easily as Garfield.

"I think they're mad at you, Margarete," Travie said.

"Well, I guess they have a right to be. I'll be extra nice to them for a while. They'll forgive me in no time, I'm sure."

"What are you doing? C'mere," Arnie said and fluttered against the screening of the travel cage. When I let him out, he flew a few bobbing and weaving turns about the room, doing a joyful aerial dance, then landed on the top perch of his aviary. After a careful scrutiny, he slid down to the bottom of his cage and walked the floor, inspecting every inch with his beak. Apparently satisfied that everything was exactly as he'd left it, he settled onto the middle perch and burst into "Mary Had a Little Lamb."

I bustled about, getting us all settled in again, while the boys began peace negotiations with the fretful felines. Even after I'd fed them, they were still snubbing me, but Sammie and Bundy had decided not to hold my betrayal against the boys. Mitzi continued to sulk under my bed.

Unfortunately, the hostility of the cats wasn't the only unpleasant part of the homecoming for me. Now that I was back, I had to face up to, and find a way of coping with, the problems I had fled briefly when I decided to take the vacation. The trip had really been a financial impracticality, but I concluded after much agonizing that I needed to get away to clear my head so I could think of a logical way out of my dilemma. From every angle, however, the handwriting was on the wall: I was either going to have to find a buyer for the Texas property within the next few months, or I was going to lose it.

Taxes on the property had more than quadrupled in the past few years and seemed destined to continue going up. Thanks in part to the storm and flood damage the area had suffered the year before, insurance rates had shot way up, and there was a big premium payment coming due at the end of summer. Worst of all, bank interest rates were hovering around the twenty percent mark, and my loan on the property was due for renewal at those new rates. Month by month, the place had been eating me alive for five years, and there was no way I could continue to cope with the spiraling costs.

Perhaps it was just as well I'd been backed into a corner and forced to face reality at last. Just two months earlier I had almost revived some of the old illusions I'd had about developing the property. Realizing that the old business debts would soon be paid off, I'd decided it was time to remodel the downstairs into another apartment, perhaps even to add the first wing onto the building. Toward that end, I had gone to the bank to apply for another loan and bought a load of recycled lumber at a bargain price. Unfortunately, the lumber had not been owned by the man who sold it to me, a fact I found out only after a day's worth of hard labor loading it onto a rented trailer—and just in the nick of time to get my money back. The bank loan hadn't gone through either, because in the face of an uncertain economy, the bank was issuing no new loans.

What had seemed to be misfortune at the time that plan fell through, however, turned out to be a stroke of good luck. I had been able to consider going further into debt only because my original dream about having a Texas oil well seemed on its way to fulfillment. Exactly as I had imagined it would happen, a man really cleanings I gave it, so I didn't dare let him see the tampering I was doing now.

"You won't notice a thing when I'm finished, Arnie," I assured him as he pecked at the screening.

"What are you doing?" he demanded.

"It's nothing you'll notice, Arnie," I said. "Trust me." I taped faster.

"Come see Arnie. He's a little bitty baby boy. Yes he is. Gimme kiss. Good'morning. Good morning!" I finished my project and backed away from the cage just as Arnie greeted my grandson.

Travie stumbled from the bedroom, rubbing sleep from his eyes. He was usually a late sleeper, and I was glad that today he was the first boy out of bed. I wanted a few minutes in private with him to let him know how much he had inspired me the night before. Waking is a slow process for Travie, however; his mind really doesn't get into gear until he's been up and around for a while. He shuffled to the couch and laid his head on the armrest, blinking his eyes and yawning. I didn't have the patience to wait for him to become alert today. The moment he lifted his head, I thrust his glass of orange juice at him and put my arm around his shoulders. "I have big news for you, Travie," I said. "We're going to do something wonderful together."

He peered at me through slit eyes and yawned mightily, indicating obvious interest with the word "Um."

"Let me explain. Remember how we talked about my money problems last night?"

"Um." It was a flat, deflated, really bored sound. His eyes closed.

"Okay, I'll skip the details and get to the interesting part. Wait until you hear about the really neat project we're going to have for this summer."

"Um?" There was a spark of infinitesimal, polite interest at last. He opened his eyes halfway.

"I'm going to use your idea, Travie. We are going

"I'll loan you the money you need," he said brightly. "I save quarters, sometimes even dollars in the bank, you know. I have lots of money. You can have it all."

"That's really very sweet of you, Travie, but I'm afraid my money problems are much bigger than your savings could ever cope with."

He rested his chin in his palm, looked thoughtful for a moment, then smiled widely. "Arnie can help you! He talks much much better this year than he did last summer. He's ready to be a star, I think. He really is Superbird, you know. Arnie can make as much money for you as the water-skiing squirrel in Florida does for his owner!"

Lost for words, I hugged my grandson, then tucked him into bed for the night. He'd given me a lot to think about as I awaited sleep that night. Arnie had come a long way in the past year. His vocabulary had expanded tremendously, and his pronunciations had achieved great clarity. Rather than being shy and hesitant to speak around people now, he was a regular ham when the whim hit him to talk. It had been a while since I'd thought of the commercial possibilities he might represent. I was probably setting myself up with another impossible dream, but maybe, just maybe, Arnie would be the way out of my dilemma.

The next morning it was difficult to restrain myself from waking the boys. They were going to be my helpers in the project I had formulated, and I was dying to tell them all about it. As excited as I was, it wasn't easy to be a thoughtful, considerate adult person. Nevertheless, I forced myself to let the children sleep. After all, there were some preparations with which I could occupy myself. Armed with a roll of masking tape, I went to work on Arnie's cage. He strained forward on his perch to get a good look at my activities. I shifted my body so he couldn't see my busy hands and talked nonsense to distract him. Arnie was very possessive about his cage. He barely tolerated the daily to let the entire world know that Arnie is Superbird! See what I've done?" I pointed to the setup I had rigged to Arnie's cage. Interested now, Travie opened his eyes all the way. "I love you. Gimme kiss," Arnie said when he heard his name. I felt a twinge of guilt that my project might somehow be tainted with immoral overtones, then decided that was nonsense. Arnie loved all the attention he could get and would be happy to help me. I plunged on.

"I taped the microphone to Arnie's cage so we can make recordings of him talking. We're also going to take photographs of him and write letters to a lot of people. Maybe we can get Arnie on television or into the movies even. The possibilities are endless. There are lots of animal stars besides the squirrel you mentioned. There's Fred the cockatoo and Morris the cat and before you were born there were famous dogs like Lassie and Rin Tin Tin; and horses like Trigger and Silver. Francis, the talking mule, did you ever hear of him? And there was Elsa, the lion. Oh, people love talented animals!" I was babbling, I knew, but I couldn't seem to stop myself. My enthusiasm was infecting Travie, too, though. His eyes were wide with interest, his face beaming with enthusiasm.

"Wow! That's neat, Margarete! Really neat! Arnie will be a movie star, and a television star, just like Miss Piggy and Kermit and Bugs Bunny and Daffy Duck!"

"Yes, Travie, maybe Arnie will be just as big as Miss Piggy and all the rest." I hugged him, but he squirmed out of my arms.

"Oh, boy, Arnie's going to be a star! I have to tell Kyle." All traces of sleep gone now, he was off the couch and running back into their bedroom like a shot. "Kyle, hey, Kyle, wake up. Wake up! We're going to help Margarete make Arnie into a movie star. Superbird is going to be a superstar. Wake up Kyle! We have to get busy. We have a lot of work to do. Our Arnie is going to be a star!"

We wasted no time beginning the project that day. I taught the boys to operate the tape recorder and assigned them the job of standing by to turn it on and off as Arnie began and quit talking. I knew it wouldn't be a professional recording, but that could be done by the experts once we had someone interested. From experience with friends, I knew the first obstacle would be skepticism, total disbelief that Arnie cold speak at all. Arnie had to be heard to be believed.

While the boys were doing the recording, I began drafting letters to the right people. "Those Amazing Animals" was first on the list, of course. Then, there was Johnny Carson; Johnny loves animals and often has oddities on "The Tonight Show." The *Guinness Book of World Records* people should be told about him, of course, for he must be breaking or perhaps establishing a record of some sort. Maybe even "That's Incredible" and "Real People" would be interested. I'd think of others later. Burning with enthusiasm, we launched into the task.

The tape recordings were all important, of course. Unfortunately, the first tape we managed to get was not of the greatest quality. Totally uncooperative, perhaps excited by the nearness of the boys, Arnie spent most of the time hopping up and down his perches, pecking on his screening with his beak, doing all manner of playful things. When we played the tape back, we had some marvelous sound effects—ka-thung, ka-thung, ka-thung, as his perches vibrated to his hopping up and down; thump-thump, thump-thump, thump-thump, with all the resonance of thunder, as he pecked on his screening; chit-chit-chit-schuss, as he cleaned his feathers. The radio or television sounded always in the background, along with an occasional fit of giggles from the boys.

Barely discernible, however, there was the unmistakable sound of Arnie talking. He whizzed through his entire vocabulary and whistled his versions of "Mary

Had a Little Lamb," Beethoven's Fifth Symphony, and "Michael, Row the Boat Ashore."

Impatient, I put the tape immediately into the mail with a letter to Johnny Carson. The recording would be good enough to get across the point, I felt certain. I wanted a better one for "Those Amazing Animals," however. That program would give Arnie his best shot at stardom, I thought, and be more inclined than anyone to give a bird a break. The boys and I would have to work to perfect our technique so we could give "Those Amazing Animals" the best possible sample of Arnie's talents. That would be no big problem. We'd have the perfect tape in no time.

Unfortunately, Arnie was not thinking along quite the same lines as were we people. He had different plans.

Arnie chose this time to pull his most shocking stunt. Abruptly, he quit talking.

XVII "Superbird's a dud," Kyle said.
Looking troubled, Travie was silent for a moment, then mumbled, "Maybe he's sick, Kyle. Maybe there's some kryptonite out in the yard. Arnie wouldn't let us down without a good reason." There was more disappointment than conviction in his voice. The boys had so wanted to make a star of Arnie. They sat on the floor near the aviary with the tape recorder between them, but they'd had no reason to press the "record" button in three days.

Arnie's only sounds lately were strictly bird noises,

and none of the pretty bird noises, at that. Nonsense like ccchhhrrrppppp and queek and prrrttt and something that sounded very much like Mitzi's best hiss were his entire vocabulary now. Listening to him, I thought of a brilliant orator suddenly reduced by a catastrophic accident to the gibberish of infancy. I was as disappointed as the boys.

Far worse than the loss of his speech, was the marked change in his personality. Despite the grand plans I had made, it would have ben okay with me if he'd simply quit speaking, but muteness was the least of his symptoms. What caused me the greatest concern was the loss of his sweet disposition. His comical mannerisms and his endearingly companionable ways were gone, and I missed them terribly. Arnie was cranky now and had developed a terrible temper. To those of us who knew him, it was as drastic a change as Dr. Jekyll transformed into Mr. Hyde.

"You might as well put away the tape recorder, boys," I said. "There must be something else you'd rather be doing."

"Nah." They shrugged in unison. "There's nothing to do."

Their playthings were scattered all over the house, but they were too restless to enjoy sedentary activities, and I wouldn't let them go outside to play. The temperature had hit one hundred and twelve degrees earlier in the day, and it wasn't much cooler now. This was the worst heat wave to hit Texas in the annals of the state's weather history, and heat strokes were becoming quite common. Besides, cases of St. Louis encephalitis and of dengue fever had been reported in nearby Houston, and I wanted to protect the boys as much as possible from the danger of insect-borne diseases.

"Why don't you let Arnie out, Margarete?" Travie asked. He wanted so badly to cuddle his little feathered friend, to comfort him, to ask him what was the matter and what we could do to help him. My own thoughts followed a similar vein; I didn't know what to make of Arnie's unusual behavior. He wasn't sick as far as I could tell, just drastically different.

"Arnie, you want to come outside?" I asked as I opened the aviary door. He didn't look very interested in the proposition. Most of his time in recent days had been spent very quietly on the top perch. Except for excursions to his food trays, he didn't seem to want to move at all. Sometimes he came out when invited and sometimes he didn't. "C'mon out, Arnie," I urged, and walked away to let him decide for himself what he wanted to do.

I heard him launch from the perch with a loud "queek." Even his manner of flight had changed. Instead of the smooth strokes he usually used when flying, his wings beat at the air with short, pummeling blows. He careened like a car without brakes and landed on the back of my chair with his talons extended and spread, looking much like a hawk descending on its prey. Hopping to the arm of the chair, he promptly stole a cigarette from the pack, then dropped it with disinterest and ripped the corner half off a paper napkin. Every movement he made was nervous and jerky, every task he set for himself incomplete, yet his agitated motions never ceased for a second. As the boys moved near, he scrambled to the top of my head, his talons pinching instead of tickling.

Travie reached for him, talking in his sweetest voice. "Hi, Arnie. Poor Arnie. I wish I knew what was bothering you. C'mere, Arnie. Oww!"

"What's the matter?" I asked.

"He pecked my fingers, Margarete!"

"Let me see. Are you bleeding?"

"No. He didn't peck that hard. Honest, it didn't hurt. I was just surprised. Don't be mad at him."

"I'm not mad at him, Travie, but I don't want him hurting either one of you boys. Ouch! Arnold!" Now he was pecking at the top of my head. Travie was right; the blows smarted, but they weren't hard enough to do any damage. Still, it was terribly aggressive behavior for my gentle Arnie. I was beginning to wonder if he might be feeling the mating urge. If so, he would certainly be frustrated at the lack of suitable candidates for his courting rituals.

"He's not very happy outside of his cage right now, boys. I'm going to put him back inside." When I reached to take him off my head, he fled with quick, slapping thrusts of his wings, flew halfway across the room sounding a series of "queeks," and circled around to come back toward me—to come back *at* me! With his talons thrust forward like claws, he barreled straight at my face. I froze in disbelief; surely Arnie would not actually attack me! "Arnold!" I snapped, raising my hand to shield my eyes. At the last moment, he swerved. He grabbed my ear, hung tightly for a moment, then clambered to the top of my head.

Grimly, I walked over to the aviary, and he fluttered inside. "I'm not going to let Arnie come outside anymore until he gets over whatever's bothering him, boys," I said. "I don't want either of you to open this door unless I say so. Okay?" That lunge he'd made toward my face was the last straw; my heart was still pounding with the fright he'd given me. It had been a narrowly averted accident, and I couldn't take a chance with two children in the house. The vision of him coming at me with his talons out was enough to give nightmares of the possiblity that he might deliberately go for someone's eyes. Those pecks that caused no damage to head or fingers could be disastrous if the target were an eye. He just couldn't be trusted anymore. I hated the idea of it, but I was going to have to keep him locked up like a criminal or a zoo animal.

"You're probably right, Margarete," Kyle said. "He might hurt himself. He sure can't fly good anymore. He's like an airplane without a pilot sometimes."

"He acts like something's hurting him," Travie said. "He flies like he's got splinters under his wings."

I stared at Arnie, perplexed. His beak was open, and he panted for air. He'd been doing that a lot lately, come to think of it. At times he seemed frightened of something, or nervous, though I couldn't imagine the cause. He scratched his head vigorously with one foot, then lifted a wing and frantically cleaned beneath it. ". . . like he's got splinters under his wings." Of course! I smiled. Why hadn't I thought of it before? If I was right, Arnie's actions were really quite understandable. For the next few days, I watched for other signs.

The change crept upon him gradually. It began with the shedding of a small feather here and another small feather there. I found a tail feather in the bottom of his cage one morning, then another in the afternoon. As I watched him cleaning himself one day, a wing feather slid neatly out. Grasping the feather in his mouth, Arnie stared down his beak at it as though wondering where it had come from. "Queek?" he said. After that, he lost so many breast feathers that he began to look naked. His body became a patchwork of oddly missing main feathers, bare spots, and protruding feather shafts jutting out like arrows. Each day when I cleaned the aviary, the bottom of it was filled with an increasingly thick blanket of feathers: tokens of his nondescript mousiness; portents of things to come; the sheddings of his childhood.

Arnie was a year old. He had gone into his first molt. Perhaps it would have been easier on him if he had a mother bird capable of explaining the natural phenomenon to him, of easing the trauma of change with soothing chirps of sympathy and understanding. But Arnie was bewildered and terrified. His old feathers were falling out, his new feathers were pricking their way through his skin, and he had no idea what was happening to him, or why. Feather shafts poking through the skin beneath his wings must have made flying very uncomfortable, indeed. His body must have felt like a pincushion. No wonder he had quit speaking and had changed the entire pattern of his behavior. He had felt his molt beginning long before it became obvious to me.

I didn't blame him for being frightened. The first time I saw a bird molting I thought it was dying of some terrible disease. Humans shed old skin and hair constantly, but gradually, so we don't notice our renewal process very much. I wonder how we would feel if we went bald in big patches and sloughed off large areas of our skin at the same time, and how frightened we would be if we didn't know why it was happening. Frankly, if you ask me, molting is one of nature's inefficiencies, but that's the way birds get their new coats.

Although the wild birds outdoors seem to cope quite routinely with molt, I suspect that's because they're too busy surviving to have time to give it much attention. Every indoor bird I've known has always taken it quite hard, however. Their dispositions invariably change for the worse, and they lose interest in almost everything except their own bodies. The process must be painful, at least to some degree, since the birds I've known frequently uttered pathetic little cries during the entire time they were growing new feathers. Molt is a time of misery.

Arnie certainly left no doubt in my mind about just how miserable he felt. He was taking his first molt far worse than any other bird I'd known. Totally self-absorbed, he spent all of his time frantically picking at his feathers and scratching his body. He articulated his discomfort constantly with Bronx cheers and queeks and hisses, sounding at times almost like a baby whimpering. Loud noises and abrupt movements by either the boys or the cats earned them a scolding "ttrrrupptt" sound from him. He had no time or attention to devote to talking or whistling. The boys and I cringed to see him so unhappy.

"Do you think he'll ever talk again, Margarete?" Travie asked.

"Oh, I'm sure he will." I hoped I was right. I missed his chatter most of all early in the day and sorely longed to hear his "good morning." I've always been one who bounced out of bed early in the morning, ready to tackle the problems of the world. Unfortunately, I've lived my entire life surrounded by late, slow starters. Even the cats didn't bother to stretch and rise until I had completed my waking rituals. Before Arnie learned to say it, I'd never heard my first "good morning" until my mornings were half over. That silly little starling had been the best thing to happen to the beginning of my day since I learned to like coffee. I think I would have missed the coffee less than I missed his voice now.

"Boy, he's sure not very friendly anymore," Kyle commented.

"I guess we can't make him into a superstar now," Travie said.

As though sensing their disillusionment and wanting to punish Arnie for having let down his friends, Vagabond acquired a new habit that I could not seem to stop no matter what I tried. With full momentum, he would run past the side of the aviary, jump up with an outstretched paw, and bang at the screening near where Arnie perched. He did it each time he had to go near the aviary for any reason whatsoever. Needless to say, that always startled Arnie out of his preoccupation with emerging feathers. He frequently fell off his perch and tumbled to the bottom of the aviary before his flailing wings could get a grip on the air. As far as Arnie was concerned that was the end of his friendship with one black cat. I think Vagabond eventually regretted his bratty behavior, but the damage could not be undone. Arnie never trusted him again.

It was a terrible summer all around. Temperatures continued to soar as though intent upon breaking a new record each day. There wasn't a drop of rain, and a state of drought was officially declared as the ground began to crack with long, running fissures. The leaves of the trees turned brown and fell to the ground. The air was so still it seemed the very breezes had gone on vacation. Fleas and roaches invaded the house in search of water, while fire ants and mosquito larvae took over the wading pool the boys had only been able to use twice.

Arnie could not have been subjected to the first molt in a worse year. Even within the air-conditioned house, we all felt something of the weather outdoors. Part of our biology is always geared to the natural, no matter how we work at isolating ourselves from the unpleasant aspects of weather. The boys and I perspired despite the cooled air, and our nerves were on edge. The cats spent most of their time lying down, motionless, their tongues lolling, their bodies heaving with short, panting breaths. Arnie, when he wasn't busy plucking and poking at himself, perched as unmovingly as a statue, his remaining feathers fluffed as much as possible, his beak opened so widely it seemed about to unhinge.

To make things as bad as they could be, the compressor unit of my air conditioner kept breaking down. It had always been a lemon, and I'd frequently been tempted to send it back to the dealer. However, once something the size of a small car has been delivered, it's easier to send for repairmen. This year, I cheerfully would have put a stick of dynamite under it and hauled off the pieces, but we needed it too badly. Unfortunately, that kind of heat had created a rash of air conditioner breakdowns; swamped repairmen could not come very promptly.

The boys and I climbed into the car and went in search of relief. At the beach, the air shimmered above the sand as I'd only seen it do in a desert before. The murky waters of the Gulf of Mexico were so smoothly unrippled, so eerily quiet in their yawning vastness, as to evoke haunting images of the Ancient Mariner's setting. For once, the boys didn't care to go into the water, saying it was "scary," an opinion with which I had to agree. We built sand castles instead, pretending to have fun, until we could endure the sun no longer. Fishing and crabbing were fruitless activities: the crabs had scuttled to deeper, cooler water, and the fish seemed to have migrated north for the summer. Visiting friends and sitting in the movies, we worried about the animals.

"Poor kitties, poor Arnie," the boys soothed each time we arrived home again. Though I opened all of the windows for ventilation and turned on a fan to circulate the air, the animals were absolutely miserable. It certainly was a bad time to have to wear a fur coat, as the cats did. They were permanently prostrate. Arnie shivered on his perch as though he were cold, the gently fanning motion of his sparse feathers serving to cool him somewhat. I gave them all cold baths. Arnie thought the baths a great treat, while the cats screamed and hissed their fury, never seeming to notice that the water cooled them.

The weather seemed to set the tone for everything that summer. Everyone has an occasional day when Murphy's Law rules: the coffee maker breaks down in the morning, the kids miss the school bus, the car won't start, a neighbor's dog scatters the garbage, etc., etc., etc., until everything that can go wrong in any one day has done so. Bedtime is embraced with great relief on days like that. I began to wonder why Murphy had such a special interest in legislating so much of my life that year. When the household air conditioner settled down to running reliably, the one in the Blazer broke down; then antifreeze backed up in a hose and ran through a heating duct to flood the floorboard. Trying to stay on top of the bills, I sold the classic convertible with which I'd had a love affair for more than ten years. The young man who bought it delivered only a couple of small payments before I gave him the title. I never heard from him again. Another property revaluation arrived from the tax office. "Sorry, we made a mistake," was the explanation I got after a city worker mowed to the ground a hundred and fifty feet of the hedge I had babied for three years. The list went on and on throughout the summer. I really should have saved some of that depression I'd conquered for this year, I thought. When the nine-month-old refrigerator quit refrigerating for the second time, I sat down and had a good crying laugh. Surely, Murphy's Law had to expire soon.

Hearing the sounds of my hysteria, Arnie quit scratching himself, cocked his head to the side and stared at me curiously. He worked his throat muscles as though trying to regurgitate, opened his beak, and said, "Good morning." His voice cracked like an adolescent male's. The boys ran out of their bedroom, excitement shining in their faces. "Was that Arnie? Is Arnie talking again?" His voice cracking once more, he answered their questions himself with another "Good morning."

As though Arnie had broken a jinx by speaking again, everything ran smoother after that. Gradually, his full vocabulary returned, and he began stretching it with an occasional new phrase. In time he told me "Good night" as well as "Good morning." He added a phrase to his most affectionate term, making it more emphatic, and now said "I love you, yes I do!" The single word "Good!" became his way of praising everything from the joy of bathing to the flavor of orange juice. When I dashed from bathroom to bedroom clad only in a wraparound towel, he flattered me with a very human wolf whistle. Words he'd had trouble pronouncing before the molt were no longer a problem; he spoke so clearly now anyone could understand him.

Of course, improved speech was only one part of Arnie's change that season. Each day he looked a bit different as his juvenile coat was shed forever. Superbird was acquiring a new identity. Travie and Kyle were absolutely fascinated with the transformation. And so was I. It took Arnie all summer to molt completely, and during that time his appearance altered dramatically.

His new plumage unfolded like ebony rosebuds opening petal by languid petal. Each individual feather was filigreed with intricate artistry: a delicate brown edging on wings and back and head, a bold white tipping on chest and belly. Beneath his lower mandible, the plumage was arranged so finely it created the illusion that Arnie sported a black mustache that drooped past the sides of his mouth to lie in stark contrast on a snow-white beard. Beginning at the point nearest his nostrils, his beak began to turn very bright yellow. Smudged at the edges as it progressed, the new color crept daily down the length and across the breadth of his beak until there was only a spot of black left at the tip of his upper mandible. The pale legs I'd worried so much about slowly acquired a pinkish tinge.

When the molt was finished, there was no trace of the nondescript, mousy, brown-gray little bird he'd been. As Arnie preened proudly in the sunlight, his fully unfurled feathers made a rainbow of iridescent colors ranging from glossy green to prancing purple to blazing blue. His facial expression had changed from babyhood sweetness and gentleness to sternly frowning maturity. Now, when he peered down his beak at me, those beady black eyes always looked fierce. At such an angle, he looked every bit the bird of prey—an eagle or hawk or owl gazing upon the world with the no-nonsense attitude necessary to a predator. He was entirely too serious now to engage in childish, comical behavior.

I began to miss my little clown. Like a parent witnessing the transformation of an offspring from youth to maturity, I was dismayed by the loss of the child.

Too late, I was sorry for all the photographs I hadn't taken to freeze his precious baby image forever. I had no remnant of Arnie's childhood except what my memory retained.

Even as I mourned the loss of the baby, however, I was intrigued with the emergence of the adult. The ugly duckling had become a swan. He had matured into such magnificent radiance, I'm certain his real mother would have been bursting with pride. His adopted mother certainly was. He was beautiful! Absolutely gorgeous! The Adónis of the avian world!

"Boy, I'll bet every girl starling in the whole state would chase after him now, Margarete," Kyle said.

"Don't forget, Kyle, he's Superbird," said Travie. "Just like Superman, he'll never get married, no matter how many girls chase him."

Their words gave me pause. Once again, I was reminded that Arnie had been hatched as a wild bird. I hadn't thought of him that way in many months. Where the baby had been content among a foster family, would the fully-grown bird want to return to the wild? Would he yield to the strength of nature's call and go in search of a wife? With a jar, I realized it was entirely possible. Like any bird parent, I must prepare now for the final leaving of the nest; the proud moment in which he would truly unfurl his wings and fly away in search of a kindred mate to share the rest of his life. I wondered if he would remember to say "Bye-bye."

XVIII

Dear "Tonight Show" Viewer:

Many thanks for your recent letter concerning an appearance on "The Tonight Show."

Your suggestion has been given full consideration by our production staff, and although it was found to be most interesting, we are unable to schedule an appearance at this time.

Thank you for your interest, and we hope you continue to enjoy "The Tonight Show."

"Well, Arnie, what do you think of that?" I said after

I'd read the words. "I have a feeling they didn't believe in you."

"Good!" he said.

"Maybe you're right," I agreed, laughing. I had forgotten all about the letter I sent to Johnny Carson by the time the reply arrived. The preprinted form letter, signed by a "Tonight Show" correspondent, seemed to nip Arnie's show business career in the bud. Fortunately, Travie and Kyle were back in Florida when the mailman delivered the note; they would have been terribly disappointed.

I was happy to find that the letter only bothered me a little bit. Even though "The Tonight Show" was the only program we'd gotten around to writing to about Arnie, I really didn't care to pursue the matter anymore. When he quit speaking at the onset of molt, I realized that, once again, I was pinning my hopes on a grandiose dream, and I'd done that too often in recent years. If I could just get home to Cape Cod in time for Christmas, I'd be content to confine my dreaming to the hours when I slept. I was going to do it, too! I resolved that I would make it to the Cape before first snowfall, even if it meant I had to walk off and lose everything in Texas.

Now I realized I had been clinging stubbornly to a place that no longer held meaning for me, and in doing so I had locked myself into a position of growing desperation. I thought often of those days of Suzanne, off in Colorado, making new beginnings. It occurred to me that I had been so pushy with her because I harbored such a deep-seated longing to leave for other parts myself. With no vision for the future, all I had in Texas was a building on a piece of real estate—mere things, and the things were encumbrances. Possessions, after all, must be weighed with good judgment against the personal price they cost. The personal price in Texas was becoming ever higher for me. I had to let go of the things to which I clung before I could reach out to the future.

With those thoughts in mind, I found peace. I wouldn't just throw away everything for which I'd worked so hard without trying the logical steps to a reasonable solution, of course, but I wasn't going to waste any more of my life in a place I didn't like, either. I contacted a real estate agency to sell the property. Actually, I didn't have much faith they could find a buyer; interest rates had skyrocketed so high that no one was interested in real estate. While I was mulling over my alternatives, though, I could be preparing for the move.

I didn't have to pull out many suitcases and boxes before the animals knew something unusual was going on. Maybe they were happy to see me getting ready for an adventure, or maybe they simply sensed my excitement and growing exuberance. Whatever the reason, I had never known any of them to behave as they did now. They absolutely went wild! Mitzi forgot her uppity ways and joined the other two cats in games of chase throughout the house. When they weren't running, they curled up together inside one of the open suitcases. For the first time, the three of them acted like loving siblings.

As the felines frisked, Arnie sang and talked at the top of his lungs, pausing only long enough in the course of each day to breathe and eat. When I let him out of his aviary, he explored with great enthusiasm all the hodgepodge that was beginning to clutter the floor and furniture. He stole small items from the growing piles, ripped the corners from my list of things to do, pulled Mitzi's tail when she was resting, clung to my blouse, inserted his mandibles into my mouth to get attention when I ignored him, and teased me in a dozen different ways. Stern as he looked in his new coat, he was still a clown. Once again, he persisted in cheerfulness no matter what. The molt had temporarily suspended his animation, but that's all it turned out to be—temporary. We all have bad days sometimes; he just happened to save all his bad days in a year for that one major period. Adolescent change is never very pleasant, and Arnie's transition had been compressed into a short, bewildering time.

I reveled in his rebirth. Too attached to him to tempt the fates, I did not offer him his freedom. I was afraid he might take it this time, and I was a little jealous that there might be a female starling somewhere outdoors who had been hatched as his soul mate. As though he sensed my fears, he stuck closer to me than ever, assuring me that he still loved me. He brought me gifts in the form of pieces of tissue paper, bits of lint from the floor, kernels of corn and strips of lettuce from his cage, cigarette butts from my own ashtray—all very fine gifts from a bird's point of view, I'm sure. As he perched upon my shoulder, he serenaded me softly. When he was in the aviary, he sang so loudly that I could hear him even when I went outdoors. I was so glad to have him back to normal; and I was becoming accustomed to his new appearance. He certainly had turned out handsome.

"You're the most attractive starling in the whole world, Arnie," I told him.

"I love you, yes I do!" he replied. "Kiss Arnie."

"You really are something special, little boy. I'm just as glad you weren't invited to be a guest on 'The Tonight Show.' You probably wouldn't have liked all those bright lights, anyway, but I do think Johnny would have enjoyed meeting you."

"He's a baboon," Arnie said. "He's a coo-coo."

"Shame on you, Arnie! He's a very nice man, really."

As though determined to prove how talented he could be, Arnie decided to become a rock-and-roll singer. He'd never paid much attention to the radio before, though I usually had either a talk show or music playing in the background. Suddenly, he discovered the music.

Betraying his youthful mental age, he placed disco and hard rock high on his list of favorites. It was easy to tell when he really liked a song because he sang right along with it. Anyone who's listened to untalented teenage offspring belt along with recorded music knows how I felt during that period. When aspiring musicians can't carry a tune, they compensate with volume, as Arnie did. The difference is that a teenager usually has at least a slight idea of what the proper words and tune are supposed to be. Arnie, unfortunately, was strictly a three-song musician. Upon hearing any of his favorite songs, he tried very, very hard to superimpose over them his very loud versions of "Mary Had a Little Lamb," "Michael, Row the Boat Ashore," and Beethoven's Fifth. I turned up the sound on the radio, trying to drown him out, and he switched to the loudest tune at his command, the obnoxious "Pret-ty-ty-ty-ty."

For once, it didn't bother me. Arnie's ebullience matched my own. "There's no place like home for the holidays," I sang as I packed. "You animals will love the Cape," I told them. "Just ask Mitzi. She's lived there with me before. She had friends who were squirrels and chipmunks and skunks and racoons. We'll see the geese flying over the roof of the house at least twice a day; maybe even the swans. You'll hear the biggest sea gulls in the world running around on the roof, sounding like a herd of horses. And we'll have snow in the winter instead of rain. We'll keep logs burning in the fireplace to make us cozy, and we'll never need air conditioning in the summer again. It's going to be wonderful!"

It would be, too, but I was beginning to wonder if we would make it that year. I grew more nervous as I peeled each page from the calendar. I would be towing a rented trailer filled with household articles I thought it better to keep than dispose of, and it wasn't a drive I cared to make once ice and snow began to blanket the roads. The realtor had only brought by one unenthusiastic prospect to look at the property. Would I really have the courage to leave for the Cape if my affairs weren't in order? I was getting a bad case of cold feet. Relentlessly, I forced myself to dispose of everything I didn't absolutely need.

The walls of the house began to echo every little noise within the rooms. Timbers creaked and groaned with sounds I'd never heard before. The atmosphere through which I walked began to feel empty the way temporary quarters do; the "good vibes" weren't warming me anymore. I wondered if the house was mourning. So much of me, so much of my entire household, was a part of this structure. I sometimes felt our departure would be like amputating a vital part from the building. Remembering all the very real blood, sweat, and tears with which the various parts had been anointed, I knew that if I should ever return to haunt a place after my demise, it would be this house. Already it owned a piece of my soul. "I love you, house," I said. "If I could load you onto a trailer and haul you with me, I would, but I built you in the wrong place, you see. I only feel good here when I'm inside your walls, and that's not much of a life for any human being."

"Coo-coo," Arnie said. "What are you doing?"

"What am I doing? I'm acting like a sentimental fool, is what I'm doing, Arnie. As much as I want to go home, a part of me hurts about leaving. We had some good times here, too, and people we love live here, but I can't let memories change my mind." I called the utility companies and ordered everything shut off on the fifteenth of October. That was one way to keep me resolute. Without electricity or water or gas or telephone service, I'd be so uncomfortable I'd have to leave, no matter what. I taped up the closed boxes and locked suitcases. Now I would have to make do with only enough dishes for the simplest meals and enough clothing for a week. I would hate the inconvenience that entailed, so it was a further nudging onto the path I had chosen.

"C'mere," Arnie said. "Come see Arnie. I love you. Gimme kiss." The little darling tried to comfort me the best way he knew how, talking sweetly and singing cheerfully, playing with his vocabulary in ways that made me laugh. He seemed to realize that as the time drew near for leaving, I was beginning to feel heavy-hearted for the things and people I would be leaving behind. I visited with friends more often that ever, realizing I might never see some of them again.

By the first of October, I had done all that could possibly be done, except for last minute packing. "We *could* leave the day after tomorrow," I told the animals. The cats regarded me with something less than glee. After the initial excitement wore off, they had quit frisking about. For them, bewilderment over the disappearance of so many familiar items gave birth to trepidations about what was to come next. This was, after all, the only home Bundy and Sammie had ever known, and I'm sure Mitzi really wasn't that crazy about having to adjust to a new place once again. "We're going home," I told them softly.

"Da-da-da-dum!" Arnie whistled.

There was one more important detail I had to take care of before we left, though. There was still a month to go before my old loan ran out, but there seemed little point in waiting until the last minute to renew it. "I don't think the interest rates are going to be any better for a long time," my banker told me. The rates had dropped slightly during the past couple of months, but they were still more than fifty percent higher than my original terms. I really had hoped a buyer would come along before I was forced to renew the loan, but there was little likelihood of that now, I realized.

I bowed before the realities of the nation's economic situation and signed the papers. Committing myself all over again to a mortgage on the place felt something like renewing wedding vows—at a shotgun ceremony. Once way or another, it seemed, the property would remain mine for a while longer. I wasn't going to let it keep me there, though. I debated whether to rent the place or leave it vacant while waiting for a buyer. Buildings left vacant have a way of gradually falling apart, however, as though they slowly die without people inside to give them life. I put ads in the local newspapers, offering the place for lease.

With nothing to occupy my time, I found it unbearable to sit in the almost empty house. All four animals were sulking now, so they were certainly not good company. I went outside to work in the yard, wanting to see it looking its very best when I pulled out of the driveway for the last time. Inevitably, I compared the way it was now to the way it had been when I'd first seen it. Little more than an overgrown field then, it had lured me with its promise. Those huge old trees had been its best selling point in an area noticeably short on trees. Now this piece of land was graced with thick hedges and flowering shrubs and young trees galore. They were all just beginning to show the beauty I had envisioned when I'd planted them as seedlings. I had hoped to turn over the place to someone who would feel for it all as much as I did. Darnit, how could I abandon it to strangers?

I went back inside, sat down, and cried. "I'm so wishy-washy!" I wailed to the animals. "How can I feel so deeply about a stupid old building and a plot of dirt?"

"Love's a coo-coo," Arnie said.

Sometimes, the combinations he invented for his few words made the strangest kind of sense. I knew the answer to my question very well. This place had been my home through some of the toughest years of my life, and I was going to abandon it. "Under the circumstances, I'm beginning to feel as bad as though I were leaving one of you animals behind," I said.

"Maybe we should wait until spring to leave. Maybe things will be different by then. Of course, if I put it off, we may never leave."

It began to look like that might well be the case. I found none of the prospective lessees suitable. If they weren't enthusiastic enough, I wouldn't accept them. If the animals didn't like them, then I wouldn't let them live in our home. The animals were so upset over everything being packed up that they didn't like anyone, of course. I was creating excuses and knew it. I should probably turn over the property to a real estate agent again, go through with my plans to move back to the Cape, then look for a good psychiatrist—I was acting as nutty as a fruitcake. "Good! Bye-bye," Arnie said as though reading my thoughts and agreeing with them.

"Okay, I'll call a realtor," I said. "Maybe I won't need the psychiatrist once I tear myself away from here." I reached for the telephone just as there was a knock on the door.

"Are we too late? Have you leased the place yet?" the young man asked when I opened the door. His eyes twinkled merrily; there was eagerness in his voice. "Please say you haven't let it go yet!"

"His father moved down the street a couple of years ago," said the woman with him, "and we've been admiring this place since we first set eyes on it. We love it! We can't afford to buy it, but maybe we can handle a lease. This is everything we've always wanted!" Her eyes twinkled, too.

"Hi there," Arnie said. "Hello. How are you? C'mere. Come see Arnie."

"Please come in," I said to the couple. I showed them around, and then we sat down to talk. One by one, the cats wandered into the room, checked out the couple with thorough sniffs, then settled down nearby. Arnie kept up a running dialogue.

"Can we make arrangements to buy the property

later?" the man asked. "We hope to be able to afford it in a couple of years."

"We have our own business," she added, "but it's just beginning to get off the ground. We'll be doing much better in a year or two. We really, really love this place. It would be like a dream come true if we could own it."

I believed her. I had grown tired of my unrealized dreams, but I hadn't quit believing in miracles. These two people were so perfect for the place it seemed as though providence had sent them knocking on my door. I'd do what I could to keep the terms within their means. We saw a great deal of each other during the next few days while an attorney was setting up the paperwork. I told them much of the history of their new home, and they shared with me the bright and sparkling dreams they had for themselves, their children, and the property. We grew so close it seemed we had been friends for a very long time.

On the last afternoon we spent in the house, I put Arnie into his travel cage and tipped the aviary onto its side. As I dismantled it, he became very silent and watched me with little "queeking" noises. I think it was his way of crying. The furniture was all gone, the bags and boxes were all packed into car and trailer, the cats were crouching in gaping closets. Arnie and I sat in the empty living room alone. "You'll see, Arnie, we're just beginning our lives together," I said. "I read somewhere along the way that starlings have been known to live longer than fifteen years. With me to take care of you, maybe you'll make it to thirty. You'll have lots of time for your genius to blossom, and you're going to be very, very happy for all of your life. I promise." Nevertheless, I think he went into a state of shock when he saw me carry the four panels of the aviary out the door so I could stuff them into the trailer. He didn't make another sound that night.

The next morning, I paused one last time on the

threshold. I had said a last good-bye to my close friends before the telephone went dead. The animals were all in the car. There seemed nothing left to do but lock the door of the house, get into the car, and drive away. I looked around one last time at all that had been wrought upon an empty field in a few short years. The building, the landscaped grounds—it really was all quite beautiful. At my feet was the dedication scratched into the concrete foundation: "We dare to dream." It had been inscribed at a time when hope ran too high to be chilled by the north wind that suddenly whipped at our small, starry-eyed group. Remembering the occasion, I thought now that that wind had been a portent. Things don't always turn out as planned no matter what the intentions. Such is life.

It's also life that dreamers seem to be drawn together. The family who would move into the building later in the day had their own vision of the future. I thought the property in very good hands, indeed. "May you always be home to a dreamer, good house," I said and patted the door as I locked it. Surprisingly, my heart wasn't heavy at all. I would just have to think up new dreams when I got to Cape Cod. Through convolutions of fate, I had gained more than lost in Texas, though in terms different than expected. My family was increased by two cats and one silly starling. I had learned a great deal while here and accomplished something I would never forget. The friends I had made would always be in my heart. No matter who might own the land, I would keep the mineral rights, and I still believed that oil well was going to come in someday for me. Best of all, I felt at peace, emotionally content, as I never had before.

As I walked to the car, the new tenants of the house drove into the driveway. We hugged good-bye and wished each other good luck. I invited them to visit me on the Cape, and they invited me to come back and visit them.

It was mid-October when we hit the road for home. I could hear the shotguns blasting in the marsh, signifying the height of the duck and goose hunting season. I wondered if the young man who'd delivered the TV set and helped identify Arnie had gotten in any target practice since I'd last seen him. Nickel apiece for dead starlings, indeed! Arnie was worth more to me than all the nickels and dollars in the entire world— past, present, and future. A flock of geese honked from formation high in the sky. A bit late in the morning for them to be coming in, but maybe now they'd be able to spot the hunters and avoid them. It dawned on me that we were heading for Cape Cod at a time when the migratory birds were all flying south. Arnie was probably the only wild bird in America going north for the winter.

Applying a bit more pressure to the accelerator, I reached down and turned on the radio. Appropriately, Willie Nelson was singing "On the Road Again." I turned up the volume. Arnie settled onto the top perch of his travel cage and began singing "Mary Had a Little Lamb." He harmonized better with the yowling of the three cats than he did with Willie, but I wouldn't shatter his illusion that he was a great musician. His entire repertoire was a symphony of joy. I began singing along with them. We were all going home!

Epilogue

And that was only the beginning, really, of the tale of a unique and wonderful little character. Along with Margarete and Mitzi and Sammie and Bundy, Arnie thrived in his new home on Cape Cod. Conquering hearts and captivating imaginations among an ever-growing circle of friends and admirers, he continued to expand his vocabulary and to touch people with wonder. It seemed that his story would have the non-ending of a fairy tale, that it would dance along happily forever after. Reality never works out with the simplicity of fairy tales, however.

When the manuscript for this book was almost ready for publication, Arnie developed abscesses on the bottoms of both of his feet, a painful condition, called bumblefoot, that birds sometimes contract. With infinite patience, Margarete treated him with antibiotics, ointments, soakings, dietary supplements, and tender loving care. Clearly exasperated, Arnie tolerated the necessary manhandling, making no secret of the fact that he hated every moment of his treatments. He was an incredibly cheerful patient, however, singing and talking and playing from morning until night as he stood first on one foot, then the other, trying to ease his pain. Friends called constantly, checking up on him, offering advice, wanting to help.

Arnie's feet got better, but the improvement was sporadic, and they always became infected again as soon as the antibiotics were discontinued. The veterinarians Margarete consulted were stymied—maybe Arnie had gout; but no, that wasn't it, either. It's just difficult to heal infections on the bottoms of a bird's feet. There was no choice but to continue giving Arnie the antibiotics. Unfortunately, prolonged treatment with antibiotics can cause dire complications. For one thing, it can temporarily destroy the blood's normal clotting ability.

Early one snowy, icy, cold, windy winter morning, one of Arnie's legs began to bleed copiously. Margarete was holding him at the time it happened, so there was little likelihood he'd been injured. Arnie stared up at her with a bewildered expression on his face, as though asking what on earth was happening to him. He'd begun the day happy and cheerful—after all, his feet were finally healed, and he'd been off antibiotics for several days. Margarete had no explanation for him; she was bewildered too. She tried everything possible to stanch the flow. But each time he moved, the bleeding began again.

Margarete tried to get help, but it was, after all,

quite early on a snowy, icy, cold, windy winter morning. A veterinarian's magical styptic powder did finally stop Arnie's bleeding almost three hours later. Margarete cuddled him for another two hours, soothing him, talking to him, telling him how much he was loved. For a while, it seemed he was recovering. Then, he gazed up at Margarete with love shining in his eyes, breathed a tired sigh, and rested his head against her chest. He'd been struggling with pain and misery for three months; enough was enough.

Gently as a feather floating on a breeze, Arnie slipped from this life on February 11, 1983. He would have been four years old that May. His body rests beneath a lush canopy of daisies in Margarete's yard, but in the hearts and memories of the many people he touched, Arnie's spirit is vibrantly alive and as indestructible as dandelions—and starlings.

About the Authors

Margarete Sigl Corbo, born in Munich, came to the United States as a bride after World War II. She served in the Peace Corps, was a student advisor at a college, and owned a pet clinic. Ms. Corbo raised a daughter, several dogs, numerous cats, and a large assortment of birds, including Arnie, of course.

Diane Marie Barras, born in Port Arthur, Texas, has worked as a journalist, newspaper editor, veterinary assistant, carpenter, plumber and electrician. While a journalist in the Navy, she covered John F. Kennedy's funeral and served on Lyndon B. Johnson's inaugural committee.

Margarete and Diane have been friends for many years. Both now live on Cape Cod.

The sights, sounds and feel
of AMERICA

from FAWCETT BOOKS

        TAF-15

BURDEN

- Do you experience negative feelings when your husband asks you to fix a meal?
- Do you get angry when your wife disagrees with you?
- Do you resent the fact that your husband is fulfilled sexually?
- Do you feel resentment when your wife is the center of attraction?

Whatever the questions . . . *The Measure of a Marriage* is designed to help you and your spouse not only to measure your marriage . . . but to improve it.

THE MEASURE OF A
MARRIAGE

GENE A.GETZ

GL Regal Books · A Division of G/L Publications
Glendale, California, U.S.A.

Other good Regal reading by Gene A. Getz:

The Measure of a Church
The Measure of a Man
The Measure of a Woman
The Measure of a Family

The foreign language publishing of all Regal books is under the direction of GLINT. GLINT provides financial and technical help for the adaptation, translation and publishing of books in more than 85 languages for millions of people worldwide.

For more information write: GLINT, P.O. Box 6688, Ventura, CA 93006.

Published by Regal Books Division, G/L Publications
Ventura, California 93006
Printed in U.S.A.

Library of Congress Catalog Card No. 78-53356
ISBN 0-8307-0638-0

Contents

If you are studying this book as a couple or in a group, be sure to get a copy of *The Measure of a Marriage Workbook* from your local church supplier.

If You're Interested in Marriage, This Book Is for You

Most people *are* interested in understanding more about marriage—whether married or unmarried. And most people who *are* married are interested in improving their marriage.

Today most marriages are undergoing various degrees of stress for various reasons. First, all human relationships experience strain due to the realities of life. And marriage represents the most intimate human relationship of all, and is probably affected more than any other by the "realities of life." Consequently, *every* marriage undergoes degrees of stress.

However, there is yet another reason all marriages experience stress. Our present-day societal structures are groaning and creaking from various changes that are continually bombarding our cultural foundations. Since every marriage is an integral part of the total culture, these changes—philosophical, economic and technological—all affect society generally and marriages particularly. In fact, *all* changes in society precipitate crises. How we handle these crises depends to a great extent on our physiological resources, intellectual insights, psychological maturity and—last, but not least—our spiritual perspectives.

You may or may not classify yourself as religious. Most people do. But whatever your viewpoint, you probably already know that the Bible has some very significant things to say about marriage. In fact, our traditional views about marriage in our Western culture are pretty much rooted in Hebrew-Christian thought and practice as stated in both the Old and New Testaments. For most of us our beliefs, attitudes and actions are probably more influenced by biblical ideas than we realize.

But whatever your religious heritage, this entire study is designed to help you and your spouse not only to *measure* your marriage but to *improve* your marriage. Each segment begins with a biblical idea and then proceeds to give you extra-biblical insights, both psychologically and sociologically, to help you understand more fully yourself and your marriage partner. Practical projects help you make these truths and insights a part of your day-to-day experience as a husband and wife.

You *can* improve your relationship. No matter what degree of success or failure you are experiencing you can begin at that point and move forward. And if you are contemplating marriage this book will help you to enter that relationship with a more adequate perspective on the dynamics involved.

Gene A. Getz, Ph.D.

How to Use This Book

First, you can read this book by yourself—as a married person or as a single. As a married person, even if your mate is not interested in reading it, you will gain insights that will help you to relate more effectively to your partner, consequently improving your relationship in some areas.

And remember! Improvement in *one* area tends to transfer and generalize to others. In fact, your mate may be so impressed with the changes in your life that he or she too may get involved in the study.

Second, you can study this book as a couple, working through the projects together. This is far more effective than merely reading it on your own. It will serve as a do-it-yourself marriage enrichment course.

Third, you can participate with a group of couples. In fact, the projects are designed to be used in three ways: (1) for *personal* study; (2) for *husband and wife* study; and (3) for a *couples' group* study.

AS A GROUP OF COUPLES

The projects in this book are designed to be both self-contained and/or sequential. For example, if you get involved in a group study, the Group Project is designed to be worked out *in the group* (see fig. 1, step 1). However, following each group session, you should also follow through as a husband and wife team by doing the Couple Project (step 2). And when working through the Couple Project, each of you will also need to work through the Personal Project (step 3). This of course is the ideal approach.

STEP 3 ← ━ ━ ━	STEP 2 ← ━ ━ ━	STEP 1
Personal Project	**Couple Project**	**Group Project**

Figure 1—As a group of couples

AS A COUPLE

However, not every couple can be involved in a group. Therefore, as illustrated in figure 2, you can begin with the Couple Project (step 1), which will also involve you in the Personal Project (step 2). And of course an excellent project and goal for both of you—once you've worked through the projects designed for personal and couple use—is to share this experience with a group of couples (step 3).

Figure 2—As a couple.

AS AN INDIVIDUAL

It is possible however that your marital partner may not want to participate either in a group or with you in the couple projects. Therefore, you can benefit significantly by working through the personal projects (see fig. 3) which hopefully will help you to eventually encourage your mate to be involved in the projects with you (steps 2 and 3).

Figure 3—As an individual.

A Notebook

If you're involved in this study either as a *couple* or with a *group* of couples, you will want to purchase a copy of *The Measure of a Marriage Workbook* (also published by Regal Books). This notebook is designed to accompany this book. It includes special tear-out sheets consisting of evaluation scales for both husbands and wives, as well as guidelines for goal setting. In other words, it's very important that you secure this notebook. It is not supplementary, but an integral part of both the couple and group projects.

CHAPTER 1

Becoming One

If you conducted a little survey on your own and stopped people on the street in New York or Los Angeles, London or Paris and asked them where the idea of marriage came from, most would probably tell you that it supposedly began with Adam and Eve in the Garden of Eden. This would happen even more frequently in small towns and rural communities.

Whatever your personal interpretation of this fascinating Old Testament story, the Bible simply states that the Lord God created the original man and woman and brought them together to form a unique relationship which we call marriage. And many people in our culture go back to this story when discussing the origins of marriage.

Moses, that incomparable Jewish leader who led the children of Israel out of Egypt and into the Promised

Land, recorded the intriguing event when God created Eve from Adam's rib and summarized that event with these words: "For this cause a man shall leave his father and his mother, and shall cleave to his wife; *and they shall become one flesh*" (Gen. 2:24).[1]

Many years later another Jew named Jesus Christ was asked His views on marriage by the religious philosophers and professors of His day. He mentally reached back in antiquity and quoted Moses' very words: "For this cause a man shall leave his father and mother, and shall cleave to his wife; *and the two shall become one flesh*" (Matt. 19:5; see also Mark 10:7,8). And then for emphasis Jesus added—"Consequently they are *no more two, but one flesh*" (Matt. 19:6).

It should not surprise us that Paul the apostle (author of 13 New Testament books), when discussing the relationship that should exist between a husband and wife, also quoted Moses—*and* Jesus. Calling marriage a "great mystery" (which also refers to the relationship between Christ and Christians), Paul again stated God's plan word for word: "For this cause a man shall leave his father and mother, and shall cleave to his wife; *and the two shall become one flesh*" (Eph. 5:31).

F. Foulkes wrote that, "this statement from the creation story is the most profound and fundamental statement in the whole of Scripture concerning God's plan for marriage."[2] It is indeed a logical place to begin when studying the subject of marriage in order to gain, not only a contemporary viewpoint on husband/wife relationships, but an historic perspective as well.

One in Humanness

What did Moses, *and* Jesus, *and* Paul mean when they

stated that a man and woman "become one flesh"? First of all, remember that the apostle Paul identified it as a *mystery*. Most of us who are married can verify experientially the truth in Paul's statement. There are certain dimensions to this relationship between a man and a woman that are impossible to understand and explain. However, the Bible *and* personal experience give us enough data to draw some rather impressive conclusions.

How was "oneness" illustrated in the original creation?

When God first created Adam, there was no one with whom he could truly become "one flesh." There was no other *human being* with whom he could share his life. The implication is clear. It would take another person created in God's image—and Adam's image—to fill that unique role. This is what God meant when He said that He would make a "helper *suitable*" (Gen. 2:18). This literally means "a help of his like," that is, "a helping being, which, as soon as he sees it, he may recognize himself."[3]

This was why Adam exclaimed when he first saw Eve: "This is now bone of my bones, and flesh of my flesh; she shall be called Woman, because she was taken out of Man" (Gen. 2:23).

Adam recognized that Eve was like him. Though she was uniquely female, she looked like him, talked like him, walked like him and smiled like him. She was his complement. He could relate to her as to no other living creature. She was another *human being*.

God had uniquely set the stage for this experience. Before creating Eve from Adam's rib, the Lord had arranged for him to name all of the animals that were already created. And as Adam named each creature, he did so with keen understanding of the nature of each one. In the process he discovered that there was no creature like himself (see Gen. 2:20). Consequently, when his eyes first fell on Eve—undoubtedly a beautiful and unblemished creation—there was no doubt in his mind as to their affinity. In common parlance, the "chemistry" was right, which was far more than sexual. She was a unique creation, physically, psychologically and spiritually, just as he was.

One in Sexuality

But there's more! Eve was indeed *one* with Adam because she was literally taken from his side. Part of his very physical body became part of Eve's physical body. And before they were ever joined together sexually, they were already, in God's eyes, "one flesh."

How was "oneness" illustrated after the original creation?

After God created Adam and Eve, what caused a man and woman to become "one flesh" in God's eyes? First, understand that there is a unique relationship between *all* men and women who are ever born into this world. Ever since God created the first man and woman, every male and female reflect the same unity. *Together*, we are made in God's image (see Gen. 1:27). And together we reflect His image and His creative handiwork.

But there is an even more unique relationship that God intended. Though He certainly planned for all human beings (male and female) to fellowship with one another and to relate to one another because of the ongoing "oneness" inherent in the original creation, there is yet another "oneness" referred to in the Bible—the oneness that exists between a husband and a wife. And that oneness is reflected in God's eyes when a man joins himself to a woman through the act of sexual intercourse. In this God-created consummation we see the original creation story illustrated again and again throughout history. In God's eyes a man and woman become "one flesh."

That God views sexual intercourse as a means by which a man becomes one with a woman (and vice versa) is emphasized by Paul in his letter to the Corinthians. These people were converted to Christianity out of a pagan culture where prostitution was a very real part of their religious life. Some of these new Christians initially continued in their old ways, visiting the pagan temples (and no doubt other places) where these women were readily available. Paul exhorted them in no uncertain terms against such a practice. "Do you not know that your bodies are members of Christ?" he asked. "Shall I then take away the members of Christ and make them members of a harlot? *May it never be!* Or do you not know that the one who *joins* himself to a harlot is *one body* with her?" (1 Cor. 6:15,16).

At this point Paul once again quotes Moses, *"The two will become one flesh"* (1 Cor. 6:16).

Taken in context there's no way to misinterpret Paul's statement. It is possible in God's eyes to become "one flesh" with more than one man or woman through the act of sexual intercourse, and this, the Bible teaches, is not God's will.

Isn't "oneness" more than physical unity?

The answer to this question is a definite yes. But in God's eyes, a unique unity takes place when a man and woman join in sexual union, whether it be a permanent or a promiscuous relationship. God's perfect will is that it be a *permanent* marriage, involving one man and one woman, reflecting the original creation. That is why Jesus also said to the religious philosophers of His day—"What therefore God has joined together, let not man separate" (Matt. 19:6).

One in Spirituality

What else is involved in this "oneness"?

Another facet of oneness can best be illustrated with the way the Bible describes Christian conversion. A person becomes a Christian by placing his faith in Jesus Christ for *personal* salvation. At that moment he becomes *one with Christ*. In this sense, each of us individually and all Christians collectively are "married" to Christ. Obviously, this is figurative language, but it is the very picture Paul painted in his Ephesian letter when discussing the interweaving relationship that exists between a husband and wife (see Eph. 5:22,23,32) as well as between Christ and His followers.

However, becoming "one with Christ" at conversion—when we personally receive Christ as Saviour (see John 1:12)—does not mean that our unity with Christ is *experientially* complete. It is true that God views us as *one* with Christ the moment we become a true believer. But to experience that unity in all of its fullness is yet another matter. As long as Christians are on earth we have the potential to grow in our relationship with Jesus Christ, personally and corporately, and the Bible teaches that someday we will be ultimately one with Him in heaven. The process will be complete. In the book of Revelation this ultimate experience is called the "marriage supper."

To a certain extent this process should also be true in a literal marriage, although this human relationship, according to Jesus, will terminate once we leave this earth.

We will no longer need this kind of human relationship to be fulfilled and happy. Jesus Christ will be all that we need. But while on earth our spiritual relationship with Christ illustrates our relationship with our marital partner. The act of intercourse, in God's eyes, indeed makes a man and woman "one flesh." But it is designed to be only a beginning point in a great adventure in getting to know each other not only physically but psychologically and spiritually. True *experiential* unity and oneness are yet future for a newly married couple. Like our *total* relationship with Christ, our *total* relationship with our husband or wife must be carefully nurtured and developed. Only then will we begin to *experience* true oneness.

Notes

1. Italics added. Hereafter all italics in Scripture quotations are added by the author for emphasis.
2. F. Foulkes, *The Epistle of Paul to the Ephesians* (Grand Rapids: Wm. B. Eerdmans Publishing Company, 1963), p. 161.
3. C.F. Keil and F. Delitzsch, *The Pentateuch* (Grand Rapids: Wm. B. Eerdmans Publishing Company, n.d.), p. 86.

CHAPTER 2
An Exercise in Becoming One

In our culture today more has been written about sexual unity than any other aspect of marriage. For some marriage partners, attaining mutual satisfaction physically has become a constant obsession. And usually this is attempted by experimenting with all kinds of physiological techniques found in a proliferation of sex manuals.

Don't misunderstand! Anyone who has counseled husbands and wives who are having sexual problems cannot ignore the value of learning various sexual techniques. Even in an enlightened society, there is still a great deal of ignorance regarding sexual physiology and technique. And later in this book we'll discuss some of these intimate aspects of marital life and how together you might improve your sex life.

Unfortunately, this kind of advice in itself is not the

key to unity and truly becoming one in a marriage relationship. In God's sight, when a man and woman are
joined in a sexual union they *are* one, whether or not it is
personally or mutually satisfying. But marital unity that is
total—physical, psychological and spiritual—involves a
process that takes time, insight, sensitivity and effort.
And it is in this larger context that sexual unity which *is*
mutually satisfying also takes place. Without this broader
setting, even sexual satisfaction can become meaningless
and eventually unsatisfactory. All the sex techniques in
the world, without total unity, leave a marriage in
shambles.

Because this is true the major part of this study is
designed to help you, as a couple, develop total unity in
marriage. So, let's get started!

Note: These projects are divided into three sections:
(1) for individuals; (2) for couples; and (3) for groups of
couples. However, each section builds on the other. In
other words, if you are reading and working through this
book as a *couple*, be sure to read carefully the section
written for *individuals*. If you are in a *group* be sure to
read the sections for *individuals* and *couples*.

AS AN INDIVIDUAL

If you are reading this book on your own (and you
should be, even if you are working through it as a couple
or in a group), read the following suggestions carefully.

Let's begin with a question. *How well do you really
know your present or future marital partner?*

To discover the answer to this question, structure an
opportunity to ask your mate (or future mate) some questions. Prepare yourself psychologically to really *listen* to
what your partner says—that is, don't be defensive or

emotionally resistant. Just listen, whether or not you "emotionally" agree with what is said.

Warning! This suggestion is particularly relevant for men who often tend to be more threatened and defensive than women when it comes to discussing marital problems.

Let me illustrate this point. On one occasion I was speaking at a pastor's breakfast sponsored by a Christian bookstore. The owner's wife (who also helped manage the bookstore) came to me and pointed out a paragraph I had written in an earlier book entitled *The Measure of a Woman*, which reads as follows:

"Most men find it difficult to listen to their wives share feelings of unhappiness and resentment. It is very threatening. But the fact is, it is only as the husband learns to know what his wife's needs are that he can meet those needs. There *must* be communication."[1]

"Gene," she said, "I encounter this problem more than any other in talking with women. Many husbands just will not listen to their wives when they try to share their negative feelings."

Unfortunately, she is right. But it's not just a man's problem. Some wives won't listen to their husbands either. Perhaps a woman's greatest weakness is not that she won't lend an ear, but she "listens" without *feeling* any real concern.

For example, Jane tells Bill she wants to hear about his work—his problems, his concerns, his frustrations. Her problem, however, is that she yawns while he's talking and when he's through she says, "That's too bad. Thanks for telling me," and then goes about her business or falls asleep.

Obviously, she hasn't *really* listened to Bill. And he

knows it. The problem is not defensiveness, as Bill's might be, but rather she's really not very interested. She's simply trying to use a technique that has not become a part of her internal concern and love for Bill.

If you're really going to listen to your husband or wife, you must *really* listen—nondefensively, intently, objectively and with feeling. You must not even allow yourself to think about how you are going to answer or respond. You will have plenty of time *after* you have listened to decide what you're going to say. In fact, if you are really listening, you'll be able to formulate your response more adequately *after* you have listened.

If you are not studying this book with your mate or in a group of couples, plan a time and find a place that is most conducive for asking your mate the questions that follow. Keep in mind that both of you should not be physically tired or psychologically on edge. In fact, the best time is when things generally are the most relaxed and comfortable in your marriage.

Warning: Don't be sneaky about this project. Be open and honest. You might say, "I've been reading this book entitled, *The Measure of a Marriage*, and there are several questions the author suggests that I ask my mate so as to learn more about myself and my relationship with you. I've been looking for an opportunity to ask you these questions. Do you mind if I ask them now or would there be a better time?"

These questions are arranged in a very important order. They move progressively from what are generally nonthreatening questions to more threatening ones. It's important that you follow this order. It will help the one *asking* the questions and the one *answering* the questions to be more sensitive, honest and nondefensive. (For couples, see *The Measure of a Marriage Workbook*.)

1. If you could point out *one thing* about me that pleases you the most, what would it be?

2. What would you say is my greatest strength?

3. How can I help you be a more fulfilled person?

4. What one thing in my personality or behavior pattern causes you the most emotional difficulty?

5. If you could change one thing about me, what would it be?

AS A COUPLE

If you are studying this book together as a husband and wife (or an engaged couple) you are already ahead of the game. Decide on a time and place to be alone for at least an hour.

Step 1—Take 10 minutes to silently record your answers to the following questions (Exercise 1 in *The Measure of a Marriage Workbook*).[2]

1. If you could point out one thing about your mate that pleases you the most what would it be? Why?

2. What would you say is your mate's greatest strength? Explain why.

3. How can your mate help you be a more fulfilled person?

4. What one thing in your mate's personality or behavior pattern causes you the most difficulty? Explain why.

5. If you could change one thing about your mate, what would it be?

Step 2—Share your answers with each other, using the following sequence:

Husband: Share the answers to question 1 with your mate.
Wife: Share the answers to question 1 with your mate.

Husband: Share the answer to question 2 with your mate.
Wife: Share the answer to question 2 with your mate.

Husband: Share the answer to question 3 with your mate.
Wife: Share the answer to question 3 with your mate.

Husband: Share the answers to question 4 with your mate.
Wife: Share the answers to question 4 with your mate.

Husband: Share the answer to question 5 with your mate.
Wife: Share the answer to question 5 with your mate.

NOTE: It is important that you not discuss the answers to these questions the first time through. Just listen to each other share answers. Both of you need time to reflect and develop objectivity. It is very important that you do not respond even though you want to—especially in a negative sense. Attempt to even avoid nonverbal reactions, such as looking away in disgust, or just looking away.

Alternate Suggestion: If you have extreme difficulty communicating in your marriage, you may need to simply let your mate read your answers to the questions and then wait a couple days to discuss them.

Additional Suggestion: If what your mate is saying is too painful to handle, simply extend your open hand in a ''please stop'' position indicating you cannot bear to hear more at this moment. With this nonverbal gesture you are simply asking for time to build up your emotional tolerance. You may need to wait until another time to regain your composure. As marital partners, respect and honor this request without indicating you feel it is a weakness. However, if you use this method try to never use it as a cop-out or escape from facing reality. If you do, you will never solve your marital problems.

Step 3—Now that you have shared your thoughts with each other without verbal reactions, go back and respond to each other's answers. Ask your partner for more clarification and elaboration. Be positive. Try to hear as much as you can so as to know how your mate really thinks and feels. If one or the other of you is not thinking clearly, there will be plenty of opportunity to state your own opinions in the projects to follow.

AS A GROUP OF COUPLES: Leader's Instructions

1. Separate into small groups of four or five in each group. Men and women should be in separate groups.

2. Have each group appoint a leader and a recorder.

3. Spend 10 minutes having each group of men answer the five questions for husbands and each group of women answer questions for wives.

4. Spend 20 to 30 minutes having each group recorder report the answers to the total group.

5. Agree that there will be no discussion or interaction during this first session—just reporting.

Note—There will inevitably be off-the-cuff comments that will be humorous. This is normal and helps break any tension that may exist. However, there should be no serious discussion or rebuttal during this first session.

Instruct those in the small groups to answer the following questions non-personally after going over the biblical material in chapter 1 and the first part of chapter 2. Rephrase the questions as follows:

Questions for Wives

1. If you could point out *one* thing about the *average* husband that pleases the *average* wife the most, what would it be? Why?

2. What is the greatest strength of the *average*

husband in today's culture? Why is this considered a strength?

3. How could the *average* husband help the *average* wife be a more fulfilled person? Explain.

4. What one personality factor in the *average* husband causes the most emotional difficulty in the *average* marriage? Explain why.

5. If you could change one thing about the *average* husband, what would it be?

Questions for Husbands

1. If you could point out *one* thing about the *average* wife that pleases the *average* husband the most, what would it be? Why?

2. What is the greatest strength of the *average* wife in today's culture? Why is this considered a strength?

3. How could the *average* wife help the *average* husband be a more fulfilled person? Explain.

4. What one personality factor in the *average* wife causes the most emotional difficulty in the *average* marriage? Explain why.

5. If you could change one thing about the *average* wife, what would it be?

Couple Assignment

Following the group process, assign couples to go home and *personalize* this group project in their own marriage by completing the three-step project on pages 26-28 under the title, AS A COUPLE, completing the worksheets in their own copy of *The Measure of a Marriage Workbook*.

Step 1—*Plan a Time*

As a couple spend a moment discussing with each

other a time when you can get together this coming week to work through the steps in the project for wives and for husbands for chapter 2. Find a place where you can get away from the house and the children. For example, have breakfast out and then work through the steps; or find a quiet place where you will be uninterrupted for a couple of hours.

Step 2—*Sign a Contract*

Following is a simple contract. As a couple, sign it, agreeing to commit yourselves to work through the projects together in this book. Though it may appear like a first-grade assignment, remember that some of us are still in the "first grade" in our marriages. But even as you consider yourself "in college" in your marital process, a contractual commitment of this nature is very helpful in following through when the pressures of other things tend to sidetrack us from our prior commitments.

With God's help we covenant together to attend this class on marriage and/or to work through the projects in this book.

Signed _____
                    Husband

Signed _____
                    Wife

Date _____

Notes

1. Gene A. Getz. *The Measure of a Woman* (Glendale, CA: Regal Books, 1977), p. 79.
2. *The Measure of a Marriage Workbook* (Glendale, CA: Regal Books, 1980) is available from your local church supplier.

CHAPTER 3

Leaving Father and Mother

Moses' original statement about marriage, which was reiterated by Jesus and Paul, contains another very significant principle for measuring a marital relationship. Not only do a man and woman become "one flesh" with unbounding potential for experiential unity and oneness, but the Bible also says: "For this cause a man [and woman] *shall leave his father and mother*" (Eph. 5:31).

In the most literal sense the Bible is simply referring to leaving certain established relationships with one family and starting another. It is only logical that a man and woman cannot become truly "one" in a practical sense unless they break certain ties with their parents and establish their own enduring relationship.

But this statement has profound implications beyond

just literal separation. In fact, it may be true that the real meaning is more related to "emotional" than "physical" separation. The facts are that children in biblical settings who separated from their parents did not necessarily move away from their parents. In their culture, they often lived under the same roof or right next door. The extended family was a part of their societal structures.

I remember visiting the Pompeii exhibit when it was on display in Dallas, Texas. As you'll remember, this Roman city was once a thriving metropolis before it was buried in A.D. 70 under tons of volcanic ash from erupting Mount Vesuvius. As you study the architectural designs of homes in that city—many of which have been carefully and painstakingly excavated by archaeologists—you can see how these structures reflect the concept of the extended family. One home particularly was featured, obviously owned by a very well-to-do family in Pompeii. The home included numerous rooms and sections where family members eventually set up their own housekeeping when they were married. In a sense *all* the members of the family lived under one roof, but there were also many homes within a home.

Although the trend in our twentieth-century culture is more toward geographical separation of parents and their married children, there are times, for economic or other reasons, when people do live together as multiple families. Close geographic proximity can make it more difficult to "leave father and mother" in the true and most profound sense of what that means.

Developing Unhealthy Dependence

For example, Bill and Mary are newly-married. Because Mary's parents have a large home, and because the newlyweds are trying to finish college, Mary's parents have invited them to live with them.

Is this wrong? Not necessarily. However, there's a problem. Bill, like most young men who marry early, has certain vulnerabilities. He knows Mary's parents are relatively well-to-do and are very unselfish with their material possessions. Consequently, under the financial pressures and the demands of college, Bill is becoming more and more dependent on his wife's parents to meet their material needs. Since he has not had to face the realities of life and his own responsibilities to support and care for Mary, he is not growing and maturing in this aspect of his life.

Will this turn out bad? Again, not necessarily. It all depends. But it has certain potential dangers that could eventually blow the lid off this new marriage.

For example, because of Bill's attitudes and behavior, Mary could be developing resentful feelings toward her husband which could eventually erupt. Or she could continue to harbor these feelings, never expressing them, and go into a state of depression.

Bill could also develop some very bad habit patterns both emotionally and volitionally. Life is filled with threatening responsibilities and having to face them later in life doesn't make it easier. But the temptation is always there to rely on good old Dad and Mom to help them out in financial binds.

Then, too, living with parents who are well-to-do makes it emotionally difficult for newly-married couples to eventually live in a small, sparsely-furnished apartment that is commensurate with their income. For most young couples starting out it will take a number of years—as it did their parents—to have sufficient resources to live more comfortably.

On the other hand, this does not mean that parents who are able should not be considerate of their married children and help them meet their needs. But should their help become a stumbling block in their children's marital adjustments, they must face this problem head-on. The most loving thing parents can do is to adjust *their* behavior so as to help both children "leave father and mother" and to establish their own home, responsibly and successfully. Furthermore, a young couple who sees a dependency syndrome developing should initiate the break themselves if their parents do not, regardless of how extremely painful at the time. Ultimate happiness is far more important than immediate comfort.

Immature Parents

There's another side to this problem. Sometimes close proximity brings out the immaturity in parents rather than in their children. For example, Tom and Jane are living next door to his parents. Tom is an only son and, though his mother loves Jane, down deep she has never felt there would ever be a girl quite good enough for her son (a rather common emotion for most mothers). Try as she might to overcome these feelings, she struggles with them every day. Unfortunately, close proximity visualizes Jane's inadequacies as a young bride and homemaker, and this only accentuates her mother-in-law's emotional problem.

Unfortunately, Tom's mother can't cover up her feelings. Jane is threatened by it all. Furthermore, Tom, as a young husband who also loves his mother, is slowly becoming convinced through her subtle innuendos that maybe Jane was a poor choice after all. For one thing, he can't quite seem to understand why his young working wife can't keep up the home as well as his older nonworking mother.

Obviously, this marriage is headed for serious problems because of close proximity. But again, all of us can point to children who *do* live next door or in the same house with their parents for a while with very few, if any, problems. But the principle of "leaving father and mother" is a valid one and both parents and children should face the issue immediately and make whatever changes are necessary. Generally, it is advisable in our culture to establish a certain degree of physical and geographical separation in order to avoid any potential problems. Because of the very nature of life, most of us, both parents and children, have a sufficient number of hang-ups to make us vulnerable. At this point an old adage is very appropriate: "An ounce of prevention is worth a pound of cure."

Emotions and Transference

When speaking of hang-ups it's important to realize that most of us have "emotional spillovers" from our home life that transfer to our mates and make it difficult to truly "leave father and mother." In fact, the phenomenon is inevitable regardless of how ideal our childhood experiences. All mothers and wives and fathers and husbands have many things in common.

Let me illustrate. Before he married, John's *mother* washed his clothes, made his bed, cooked his meals, and kept up the house. Now he's married and his wife, Sally, washes his clothes, makes his bed, cooks his meals and keeps up the house. Though Sally is involved in performing the same functions as John's mother used to, she does things differently. For one thing, she's not quite as efficient. She doesn't organize his socks the way his mother did, and sometimes she doesn't have the bed made up when he gets home from work. And her meal schedule is not as regular. These similar functions combined with the dissimilar procedures irritate John no end. He finds himself emotionally reacting to Sally and constantly compares her openly to his mother. This, of course, makes Sally furious. In fact, it makes her want to do the opposite.

Sally's problems are also aggravated by the fact that her husband, John, also reminds her of *her father*, who was always picking on *her* mother, putting her on a performance standard and reminding her that she did not measure up to *his* own mother.

This process is often at least partially subconscious. There are times when things irritate us about our mates that we don't really understand. Subconsciously over the years we have repressed certain feelings and emotions which we had toward our parents. Unknown to us we subtly transfer these covert emotions to a husband or wife. This can happen even though we have been reared in a relatively happy home situation.

I remember this process at work in my own life. After I was married I experienced certain spontaneous negative feelings toward my wife when she would ask me to do certain things—particularly if she expressed her desires with a certain tone of voice. It wasn't until years later while visiting my parents' home that I began to see the connection. I found myself—during that visit—reacting to my mother emotionally just as I had been reacting to my wife. I had come "full circle." Old emotional memories suddenly came to the surface. I clearly saw the source of my more recent emotional feelings and reactions toward my wife. They had been there all along at a subconscious level. In reality, when I reacted to my wife's requests I was reacting to my mother. Those reactions did not necessarily relate to whether or not I loved or respected my mother, which I did and still do. They were *natural* feelings I had not understood or dealt with properly as I was growing up.

CHAPTER 4

An Exercise in Leaving Parents

How well do you understand the emotional dynamics involved in your own marriage? To what extent have you actually "left" your father and mother psychologically? Understanding the answers to these questions is the place to start in isolating problems and then solving them. Personal insight is absolutely essential, and this chapter is designed to help you gain that insight.

AS AN INDIVIDUAL

The following evaluation scales will help you isolate areas that need attention. The statements focus on three areas: Dependence vs. Independence, Parental Maturity, Emotional Transference for the Wife and Emotional Transference for the Husband. Circle the number that best describes your personal situation.

Dependence vs. Independence

	Never	Seldom	Sometimes	Frequently
1. When I feel *insecurity* I have a strong desire to share it with my mother.	1	2	3	4
2. When I get *angry* at my mate I have a strong desire to tell my mother.	1	2	3	4
3. When I get *lonesome* I have a strong desire to visit my mother.	1	2	3	4
4. When my mate *misunderstands* me I have a strong desire to talk with my mother.	1	2	3	4
5. When I have problems with my *children* I have a strong desire to seek my mother's advice.	1	2	3	4

	Never	Seldom	Sometimes	Frequently
6. When we run out of *money* I have a strong desire to ask my mother for financial help.	1	2	3	4
7. When I feel *insecurity* I have a strong desire to share it with my father.	1	2	3	4
8. When I get *angry* at my husband/wife, I have a strong desire to tell my father.	1	2	3	4
9. When I get *lonesome* I have a strong desire to visit with my father.	1	2	3	4
10. When my husband/wife *misunderstands* me I have a strong desire to talk with my father.	1	2	3	4

	Never	Seldom	Sometimes	Frequently
11. When I have problems with my *children* I have a strong desire to seek my father's advice.	1	2	3	4
12. When we run short of *money* I have a strong desire to ask my father for financial help.	1	2	3	4

Parental Maturity

	Never	Seldom	Sometimes	Frequently
1. My mother communicates with me to see how I'm doing in our marriage.	1	2	3	4
2. My mother criticizes my mate.	1	2	3	4
3. My mother sends me money.	1	2	3	4
4. My mother criticizes me.	1	2	3	4

	Never	Seldom	Sometimes	Frequently
5. My mother is upset if I don't contact her regularly.	1	2	3	4
6. My mother is quite disturbed if we visit my mate's parents more often than we visit them.	1	2	3	4
7. My father communicates with me to see how I'm doing in my marriage.	1	2	3	4
8. My father criticizes my mate.	1	2	3	4
9. My father sends me money.	1	2	3	4
10. My father criticizes me.	1	2	3	4
11. My father is upset if I don't contact him regularly.	1	2	3	4

	Never	Seldom	Sometimes	Frequently
12. My father is quite disturbed if we visit my mate's parents more often than we visit them.	1	2	3	4

Emotional Transference
For the Wife:

	Never	Seldom	Sometimes	Frequently
1. When my husband asks me to wash his clothes I feel negative.	1	2	3	4
2. When my husband asks me to sew a button on his clothes I feel negative.	1	2	3	4
3. When my husband asks me to fix a meal I feel negative.	1	2	3	4
4. When my husband asks me to make love I feel negative.	1	2	3	4

	Never	Seldom	Sometimes	Frequently
5. When my husband asks me to overcome a habit I experience negative feelings.	1	2	3	4
6. When my husband asks me to help him with his work I feel negative.	1	2	3	4
7. When my husband asks me to run an errand I experience negative feelings.	1	2	3	4
8. When my husband asks me to keep a certain time schedule I experience negative feelings.	1	2	3	4
9. When my husband disagrees with me I get angry.	1	2	3	4

	Never	Seldom	Sometimes	Frequently
10. When my husband makes a suggestion to me I get emotionally upset.	1	2	3	4

For the Husband:

	Never	Seldom	Sometimes	Frequently
1. When my wife asks me to help with the dishes I experience negative feelings.	1	2	3	4
2. When my wife asks me to carry out the garbage I experience negative feelings.	1	2	3	4
3. When my wife asks me to help with the housework I experience negative feelings.	1	2	3	4
4. When my wife asks me to show affection toward her I experience negative feelings.	1	2	3	4

	Never	Seldom	Sometimes	Frequently
5. When my wife asks me to overcome a habit I feel negative.	1	2	3	4
6. When my wife asks me to watch the children I feel negative.	1	2	3	4
7. When my wife asks me to account for the money I spend I feel negative.	1	2	3	4
8. When my wife asks me to maintain a certain time schedule I feel negative.	1	2	3	4
9. When my wife disagrees with me I get angry.	1	2	3	4
10. When my wife makes a suggestion to me I get emotionally upset.	1	2	3	4

As an individual, study your answers on these three scales. What can *you* do to improve your marriage, even though your mate is not particularly interested?

Suggestion: Share the results of your self-evaluation with a mature friend or competent Christian counselor. Seek their advice. Have them help you evaluate your objectivity regarding your marriage.

AS A COUPLE

Step 1—Make sure both of you have completed the three evaluation quizzes, Exercises 2, 3 and 4 in *The Measure of a Marriage Workbook*.

Step 2—Use the following questions to evaluate your responses. Each of you should take at least 10-15 minutes to write your observations in Exercise 5 in *The Measure of a Marriage Workbook*.

Dependence vs. Independence

1. As a wife are there any areas where you are overly *dependent* on your mother? Your father? Are there any areas where you are overly *independent?* How does this affect your marital relationship?

2. As a husband are there any areas where you are overly *dependent* on your mother? Your father? Are there any areas where you are overly *independent?* How does this affect your marital relationship?

Parental Maturity

1. As a wife what areas of *maturity* can you identify in your parents? What areas of *immaturity?*

2. As a husband, what areas of *maturity* can you identify in your parents? What areas of *immaturity?*

3. How do these dynamics affect your husband/wife relationships?

Emotional Transference

1. As a wife are there any negative emotions you have experienced toward your parents that you are now transferring to your husband? How does this affect your husband's attitudes and behavior toward you?

2. As a husband are there any negative emotions you have experienced toward your parents that you are now transferring to your wife? How does this affect your wife's attitudes and behavior toward you?

Step 3—Share what you have written (Exercise 5 in *The Measure of a Marriage Workbook*) with your mate. Take turns sharing your answers. Ask each other whether or not you agree with the observations.

Step 4—Write out specific goals (Exercise 6 in *The Measure of a Marriage Notebook*) that relate to specific areas of need in your marriage. The following section, "Overcoming Problems," will illustrate this process.

Overcoming Problems

Isolating problems and understanding their nature is the place to start in solving them. However, you must go a step further. *Insight* is only the beginning. You must set specific goals to overcome these problems. What goals should you set in your marriage in order to help you to maturely "leave father and mother"? The following illustrations will help you in your goal-setting process:

Case 1: Jane has a consistent tendency to talk to her mother every time she feels *insecurity* in her marriage.

Her goal is to sensitively share these feelings with her husband rather than her mother. Jim, her husband, has set up the goal to listen objectively and nondefensively to Jane when she shares these feelings and to do what he can to help her overcome her insecurities.

Case 2: Jim reacts negatively to his wife every time she asks him to do something around the house. His primary goal is to volunteer to do certain things before he is asked. Secondly, his goal is to be emotionally open to his wife's requests—realizing he is subconsciously reacting to his mother. On the other hand, Jane's goal is to ask Jim to do things with a different tone of voice. She realizes she conveys her desires in a rather demanding way. So, she is trying to avoid sounding like Jim's mother.

Case 3: Both Jim and Jane realize that *his* mother tries to control their marriage. They have set up two short-range goals and one long-range goal.

First, Jim is going to talk to his mother openly but sensitively, asking her not to interfere with their marriage. He plans to talk with his father privately, sharing why he is going to talk with his mother.

Second, Jane is simultaneously going to do all she can to let Jim's mother know she really cares about her—sending her a note of appreciation, calling her periodically to carry on a friendly conversation, etc.

Third, if the problem persists, Jim and Jane are considering moving to another part of the city to avoid geographical closeness.

AS A GROUP OF COUPLES: Leader's Instructions

Step 1—Review for the group the biblical material and illustrations in chapter 3. (See pages 34-39.)

Suggestion: Read the illustrations out loud to the class under the three problem areas; that is, (1) developing unhealthy dependence; (2) immature parents; and (3) emotional transference.

Step 2—Divide the men into small groups and the women into small groups. Have each group appoint a leader and recorder/reporter. Then have each group take 15 minutes and discuss the answers to the following questions:

Questions for Husbands
1. What areas in a wife's personality can reflect *over-dependency* on her mother? On her father? How can this negatively affect a marital relationship?
2. What areas in a wife's personality can reflect an overly *independent* attitude toward her mother or father?
3. What areas of immaturity on the part of *in-laws* can create problems in their children's marriage?
4. What possible areas of parental emotional transference are apt to show up in a wife's personality, thus affecting her relationship with her husband? What are the possible negative effects in the marriage?

Questions for Wives
1. What areas in a husband's personality can reflect *over-dependency* on his mother? On his father? How can this negatively affect a marital relationship?
2. What areas in a husband's personality can reflect an overly *independent* attitude toward his mother or father?
3. What areas of immaturity on the part of *in-laws* can create problems in their children's marriage?

4. What possible areas of parental emotional transference are apt to show up in a husband's personality, thus affecting his relationship with his wife? What are the possible negative effects in the marriage?

Step 3—Have the recorders for each men's group report their answers to the whole group. Ask the women to listen carefully. Then have the women recorders report their findings while the men listen carefully.

Note: If your class is small you may have all the group members participate in the reporting.

Couple Assignment

Ask each couple to complete at home the four-step project on pages 50-51 in this book. They should use their copy of *The Measure of a Marriage Workbook* to complete the evaluation scales (Exercises 2,3,4) on "Dependence vs. Independence," "Mature or Immature Parents," and "Emotional Transference," and answer the questions (Exercise 5). Then they should set goals (Exercise 6) for overcoming problems after they have read the case studies on pages 51,52 of this book.

CHAPTER 5

Loving as Christ Loved

If someone were to ask you to identify a person in history who demonstrated true love more than any other individual, what would you say? The fact is that most people who live in our culture, if asked that question, would probably identify that person as Jesus Christ. Even people who have studied His life very little, or who would not be particularly enthused about His teachings or personal claims would still credit Him with being a man who demonstrated supreme love, far beyond any other human being.

Biblical writers—especially Paul the apostle—identify Christ quite frequently as an example of love in human relationships. They particularly uphold Christ's example in the most unique of all human relationships—marriage! But unfortunately, some students of the Bible have attempted to interpret scriptural directives about these marital relationships without considering directives to *all* Christians regarding their overall relationships with one another. This often leads to erroneous conclusions regarding husband and wife roles. And today, these erroneous conclusions are most often reflected by religious leaders who are dispensing simplistic and almost dogmatic solutions to marital conflicts and problems.

It's imperative that we realize that the instructions which the New Testament gives us, particularly in the letters written to various churches in the first-century world, were in the most part written to *all* Christians. It is true, however, that within this larger context there are some specific instructions given to certain individuals within these churches—such as husbands and wives. But if we attempt to isolate instructions directed to these individuals, we will come up with interpretations that are indeed narrow, restrictive, simplistic and in some instances totally unworkable.

Let me illustrate. Often we have zeroed in on Paul's statements in his letters to the Ephesians and Colossians that husbands are to love "as Christ loved" (see Eph. 5:25; Col 3:19), and wives are to "submit to [their] husbands" (see Eph. 5:22; Col. 3:18) without considering the larger context of these statements. Consequently, we have come up with conclusions regarding husband and wife relationships that are in some respects unscriptural and often offensive to those who understand more thoroughly the dynamics of human personality and interpersonal relationships, particularly from a sociological and psychological point of view.

To love "as Christ loved" is probably one of the most foundational directives and principles in all of Scripture.

It was Christ's "new commandment" to the apostles. "Love one another," He said, "even as I have loved you" (John 13:34). It is stated as the greatest mark of maturity among followers of Christ, "But now abide faith, hope, love, these three; but the greatest of these is love. Pursue love" (1 Cor. 13:13; 14:1).

To love is either directly or indirectly given as an imperative in Scripture more than any other directive. And it is the key to unity and harmony in human relationships (see John 17:20-23). By obeying God in this area of our lives, we can fulfill the whole law of God (see Rom. 13:10; Gal. 5:13,14; and Jas. 2:8).

If loving "as Christ loved" is foundational in enabling *all* of us to become one, how much more so in a marital relationship. It certainly provides the broad frame of reference, or to put it another way, it becomes the overarching principle for keeping all other scriptural directives in proper focus.

Focusing on Others

What does it mean to love "as Christ loved"? Perhaps the most graphic illustration is given by Paul in his letter to the Philippians. Initially, Paul gave a specific exhortation: "Do *nothing* out of selfish ambition or vain conceit, but in humility consider others better than yourselves. Each of you should look not only to your own interests, but also to the interests of others" (Phil. 2:3,4 *NIV*).

Just reading this paragraph from Paul's letter makes it quite clear how this directive will affect a marital relationship. The principle of loving "as Christ loved" puts the focus immediately on our partner's needs, not on our own. In *everything* we do, our goal should be to consider the other person's needs and concerns first.

Paul goes on to spell out how Christ demonstrated these attitudes and actions toward us.

First, he said, there's to be an attitude of unselfishness. "Your attitude should be the same as that of Christ Jesus: who, being in very nature God, did not consider equality with God something to be grasped" (Phil. 2:5,6, *NIV*).

In other words, Christ did not cling to His heavenly position with His Father, but was willing to lay it aside to come into this world—the world He made. And in His incarnation He identified with our fallen condition, though He, of course, did not personally participate in sin. He did, however, give up the glories of heaven to live among men. And when He did so He was demonstrating an unselfish attitude that is unparalleled in the universe.

Second, Christ's love was demonstrated by an attitude of humility (see Phil. 2:7). Christ, who was "in very nature God" (v. 6), voluntarily "made himself nothing." He who created all things temporarily laid aside His heavenly glory. He who was and is God took upon Himself "the very nature of a servant." He who made man took upon Himself "human likeness." This, of course, is ultimate humility personified.

Third, Christ demonstrated an attitude of sacrifice and self-giving. His actions illustrate the greatest act of love ever known to mankind. "Being found in appearance as a man, he humbled himself and became obedient to death—even death on a cross!" (Phil. 2:8, *NIV*). Jesus Christ died that we might live eternally. Because man's sin demanded the penalty of death, Jesus Christ died for every man, even His enemies. Thus, when they nailed Him to the cross, He prayed, "Father, forgive them, for they do not know what they are doing" (Luke 23:34, *NIV*).

Paul wrote these words in Philippians to all Christians who are supposed to emulate Christ in their relationships with others. But it is also a powerful demonstration and elaboration for both husbands and wives of what it means to love "as Christ loved."

Focusing on Husbands

Why did Paul zero in on husbands when a wife is also to love "as Christ loved"? The answer is clear when we understand the specific temptation that most men face—the temptation to focus on their own needs and to "use" women selfishly. This was particularly true in the first-century world. Culturally, women were commonly treated like slaves and second-class citizens. These men, converted to Christianity out of a pagan life-style, needed to be told what their proper attitude toward their wives was to be.

But it is also true that men in *all* cultures and in any given moment in history need this emphasis. There is within men a tendency toward selfishness that seems to be uniquely male. This is particularly true in the area of sex. It is very easy to be naturally demanding, insensitive, selfish and manipulative. Paul—a man—knew that. Consequently, he bore down on this injunction for husbands.

Furthermore, the very authority and responsibility God has given husbands makes this emphasis necessary. *First, like Christ, they are to have an attitude of unselfishness.* Like Jesus, a Christian husband should not grasp and hold on to his position of authority, using it as a manipulative device to get what he wants. True, there may be times when he must make decisions and judgments that will cause a certain amount of resistance and even emotional pain, but he must always use the authority for the benefit of his mate. Whatever he does must be done to protect his wife and to assist her in her personal growth. Christ's goal for the church is to "make her holy, . . . to present her to himself as a radiant church, without stain or wrinkle or any other blemish, but holy and blameless. In this same way," continued Paul, "husbands ought to love their wives as their own bodies. He who loves his wife loves himself" (Eph. 5:26-28, *NIV*).

2. *Second, a husband, like Christ, should have an attitude of humility.* Though God has given man a position of headship and authority, he must realize that he is also a servant. He must never lord it over his wife, using his male ego as an excuse for insensitivity and personal defensiveness that is purely self-protection.

Furthermore, he must identify with his wife—her pain, her heartaches, her struggles, her weaknesses, her anxieties, her stresses, her needs, as well as her joys, her successes, her achievements. Remember that Christ's love caused Him to identify with us. To love our wives as Christ loved the church means physiological, psychological and spiritual identification with them.

3. *Third, a husband who loves "as Christ loved" must demonstrate an attitude of sacrifice and self-giving.* This is one of the most difficult facets of Paul's teaching. When it comes to sacrifice, most of us, men and women, operate at a very superficial level. Much of what we do, if we're not careful, is for ourselves. It may appear on the surface to be for the benefit for our mate, but a closer look into the depths of our psychological nature often reveals a selfish person. But the challenge is still there. Though we are imperfect human beings, we must set as our goal pure motives—to love as Christ loved—demonstrating a sacrificial and self-giving spirit.

CHAPTER 6

An Exercise in True Loving

To love "as Christ loved" is probably one of the most difficult challenges facing any couple. It calls for attitudes and actions that run contrary to our natural inclinations. It is much easier for most of us to receive than to give; to be self-centered than to focus on others; to be ministered unto than to minister. And indeed we must be able to receive, to have our share of attention and to be ministered unto. But to focus on ourselves primarily destroys that unique process that *must* put others first if we are to follow Christ's example. The following exercise will help you develop these qualities in your own life first—and then in your marriage.

AS AN INDIVIDUAL

Evaluate your relationship with your mate in light of

Christ's example of unselfishness, humility and sacrifice and self-giving. The following evaluation scales will assist you in this process.

Note: It is true that there are circumstances making some of the following attitudes and actions appropriate and essential. But generally, these statements represent behavior that is basically selfish, proud and unsacrificial. In short, they do not reflect Christ's example of love.

A Quiz for Husbands

Instructions: Circle the T to indicate that you feel the statement is *mostly* true regarding your behavior. Circle the F to indicate the statement is *mostly* false regarding your behavior.

☐ 1. When I come home from work I immediately seek a place of privacy where I can do my own thing.   T   (F)

☐ 2. When I come home from work I want my wife to be available immediately to listen to my problems.   T   (F)

☐ 3. I resent it when my wife is running behind schedule with her meal preparation.   T   (F)

☐ 4. I do not expect to help with the children when I'm home.   T   (F)

☐ 5. I seldom think about the burden my wife carries when she is home all day with the children.   T   (F)

☐ 6. When I want to have sexual relations with my wife, I seldom think about her personal schedule.   T   F

☐ 7. I resent it when my wife gets attention.   T   (F)

☐ 8. I seldom thank my wife for cooking meals and taking care of the home. (T) F

☐ 9. I seldom suggest to my wife that we eat out. T F

☐ 10. I resent it when my wife sleeps late in the morning. T F

☐ 11. I resent it when my wife stays up late to get things done around the house. T (F)

☐ 12. I seldom ask my wife what I can do to help her with her work. T (F)

☐ 13. When I have a day off I usually plan to spend it with my male companions. (Golfing, playing tennis, etc.) T (F)

☐ 14. When I have a choice between spending time with my wife and my friends, I usually choose to spend time with my friends. T (F)

☐ 15. When I have a choice between spending time with my wife or my children, I usually spend time with my children. T F

☐ 16. I seldom call my wife during the day and tell her I miss her and love her. T (F)

☐ 17. I seldom think about how to encourage my wife when I come home from work. (T) F

☐ 18. I seldom think about my wife's personal needs. T (F)

☐ 19. I seldom think about how to be a creative lover. (T) F

☐ 20. I expect my wife to initiate sexual relations. T (F)

☐ 21. I seldom think about my wife during the day. T (F)

☐ 22. I seldom make an effort to know what my wife is doing during the day; that is, to become aware of her personal work schedule.   T (F)

☐ 23. I'd rather spend most of my time by myself.   T (F)

☐ 24. When I know I'm going to be coming home later than normal I usually do not call my wife to explain.   T (F)

☐ 25. I seldom ask my wife for permission to do things.   T (F)

☐ 26. I resent having to spend money on my wife.   T (F)

☐ 27. If I had it to do over again, I'd rather not have children.   T (F)

☐ 28. I seldom express appreciation to my wife for her ministry to me and my children.   T (F)

☐ 29. I resent having to work to earn a living for my family.   T (F)

☐ 30. I seldom postpone my desire for sexual activities.   T F

☐ 31. I seldom spend time preparing my wife emotionally for our sexual experience or helping her reach a sexual climax.   T (F)

☐ 32. I seldom write love notes to my wife.   (T) F

☐ 33. Most of the time when I say, "I love you," is when I'm having sexual relations with my wife.   T (F)

☐ 34. I resent the children's demands upon my wife when I want to spend time with her privately.   T (F)

A Quiz for Wives

Instructions: Circle the T to indicate you feel the statement is *mostly* true regarding your behavior. Circle the F to indicate the statement is *mostly* false.

☐ 1. When my husband comes home from work I immediately ask him to sit down and listen to my problems.   T (F)

☐ 2. When I see my husband has a few spare moments at home I present him with a list of things that I want him to do around the house.   T F

☐ 3. I resent it when my husband sits down in the family room and watches television—especially when I'm preparing the meal.   T (F)

☐ 4. I expect my husband to take care of the children while he's home.   T (F)

☐ 5. I resent the fact that my husband is away from the children during the day and I have to take care of them.   T (F)

☐ 6. I find myself quite frequently emotionally resistant when I know my husband has sexual interests and needs.   T (F)

☐ 7. I resent the fact that my husband gets more attention from others than I do.   T (F)

☐ 8. I resent having to cook meals and take care of the home.   T (F)

☐ 9. I want to eat out most of the time.   T (F)

☐ 10. I sleep late most days, getting up after my husband leaves for work.   T (F)

☐ 11. I usually stay up late to do things after my husband goes to bed.   T (F)

☐ 12. I seldom ask my husband what I can do   T (F)
to help him with his work.

☐ 13. I spend more time with my friends than   T (F)
with my husband.

☐ 14. When I have a choice between setting   T (F)
aside time to be with my husband or
my friends I usually set aside time to be
with my friends.

☐ 15. When I have a choice between setting   T (F)
aside time to be with my husband or
my children I usually set aside time to
be with my children.

☐ 16. I seldom call my husband at work and   T (F)
tell him I miss him and love him.

☐ 17. I seldom plan how I can make my   T (F)
husband feel welcome when he comes
home from work.

☐ 18. I seldom think about my husband's   T (F)
personal needs.

☐ 19. I seldom think about how to be a crea-   T (F)
tive lover.

☐ 20. I seldom initiate sexual relations.   T F

☐ 21. I seldom think about my husband dur-   T (F)
ing the day when he's not home.

☐ 22. I seldom make an effort to know what   T (F)
my husband is doing during the day;
that is, his personal work schedule.

☐ 23. I'd rather spend most of my time by   T (F)
myself.

☐ 24. If I'm going to be gone when my   T (F)
husband comes home, I usually do not
leave a note or call him and explain
changes in my personal scheduling.

☐ 25. I seldom ask my husband's permission to do things.   T (F)

☐ 26. I resent the fact that I don't have a separate bank account.   T (F)

☐ 27. If I had it to do over again, I'd rather not have children.   T (F)

☐ 28. I seldom thank my husband for his commitment to his job and for providing materially for my personal needs.   T F

☐ 29. I resent having to care for the children, keep up the home, prepare meals, etc.   T F

☐ 30. I resent my husband's sexual requests.   T (F)

☐ 31. I resent the fact that my husband is fulfilled sexually.   T F

☐ 32. I seldom write love notes to my husband.   T—F

☐ 33. I seldom tell my husband how much I love him.   T (F)

☐ 34. I resent the children's demands upon my husband when I want to spend time with him privately.   T—F

Having worked through the particular scale designed for you, go back over your T and F responses. Wherever you find a T, put a check (✔) in the box provided at the beginning of each item. These checks will identify areas that *may* (but not always) represent areas of selfish and unloving attitudes and actions on your part in your relationship with your mate. Use these areas to write out some specific goals that you want to achieve that will cause you to love more as Christ loved! Hopefully, this will help your mate to reciprocate.

Note: If your mate is open to making this a reciprocal

process, move on to the couple project and work through the evaluation scales together.

AS A COUPLE

Step 1—As a husband and wife, complete the evaluation scales designed for each of you, Exercise 7 in *The Measure of a Marriage Workbook*.

Step 2—Now that you've completed the evaluation scales designed for each of you, fill out the one designed to evaluate your mate, Exercise 8 in *The Measure of a Marriage Workbook*.

Step 3—Compare your evaluation of your mate (Exercise 8) with your mate's self-evaluation (Exercise 7). To isolate areas of discrepancy as well as areas of agreement, record your answers and your mate's answers in Exercise 9, in *The Measure of a Marriage Workbook*, which is designed for a comparative study.

Step 4—Now that you have recorded your answers on the forms designed for a comparative study, isolate the areas of discrepancy by placing a check (✔) in the box provided before each statement in Exercise 9. Then discuss the areas of discrepancy and why you think they exist. Do so as sensitively and as nondefensively as possible.

Step 5—Following your discussion of the comparative study, each of you should go through the *original* evaluation scale, Exercise 7, designed for each of you and place a check (✔) in the box provided by each item which you marked T for mostly true about yourselves.

Note: Answers you've marked T about yourselves indicate areas of life that usually (but not always) focus on oneself rather than the other partner. Utilizing your observations from both the comparative studies as well as your personal scales, set up personal goals for your marriage.

Caution: Each marital partner is entitled to his own rights in a marriage. To say we have no rights is an oversimplification. For example, a wife needs a husband who will sit down and listen to her problems; also, a husband needs the same attention. However, if we consistently demand this right, we have put the primary focus on ourselves rather than on our mate. To do so, violates Jesus' example who came to "minister" rather than to be "ministered unto." God's will is that both mates reach out to the other to meet each other's needs. When we do so, our own needs will be met. The relationship is then in proper focus.

Step 6—Utilizing the observations you've both made as a result of the foregoing process, write out specific goals for yourselves as marital partners. (Exercise 10 in *The Measure of a Marriage Workbook*.)

AS A GROUP OF COUPLES

First, review with the group the biblical material presented in chapter 5. Then divide up into small groups with men and women in separate groups. You may wish to maintain the same groups from session to session. Feel free, however, to mix them up if you feel this is necessary.

Step 1—Have each group of women read through the evaluation items for wives on pages 29-30 in the Workbook and put a check (✔) in the box provided if they feel this is a problem area for the *average* woman. In other words, have them check the item where the average wife would probably have to admit this particular item is "mostly true." Have the men's group go through the same process for their own scale on pages 31,32 in the Workbook.

Step 2—Have each group work through their evaluation scale, noting the checked items and make a statement on a separate sheet of paper as to *why* they believe that is a particular problem for the *average* wife or husband. Appoint a recorder to list the statements.

Step 3—Have each group briefly report their observations. Hear first from the women. Ask the men to listen carefully and as objectively as possible. Then give them a brief period of time to voice their opinions as to whether or not they feel the women are making valid observations.

Then repeat the same process for the men. First have them report and then have the women respond to what they hear.

Note: If you have several groups, ask reporters not to repeat observations another group has shared.

Couple Assignments

Assign couples to complete Exercises 7—10 in *The Measure of a Marriage Workbook*. This time they will use the "mostly true" or "mostly false" approach as it applies to their own marriage.

A Final Thought

All people everywhere have the *potential* to love as Christ loved. But all cannot satisfactorily practice this kind of life-style in their marriages or in any other relationships without knowing personally the One who exemplified this kind of sacrificial love.

This implies more than simply trying to follow His

example. It means coming to know Jesus Christ in a personal way as Saviour and Lord. It is then that He will help each of us love as He loved.

Do you know Christ personally? Have you received Him as your Saviour from sin? If not, you can. Sincerely take the following steps and you will add a dimension to your marriage that you have never known before.

Step 1—Acknowledge before God that you have sinned—that is, you have fallen short of God's divine standard (see Rom. 3:23).

Step 2—Accept the fact that Jesus Christ offered Himself for your sins on the cross and paid the supreme penalty for sin—death (see Rom. 6:23). Believe also that He arose from the dead and because He lives, you too can live eternally with Him.

Step 3—Receive Jesus Christ as your personal Saviour from sin; that is, believe that He not only died and rose again for the sins of the world, but that He died and rose for you (see John 1:12; Rom. 5:1).

Step 4—Confess Jesus Christ before others; that is, let someone know what steps you have taken (see Rom. 10:9,10). Above all, begin to demonstrate with your lifestyle that you are a follower of Jesus Christ. The best place to begin is in your marital relationship as you begin more than ever before to love "as Christ loved."

CHAPTER 7

Submitting to Each Other

No aspect of marriage has been given more universal attention than wifely submission. And of course it is a very controversial subject at this juncture in our present-day cultural journey—particularly among those who classify themselves as feminists or at least are sympathetic to feminist ideology.

The very word "submission" is threatening. One reason is that we haven't understood its meaning as we should. We sometimes think of submission as allowing another person to dominate and control us. And all of us resist that kind of relationship.

In God's scheme of things, the concept of submission was never to be applicable to only one person in a given relationship. It was to be reciprocal and mutual.

It must be added that there are times when a marital partner (or a person generally) may need to submit under conditions that are not reciprocal. But God never intended this to be the normal rule for any human being, particularly since Christ came and introduced a whole new way of life.

What the Bible Says

The fact is that the Bible *does* teach submission, but not only for wives. It is a quality of life that should characterize *all* of us in our relationships with others. Thus, Paul, before exhorting wives to be submissive to their husbands (see Eph 5:22), exhorted *all* believers to be "subject [to submit] to one another in the fear of Christ" (Eph 5:21).

It's interesting that Paul did not use the word "submission" in his statement to wives. Rather, he based his directive for wives to "submit" on his use of the word in verse 21 when he was speaking to all the followers of Christ in Ephesus. In other words, Paul told all of these people they were to *submit* to one another (Eph. 5:21)—which, he said, includes wives to husbands (5:22), husbands to wives (5:25), children to parents (6:1), fathers to children (6:4), servants to masters (6:5) and masters to servants (6:9). Put another way, Paul's statement to "submit to one another" in verse 21 is the basic concept on which he builds his specific exhortations to the other people mentioned in the remaining part of his Ephesian letter.

That Paul believed that husbands should submit to their wives is clearly illustrated in the fact that they are to love as Christ loved. As we've already seen from Philippians, Christ demonstrated His love by becoming a *servant*, and it is impossible to be a servant without being submissive. Inherent then in Paul's statement to love "as

Christ loved" is a submissive attitude and spirit.

Why, then, does Paul specifically direct wives to be submissive to their husbands? The answer is that it is not in God's will for a wife to dominate, control or manipulate her husband. In fact, it is not within God's will for *any* Christian to dominate, control or manipulate any other human being. You see, the opposite of submission is control, resistance, domination. There's really no in-between. Either we are submissive, or we are non-submissive. There is, practically speaking, no neutral ground. Either we are teachable, willing to listen to someone else's advice and correction and willing to put the other person first, or we are resistant, unwilling to listen to another person's advice and correction and unwilling to put the other person first. Even a neutral attitude usually represents passive resistance, which is the opposite of having a submissive spirit.

Don't misunderstand! Discussion and dialogue and even disagreement are not necessarily synonymous with a non-submissive attitude. It depends on *how* it is done. Those who classify *all* resistance as non-submissive do not understand the communication process. God forbid that a man never allows his wife to disagree with him. If he does he, at that moment, also becomes non-submissive and certainly is not loving "as Christ loved." Unfortunately, some husbands have interpreted Paul's injunction to wives in this narrow way—which is incorrect and quite frequently rooted in personal pride and insecurity. In short, it reflects a male ego that has not been brought into conformity with Christ's example of love and way of life.

A Larger Perspective

Some theological, historical and cultural background

will help clarify further why Paul emphasized submission for women generally and wives particularly. First, God created Eve for Adam. She was *not* to be his subordinate but his equal. However, when sin entered the world, Eve (and all women following her) had to bear a special burden because Eve was first deceived (see 1 Tim. 2:13,14). If we are to accept the biblical account at all we cannot deny these facts. This is not just merely a Pauline interpretation but rather this concept can be traced all the way through the Bible. Furthermore, history verifies this reality.

However, with the coming of Jesus Christ something unique happened regarding a woman's role. As Christians, a man and wife have the potential to experience a unity and oneness that can grow constantly deeper and more meaningful day by day. From God's eternal and spiritual perspective, there's total equality (see Gal. 3:28). But since marriage is not an eternal relationship and is limited to time and space, man was appointed to be the head (as Christ is the head of the church) and the woman is to recognize his God-given authority. Becoming Christians does not eradicate sin. But in Christ, if a husband and wife continually love each other as Christ loved them, and regularly fulfill their God-ordained responsibilities and trust each other, they have the potential to experience a growing unity and oneness that can actually be a foretaste of heaven on this side of glory. Have you experienced some of this unity in your marriage?

A Psychological Reaction

In the New Testament world Paul had to deal with the problem of women who, once set free from the demands of their pagan religions, began to use their freedom in irresponsible ways. Naturally, the first area where it would be most observable would be in their relationships with their husbands. Having been put down for years and treated like slaves, they found themselves now with the opportunity for dominance and control.

This we ought to understand. Any group of people who has been mistreated and kept in bondage, once set free, will normally overreact. People like this often do not know *how* to handle this freedom.

This has been obvious in our own culture. Some minority groups have had to learn to handle freedom since for years they were mistreated, kept ignorant and in bondage. It takes time to overcome these social restrictions and our tendencies to overreact.

Some women today who are experiencing new freedom are likewise overreacting. For years in *our* culture many women have been mistreated. In the non-Christian world particularly, men have been notorious for using women for their own ends. On the current scene we see the "Playboy philosophy" that views women as toys, as playthings, as a means to selfish pleasure. It is no wonder that most thinking women react against this self-centered philosophy. Today, more than ever before, women are used for materialistic purposes. Sex sells anything, and women of course are the primary targets for this abuse. Again, it should not be surprising that many women react against such selfish exploitation.

Women also react to the general male selfishness that permeates the whole society in which we live. They have often been treated as inferior personalities, incapable of certain roles. They've often been kept "in their place" primarily because men have been threatened by the wo-men's abilities. Again, it should not surprise us that women can see through such egocentric behavior.

But where can these women turn? What is their source of authority for what they do? Unfortunately, many do not have or they reject any divine perspective. Motivated by the same sinful nature that motivates men, they are seeking liberation without God's principles. They do not realize that without Jesus Christ's attitudes they can never know true freedom. Consequently, they overreact, moving first in one direction and then in another. Being non-submissive certainly will not set them free any more than it sets a man free. No wonder the world is filled with frustrated people, many sincerely trying but never coming to a knowledge of these principles and the secret to what they are looking for.

The only answer to this overreaction is to follow Christ's example and instructions. Then husbands can love their wives as Christ loved the church—which includes submission. And wives can submit to their husbands as the church is subject to Christ—which certainly includes loving "as Christ loved." In fact, Christ's love is the basis for mutual submission. And mutual submission is possible without eliminating the husband's "headship." Applying these biblical principles is the *only* way to experience *functional* egalitarianism and still maintain the husband/wife roles specified in Scripture.

CHAPTER 8

An Exercise in Submitting

Marriage, more than any other relationship, includes many areas calling for mutual submission. What are these areas? To what extent are you submissive? Why are you having difficulty submitting? In what ways do you make it difficult for your mate to submit to you? How can you become a more submissive person?

This chapter is designed to help you answer these questions.

AS AN INDIVIDUAL

Following is a list of those areas in marriage that commonly create difficulty in submitting to each other. There's also room to add any that are not listed but are problem areas for you.

Step 1—Circle the number in the scale following each item to indicate the degree to which there is a problem in submitting to your mate. If it is *never* a problem circle number 1; if it is *always* a problem, circle number 7; or, circle any number between 1 and 7 that indicates the degree to which you have trouble in submitting to your mate in your marriage.

I find it difficult to submit when:	Never a Problem				Always a Problem		
☐ 1. My mate asks me to do things that are routine and boring;	1	2	3	4	5	6	7
☐ 2. My mate asks me to be more frugal in spending money;	1	2	3	4	5	6	7
☐ 3. My mate asks me to be more neat in personal grooming;	1	2	3	4	5	6	7
☐ 4. My mate asks me directly or indirectly to meet sexual needs;	1	2	3	4	5	6	7
☐ 5. My mate asks me to break a personal habit;	1	2	3	4	5	6	7
☐ 6. My mate asks me to be more orderly in my personal life;	1	2	3	4	5	6	7
☐ 7. My mate asks me to give up something I plan to do in order to do something my mate wants to do;	1	2	3	4	5	6	7

			Never a Problem				Always a Problem		

☐ 8. My mate asks me to set goals for my life and family;   1 2 3 4 5 6 7

☐ 9. My mate asks for a period of time to communicate;   1 2 3 4 5 6 7

☐ 10. My mate asks me to do something immediately when I plan to do it later;   1 2 3 4 5 6 7

☐ 11. My mate asks me to do something I usually do anyway;   1 2 3 4 5 6 7·

☐ 12. My mate asks me directly or indirectly to be more creative in our lovemaking;   1 2 3 4 5 6 7

☐ 13. My mate asks me to do something I feel is my mate's responsibility;   1 2 3 4 5 6 7

☐ 14. My mate asks me to help with the children;   1 2 3 4 5 6 7

☐ 15. My mate asks me to help with his or her work;   1 2 3 4 5 6 7

☐ 16. My mate asks me to explain my personal schedule;   1 2 3 4 5 6 7

☐ 17. Other _____   1 2 3 4 5 6 7

Step 2—Now that you have indicated the degree to which this is a problem in submitting to your mate, go through the items again and print an initial in the box provided at the beginning of each statement to indicate who you feel is primarily at fault. If you feel it is primarily your husband's fault that you have difficulty submitting to him, print an H in the box. If you feel it is primarily your wife's fault that you have difficulty submitting to her, print a W in the box. If you feel the fault is about evenly divided, print a B in the box.

Remember: Marriage is a two-way street. You may have difficulties submitting because of your partner's attitudes and behavior. On the other hand, you may be as much or more to blame than your mate.

Step 3—Sit down with a close friend of the same sex who is mature, happily married, and who is aware of your marital relationship and who will not favor your point of view just because he or she is your close friend. Ask your friend to evaluate your answers and to indicate the extent to which he or she thinks you have been objective in your responses. Also, seek your friend's advice as to *why* you may be having difficulties in certain areas of your relationship.

Note: If your friend believes that the problem is mostly your mate's, you may need to seek counsel from your pastor or some other competent marriage counselor. If your friend indicates it appears to be mostly your own attitudes and behavior, you may be able to handle the problem with your friend's advice, help and support. If not, do not hesitate to seek counsel from someone who specializes in helping people overcome marriage problems.

AS A COUPLE

Step 1—As a husband and wife, complete the "Submission Scale for Husbands" and the "Submission Scale for Wives" (Exercise 11) in *The Measure of a Marriage Workbook*.

Step 2—After evaluating yourself in terms of submission, evaluate *each other*. Complete the two scales in Exercise 12.

Step 3—Now that you have evaluated yourself personally as well as each other, compare your answers. To do this, fill in the blanks by each item on the comparative forms (Exercise 13).

Step 4—Compare your answers by placing a check in the box provided by each item in the scale, Exercise 13, where there are two or more points of difference in your evaluations. Then discuss with each other why you believe this variance exists. Take turns sharing and listening to each other. Discuss together as objectively as possible how you can help each other more easily submit to each other's desires.

Note: If you cannot work through this project satisfactorily, arriving at a degree of mutual understanding and concern for each other, you no doubt need to seek help from a professional marriage counselor. The sooner you do so, the better.

Step 5—Write out several personal goals that result from your discussion (Exercise 14).

AS A GROUP OF COUPLES

Step 1—Pass out sheets of paper and ask each individual to anonymously record *three* areas in his or her marriage that present the greatest difficulty in being submissive to the other marital partner.

Note: Ask each person to identify at the top of the sheet whether he/she is a husband or a wife.

Step 2—Collect the answer sheets. As a group leader, share what the wives have recorded and then share what the husbands have recorded.

Note: Ask a woman to record the results of the wives reports and a man to record the results of the husbands report. Ask each recorder to tabulate the number of times an area of difficulty is repeated.

Step 3—As previously, divide the total group into smaller groups (men with men and women with women). Each group should select a leader and recorder and then answer two questions regarding the two areas of difficulty that were mentioned the most. The questions are:

1. *Why* is this a problem?
2. *What* can be done specifically to overcome these problems?

Note: This process will take at least 10 minutes.

Step 4—Have each group recorder report the results of each group's discussion.

Note: Ask each recorder to avoid repetition in their reports.

Couple Assignments

Complete the project for couples outlined in this text, using Exercises 11, 12, 13 and 14 in *The Measure of a Marriage Workbook*.

CHAPTER 9

Learning to Love

A couple I knew were having serious problems in their marriage. One of the pastors in our church met with the husband one day for lunch and very pointedly asked him if he loved his wife.

"Yes," he responded, "I love her."

"May I read something to you?" asked the pastor. He opened his Bible and read from 1 Corinthians 13, which outlines the qualities which Paul defined as love:

- Love is patient
- Love is kind
- Love does not envy
- Love does not boast
- Love is not proud
- Love is not rude
- Love is not self-seeking

- Love is not easily angered
- Love keeps no record of wrongs
- Love does not delight in evil
- Love rejoices in the truth
- Love always protects
- Love always trusts
- Love always hopes
- Love always perseveres.

After the pastor had read this list from 1 Corinthians 13:4-8, he asked the question again: "Do you really love your wife?"

Without a moment's hesitation the husband responded: "No, I really don't love my wife—not that way!"

You see, the man's first response was based on our contemporary culture's definition of love—often primarily sexual feelings. And in this case, which can be multiplied again and again, what this man defined as "love" was probably not love at all.

Unfortunately, our Western culture particularly has propagated the idea that *feelings* of attraction and particularly *sexual* feelings are the essence of love. This is a very superficial and inadequate explanation of what keeps a marital relationship on track. In many instances what is initially classified as "love" is a *selfish* feeling—a *desire* to have the other person satisfy a personal need.

Let's look at another example. Tom and Diane were intensely attracted to each other during their dating and courtship experience. They were so emotionally involved that they engaged in various kinds of sexual activity. Both of them felt guilty about their behavior, but it didn't seem to diminish their "feelings" for each other, so they continued to be intimate prior to marriage.

Shortly after they were officially married, something began to happen. They discovered that living together 24 hours a day was quite different from seeing each other several times a week. They became aware very quickly that marriage involves far more than dinner out, dim lights, quiet music and a carefree evening together. In fact, Diane's attitude toward sexual involvement changed, which confused her and Tom. Right now both are going through a state of disillusionment. Unknown to both of them, neither has really learned to love each other.

More than ever before we need a more adequate view of premarital and marital love. I believe the Bible provides that view. There is no other source that provides a better perspective. All other approaches are limited, unsatisfactory and ultimately disillusioning.

Agape Love

The words *agapao* and *agape* are used most frequently in the New Testament to describe love. In most instances these Greek words are used to portray loving acts—that is, behaving in certain ways because it is the *right thing* to do. Though *agape* love should normally be combined with positive feelings, it is the kind of love that should cause me to meet my mate's needs, no matter how I personally feel about it.

Jesus Christ demonstrated this love dramatically when He voluntarily suffered on the cross, even though, at the *feeling level*, His *human* desire was to escape the agony that lay before Him. In spite of His painful ambivalence He did what He totally believed was the will of God.

Experience bears out why this kind of love *must* form the foundation for every marriage. If we performed our responsibilities to each other only when we *felt* like it, we would frequently leave undone many important things that contribute to marital harmony. For example, a man who faces a really tough day in the office in order to earn money to provide for his family does not always—at least at that moment—attack his responsibilities with strong motivation and positive emotions. But, *if* he really behaves toward his wife and family as Christ loved him, he'll do what is right, in spite of his negative feelings.

The same is true of wives and mothers. Washing clothes, preparing meals, and cleaning the house are not always the most exciting responsibilities. And it is even less exciting for a husband to lend a helping hand when he has just faced a day at the office that has been difficult and draining. And when a husband asks his wife—who has had a difficult day at home—for help with some of his office work, her own emotions don't usually cry out with anticipation to cooperate.

Husbands and wives who are mature intellectually *know* there are difficult moments in marriage. And because they are mature psychologically and spiritually, their love for each other ultimately transcends their selfish tendencies. They often perform responsibilities for each other in spite of their negative feelings. In fact, meeting the needs of each other in times like these is the fastest way to ''feel good'' about ourselves and our marital role.

On the other hand, *agape* love also causes husbands and wives to be sensitive to each other's emotional moods. There are times when the most loving thing to do is not to place demands on our mates. And, at the same time, the most loving thing to do in response may mean not taking advantage of our mate's willingness to forego a need, be it emotional, social, spiritual or physical. Men and women who indeed love according to God's perspective and Christ's example are able to work through these situations with sensitivity, maturity and good balance. They're very much aware that marital life is not always a rose garden.

Phileo Love

The Greek word *phileo* is often used interchangeably in the New Testament with *agapao*, but seemingly is also used distinctively to refer to love that is emotionally positive in nature. It is associated with true friendship. It involves delight and pleasure in doing something. Perhaps one of the best definitions of this kind of love is "a deep emotional feeling of trust generated from one person to another person."[1]

This is the kind of love Paul is referring to in Romans 12:10 when he writes: "Be devoted to one another in *brotherly love*." The Greek word translated "brotherly love" is *philadelphia*. It involves the idea of *phileo* love toward family members. But in this context Paul was using the kind of loving relationships that should exist among family members to illustrate the kind of relationships that should also exist among members of God's family.

In Christ, husbands and wives are also brothers and sisters. They too are to "be devoted to one another in brotherly love." And this is a special kind of love. Paul made this clear when he used the phrase "be devoted," which literally refers to the mutual affection that should exist between husbands and wives as well as other family members. Consequently, the *King James Version* reads, "Be kindly *affectioned* one to another in brotherly love," and Beck translates, "Love one another *tenderly* as fellow Christians."

This leads to a very important observation. The Bible uses different words to describe love. Though they are not always mutually exclusive in meaning, there are some important distinctions that relate to the subject before us—learning to love.

This distinction seems to be most clearly seen in Paul's instructions to women in Titus 2:3,4. "Likewise," Paul wrote, "teach the older women" and "then they can train the younger women *to love their husbands*" (*NIV*). This phrase is translated from the basic Greek word *philandros*.

Note that Paul assumes in these instructions to women in his letter to Titus that *phileo* love can be learned. In other words, we can engage not only in proper behavior toward our mate, but also develop positive feelings, particularly when we have positive models in other people.

Erao Love

There's another word for "love" that was used by Greek-speaking people in the first century—the word *erao*. Usually it referred to sexual love. Interestingly, this word is never used by New Testament authors. This does not mean that sexual love is wrong or improper, or is never referred to in the New Testament. However, biblical writers no doubt avoided this word because it was so frequently used in their culture to describe illicit sexual activity. Though it is not totally an accurate comparison, there are certain words for sexual expressions in our present-day culture that we avoid in most proper public discussions of sexual love. Though these words are frequently used by people to describe and talk about illicit sex in literature, movies and jokes, they're considered unacceptable, particularly by those who consider sex sacred.

Erotic experience, nevertheless, is an important part of marital love. Without it, marriage can never be what God intended it to be. It's that dimension of our personalities that enables a man and woman to be emotionally attracted to each other in ways that go beyond feelings of friendship. It enables a husband and wife to enjoy each other at levels of communication that are biblically off limits among men and women generally and family members particularly.

This does not mean that erotic feelings will not emerge under certain conditions leading to improper sexual behavior. The same human capacities that are designed by God to be used properly sometimes lead to premarital sexual activity, extramarital affairs, homosexual relationships and even incest. The important point is that when a man or woman engages in erotic lovemaking, they do so according to God's will. They should avoid conditions that lead to illicit sexual behavior. And if, on occasion, sexual feelings emerge (which in themselves are not wrong), they should avoid the inappropriate mental and physical actions that can easily follow.

As stated earlier, our present culture often defines love in emotional and sexual terms. For example, the words of most popular songs that speak of male and female relationships are clearly focused on sexual feelings. The theme of most movies, books and magazines that feature relationships between men and women also focus on this kind of love. Consequently, when a man says to a woman, "I love you," and the woman says, "I love you, too," the essence of their feelings at that moment are frequently sexual. And more recently in our own culture this kind of definition of love is openly featured in homosexual relationships.

This confuses many people, both men and women, old and young, married and unmarried. This was Tom and Diane's problem who were mentioned earlier. Victims of the twentieth-century culture, they thought they were in love. To a certain extent they may have been, but actually their relationship was based primarily on sexual or erotic feelings which God designed to be a vital and legitimate part of *agape* and *phileo* love. But in their case, sexual feelings were operative in a context void of a mature understanding of love that keeps the ebb and flow of erotic feelings from causing disillusionment and confusion. To keep their marriage intact they only had one choice. They must now really learn to love each other.

A Total Perspective

The Scriptures present the concept of love as three-dimensional. In its broadest meaning it involves attitudes and actions that are right and proper, no matter how we feel (see fig. 1, p. 94). *Agapao* love rises above feelings that may be more negative than positive. As previously stated, this is the kind of love Jesus Christ demonstrated when He with an act of His will chose the cross. In His humanity He agonized over this decision. He actually prayed that He might be released from the suffering that lay ahead (see Luke 22:42). However, He knew what His Father's will was and He died on the cross, though every ounce of human emotion within His being cried out for deliverance. He willingly gave up His life for others.

This is the ultimate in *agape* love. And it is God's will for all Christians in *all* relationships to "live a life of love, just as Christ loved us and gave himself up for us as a fragrant offering and sacrifice to God'' (Eph. 5:2, *NIV*). This particularly applies to marriage partners.

Phileo love involves positive feelings and should always be a part of and guided by *agape* love (see fig. 1, p. 94). In fact, it is *agape* love that keeps feelings of affection from becoming selfish and demanding. Many friendships have been destroyed by people who try to keep a relationship purely to themselves.

This also happens in marriage. Both husbands and wives need friendships with other men and women. A jealous spouse can literally destroy and crush a relationship, turning it into a nightmare of emotional pain. On the other hand, marital partners who indeed love according to God's standards, will never allow friendships outside the marriage to interfere with their own marriage. Mature Christians who are guided by *agape* love, as it is defined in the Bible, will maintain this intricate balance.

Erotic feelings and actions are also a part of the circle of biblical love. *Erao* love has been designed by God to be used and enjoyed fully, but it is always to be expressed within the boundaries of *agapao* and *phileo* love (see fig. 1, p. 94). It is this larger context that keeps a relationship morally on track. And it is only this larger context that will keep these feelings from being used in purely selfish ways, even in a marital relationship. Furthermore, it is this larger context that helps a married couple keep their emotional equilibrium during the many times when married life is difficult and demanding.

Note

1. Mort Katz, *Marriage Survival Kit* (Rockville Centre, NY: Farnsworth Publishing Company, Inc., 1974), p. 44.

THE CIRCLE OF BIBLICAL LOVE

Doing what is *right* and *best* for someone, even if it involves negative feelings.

Responding to someone's needs affectionately and with positive emotions, but always within the guidelines of *agape* love.

Becoming both emotionally and physically involved with another person sexually, but always within the guidelines of *agape* and *phileo* love.

Figure 1

CHAPTER 10

An Exercise in Developing Action Love

There is no simple formula for learning to love another person in a total sense. First of all, it requires being obedient to God (see John 15:10-12) and many times that is a difficult assignment emotionally.

First Corinthians 13 probably outlines the dimensions of *agape* love more completely than any other passage of Scripture. The scale on page 96 will help you measure your growth in expressing *agape* love toward your mate.

AS AN INDIVIDUAL

In the exercise on page 96, indicate on a scale of 1 to 10 the degree in which you love your mate in each of the areas. Then, when you have completed the evaluation scale, follow steps 1 through 4.

My dimension of agape love   *Degree of love*

1. Patience toward my mate   1 2 3 4 5 6 7 8 9 10

2. Kindness toward my mate   1 2 3 4 5 6 7 8 9 10

3. Lack of envy and jealousy   1 2 3 4 5 6 7 8 9 10

4. Lack of boasting (putting my mate down)   1 2 3 4 5 6 7 8 9 10

5. Lack of pride (competing with my mate)   1 2 3 4 5 6 7 8 9 10

6. Lack of rudeness   1 2 3 4 5 6 7 8 9 10

7. Not self-seeking (selfish behavior)   1 2 3 4 5 6 7 8 9 10

8. Not easily angered   1 2 3 4 5 6 7 8 9 10

9. Not keeping a record of wrongs   1 2 3 4 5 6 7 8 9 10

10. Not delighting in evil (insisting my mate participate in sinful actions)   1 2 3 4 5 6 7 8 9 10

11. Rejoicing in the truth (in doing God's will)   1 2 3 4 5 6 7 8 9 10

12. Protecting my mate   1 2 3 4 5 6 7 8 9 10

13. Trusting my mate   1 2 3 4 5 6 7 8 9 10

14. Seeing the best in my mate   1 2 3 4 5 6 7 8 9 10

15. Persevering in doing what is right   1 2 3 4 5 6 7 8 9 10

Step 1—Note the areas where you are *strongest*. Give yourself credit where credit is due.

Step 2—Note the items where you are *weakest*.

Step 3—Isolate the situations in your marital relationships where you demonstrate that weakness most.

Step 4—Set up one specific goal for each situation. For example, if you are quite frequently impatient, complete this sentence: This week I am going to demonstrate more patience toward my mate when . . .
Note: There may be legitimate reasons for your impatience. However, do not allow a two-way problem to keep you from working on your own negative reactions. If you begin to change, it often causes your mate to change too.

AS A COUPLE

Step 1—Each of you should complete the evaluation scales, Exercise 15, in *The Measure of a Marriage Workbook*.

Step 2—Each of you should also fill out the evaluation scale about your mate, Exercise 16.

Step 3—Compare your responses by filling out the comparative evaluation worksheets, Exercise 17. Put a plus (+) or a minus (−) in the box by each item to indicate if your mate rates you higher or lower than you do.

Step 4—Isolate areas of strength and weakness:
    A.   Look for discrepancies between "personal evaluation" and your "mate's evaluation of you." The items by which you placed a minus (−) will indicate the areas of discrepancies where you will need to concentrate. Plus (+) items indicate that you are harder on yourself than your mate is. Be encouraged!

Note: To be a significant discrepancy there should be two or more points difference. For example, if your mate circled number 5 regarding your "degree of patience" and you gave yourself a 6, consider this equal. However, if there's a two-point spread, consider this an area to look at carefully. Obviously, the greater the spread the greater the significance in difference and the more attention you should give that particular item.

B. In isolating areas of need, look for those items that are circled from 1 to 6; on a 10-point scale, consider 7 or above a very good score. However, if your scores mostly range at 7 or above, there is still room for improvement; but realize that if you rate this high with each other you are making great progress in learning to love.

Step 5—Each of you should record the answers to the questions listed in Exercise 18 in *The Measure of a Marriage Workbook.*

Step 6—Share what you've written with your mate either silently by letting him or her read what you have written or sharing it aloud.

Note: Decide together which approach you would rather use.

Step 7—Discuss together what you can do to help each other improve in your areas of weakness. Then write out specific goals in *The Measure of a Marriage Workbook*, Exercise 19.

AS A GROUP OF COUPLES

After reviewing the biblical material in the first part of this chapter, divide the total group into small groups. This time, however, include both men and women in each group, but have husbands in a different group than their wives. Have each group appoint a leader and a recorder.

Step 1—As a group answer the following questions which are based on the "dimension of *agape* love" scale on page 96.

1. What factors cause the most difficulty in the average marriage in keeping marital partners from demonstrating *patience* toward each other?

2. What factors cause the most difficulty in the average marriage in keeping marital partners from demonstrating *kindness* toward each other?

3. What causes *envy* in the average marriage?

4. What causes a marital partner to engage in *boasting* that has a negative effect in a marriage relationship?

5. What causes hurtful *pride*?

6. What causes *rude behavior* in a marital relationship?

7. What factors cause marital partners to be *selfish*?

8. What factors trigger hurtful *anger*?

9. Why do some marital partners keep *records of wrong*?

10. Why do some marital partners *delight in evil*?

11. What keeps a husband or wife from *rejoicing in the truth*?

12. Why do some marital partners *not protect* one another?

13. What destroys *trust* in a marriage?

14. What keeps marital partners from *seeing the best* in each other?

15. Why do some couples stop *persevering in doing what is right*?

Note: Allow about 15 minutes for this process. If you have several groups, have them divide up the questions. For example, half the group may start with question 1 and the rest of the group may start with question 15 and work backwards.

Step 2—Have the recorder share the group's observations and conclusions with the total group. If you have a number of groups, have each group recorder report on only one or two questions.

Couple Assignment

Ask each couple to work through the couple project outlined in the section for couples, and to complete Exercises 15, 16, 17, 18 and 19 in *The Measure of a Marriage Workbook*.

CHAPTER 11

Understanding Each Other

All human beings are unique—primarily because we are made in God's image. But beyond that, each of us is an individual. And as individuals we have *unique* needs, concerns, interests, talents and potentialities.

But there is yet another difference. We are uniquely male and female. Though both men and women reflect many similarities, we are indeed different in certain respects. And in order to meet one another's needs, we must understand one another, not only as individual human beings but as men and women.

Understanding Your Wife

The apostle Peter spoke directly to this issue in his first letter when he exhorted: "You husbands likewise, live with your wives in an *understanding way*" or literally, live with your wives "according to knowledge" (1 Pet. 3:7). From a practical point of view, Peter was saying that husbands are responsible before God to become *students* of their wives; to make a special effort to understand their particular uniqueness. This involves not only understanding them as individuals because they are human beings, but also as special people. Peter goes on to make this clear.

Your wife is "a woman." Live with your wife in an understanding way, continued Peter, "since she is a *woman.*"

Today, some people are attempting to eliminate unique distinctions between men and women. This is not only biblically unsound, but cannot be demonstrated pragmatically. True, there have been differentiations over the years that are absolutely absurd, unfair and unfounded. But certain distinctions are there nevertheless, even though men, particularly, have widened the gap far beyond reality. Though Adam first recognized Eve's humanness because of her *similarities* to him, he then discovered that she was uniquely *different* from him. She was a "woman" (Gen. 2:23).

Your wife is a "weaker vessel." Peter also stated something in this verse of Scripture that causes some women to actually see red. "Live with your wives in an understanding way," wrote Peter, "as with a *weaker vessel*" (1 Pet. 3:7).

One day I was lecturing on this subject in a well-known institution of higher learning. In the process a bright young woman put up her hand and asked, "Are you sure this is not some kind of translation error? Does the original language in the New Testament actually read 'a *weaker* vessel'?"

My answer had to be first no and then yes. No this is not a translation error. Yes it does mean a "weaker vessel" in the original New Testament text. In other words, this is what Peter actually said.

The problem is that some Bible interpreters have made Peter say far more than he meant. In fact, one very uninformed and prejudiced male once wrote, as he interpreted this phrase: "Women are weak in point of sex, the constitution of their body, mind and judgment, art, aptitude and wisdom in the conduct of affairs."

As a man, this statement embarrasses me. In fact, I hate to admit he is a fellow Bible interpreter. But unfortunately, some men actually believe this. But it is particularly true among men in non-Christian religions. For example, some Muslims actually believe that a woman does not have a soul. But how tragic when people who claim to believe the Bible teach such nonsense. The facts are that women often excel men in mental abilities, psychological and physical (women live longer) endurance, and in both scientific and artistic achievements.

What then does Peter actually mean? The answer is really quite simple. The apostle is referring to the degree of physical *strength* that women *normally* have when compared with men. Though there are exceptions, men by creation have more brute strength. This is easily observable in certain kinds of athletic activities today. Though women can often compete equally, and even exceed men in some sports—such as skiing and skating, you seldom see women able to hold their own against men in the more physically demanding sports such as basketball, football and hockey. Women, in this respect, are the "weaker vessels."

But some believe there is yet a deeper meaning in

Peter's statement. *Your wife is a sexual partner*. Some believe that the most basic and literal meaning of this verse has to do with "weaker vessel" in sexual intercourse. In other words, when Peter wrote, "*Live with* [dwell together with] your wives in an understanding way," he was first and foremost referring to the sexual relationship. Thus Peter would be saying, "Husbands, when you have sexual relations with your wives, do so with understanding and sensitivity remembering that she as a woman is not as strong as you are."

Personally, I would not restrict what Peter had in mind to this interpretation, though this kind of understanding is certainly inherent in what he says. Any Christian husband who is insensitive to his wife's physical capabilities in this most intimate area of life is indeed selfish and *not* understanding. And of course there's a great deal of variation among individual women in terms of actual physical strength and sexual responsiveness. This, too, must be considered if a Christian husband is to obey God and "live with his wife in an *understanding* way."

But just as important, if not more so, as understanding a woman's physical makeup is understanding her emotional needs. This certainly must be included in Peter's injunction. I say this because observations verify the importance of this again and again. I personally have seen many situations where a wife has been treated insensitively over a period of time, usually for several years. In turn she has attempted to tolerate the situation as best she could. Finally, however, her *feelings* of love die and either become numb or negative. In some instances she suddenly turns and walks away from the marriage, leaving her husband dumbfounded. When he asks her *why*, he discovers for the first time she has been feeling hurt and resentment for years because of his insensitivity to her feelings. "Why didn't you tell me?" he asks. "I tried to," she replies. "But you wouldn't listen. Now it's too late."

Unfortunately, when a woman really believes it's too late, it's very difficult to change her mind.

Obviously, most of these situations are two-way problems. The fault lies on both sides. But it does underscore *why* a husband *must* understand his wife.

Understanding Your Husband

Though Peter does not specifically tell wives "to live with their husbands in an understanding way," it is definitely implied in what he *does* say.

In chapter 3 verses 1-6 Peter specifically deals with a Christian wife's relationship to a non-Christian husband. This was a particular problem among those to whom Peter was writing. Evidently a number of women were becoming followers of Christ whereas their pagan husbands were not responding to the message of Christianity. Peter exhorted these women to be submissive to these men— that is, don't resist them or rebel. Furthermore, they were primarily to demonstrate the realities of Christianity with their life-style rather than with theological statements. They were definitely to be loyal to these men sexually, though some certainly were tempted to become involved with Christian men who would be more understanding and sensitive. And, rather than emphasizing *external* adornment, they were to demonstrate true *inner* qualities—"a gentle and quiet spirit."

Peter's specific instructions to these women involves behavior on their part that reflects keen insight into the unique male personality. Ironically, men have often been classified as being superior to women. In this passage Peter implies that in at least one area of life men seem to be inferior, particularly in terms of ego strength.

The male ego is a very sensitive dimension in every man. Though it often reflects strength, it is frequently a cover-up for weakness and feelings of insecurity. A woman who either attacks a male ego or ignores it is only aggravating the problem. She certainly is not living with her husband in an "understanding way."

Peter, it seems, was by implication treating this aspect of the male personality. He exhorted these women to be sensitive to this unique problem. Just as a husband is to be sensitive to a woman's lack of *physical* strength, so a woman is to be sensitive to a man's lack of *ego* strength.

This observation has been verified again and again in my own counseling experiences with couples who are having difficulty in their relationship. A woman who attacks or ignores a man's ego needs can in some instances actually incapacitate him. For example, he may not be able to perform sexually; or if he can perform, he is not able to do so sensitively and compassionately. Furthermore, he may become withdrawn and uncommunicative; or he may become angry or resentful, which interferes with his ability to be emotionally sensitive and understanding.

In these situations a man is also extremely vulnerable. He is easily tempted into an extramarital affair by a woman who *understands* his ego needs. Ironically, most successful prostitutes are masters at understanding men in this area of their lives. And this also explains why some men—even Christian men—will give up everything—a good Christian woman, children, a home, position and finances—to live with another woman. At that moment in his life, more important to him than anything else in the whole world, even his Christianity, is that his ego needs be met. This is tragic but true! I've seen it happen to some of my acquaintances.

A vital relationship with Jesus Christ can of course change a man. But conversion to Christianity and a desire to live according to God's will does not automatically eliminate the problem every man has with his nature which he inherited from Adam. This was why Peter turned next (3:7) to *Christian* husbands and exhorted them to live with their wives in an "understanding way" and to grant them "honor as a fellow-heir of the grace of life."

But as with every relationship in life, this is a two-way street. Every man needs a woman who understands more than anything his ego needs. And every woman needs a man who understands her uniqueness as a woman. And through mutual understanding they can grow together, meeting each other's needs, whatever those needs might be.

Peter concluded his instructions to people in general and to husbands and wives in particular: "To sum up, let all be harmonious, sympathetic, brotherly, kind-hearted, and humble in spirit; not returning evil for evil, or insult for insult, but giving a blessing instead; for you were called for the very purpose that you might inherit a blessing" (1 Pet. 3:8,9).

CHAPTER 12

An Exercise in Developing Feeling Love

We have already considered three dimensions of love which are discussed and illustrated in the Bible (see fig. 1, p. 94). Generally speaking, *agape* love involves doing what is right and best for someone even if it involves negative feelings. *Phileo* love often refers to that dimension of love that involves responding to someone's needs affectionately and with positive emotions. *Erao* love involves sexual response.

Though there are many instances when we must demonstrate love at the action level even when we don't feel like it (that is, if a marriage is to work), it is not God's will that our lives together as husbands and wives be characterized primarily by negative feelings. Rather, we are to *enjoy* each other; not merely endure a painful relationship.

Probably 99 percent of all men and women in our culture enter marriage with very positive feelings. Unfortunately, these feelings are often more physically oriented rather than reflecting a love that is comprehensive and based on mature understanding and feelings. Fortunately, many of these couples soon learn to love each other at a deeper level. On the other hand, what began as a strong physical attraction, in some instances, subsides rather quickly or very quickly turns to feelings of resentment and anger.

How can a marriage, no matter at what level it began in terms of love, grow and mature at the *feeling* level? The answer to this question is to live together in an understanding way. It is only as we come to know each other emotionally that we can minister to each other emotionally. This involves learning to communicate at the *feeling* level. The following exercise is designed to help you accomplish that goal.

AS AN INDIVIDUAL

If your marital partner is uninterested in communication at this level, you have before you a difficult challenge. But don't give up until you give it your best shot. Maybe your mate does not understand your feelings because you don't understand his or hers.

Step 1—Determine what areas create the most difficulty in your marital communication. Respond to the following questions as honestly as possible:

1. Write down several areas where you communicate well with your mate. That is, you can discuss matters together and reach conclusions objectively, clearly and with understanding.

2. Write down several areas where you have difficulty communicating with your mate. That is, you feel these areas usually create misunderstanding and emotional difficulties.

3. Write down areas where you feel you communicate with your mate very superficially or not at all.

Step 2—Analyze your communication style. How do you come across to your mate? Are you a *positive* or a *negative* communicator? The following exercise will help you with this personal evaluation. Check the box in front of each statement to indicate which approach more frequently characterizes your communication style.

When You State Your Opinions or Desires . . .[1]

Do you say:	or	*Do you say:*
☐ Pick up your …		☐ Would you please be kind enough to …?
☐ Why don't you…?		☐ Have you thought about trying …?
☐ Let's go …		☐ How would you feel about going …?
☐ There must be a better way to do that.		☐ Perhaps you would do better if you …
☐ You sure know how to hurt me.		☐ I'm glad you let me know exactly how you feel.
☐ Don't pry so much.		☐ I'm glad you feel free to ask that kind of question even though it is painful for me.
☐ Thanks for doing …		☐ You certainly did a good job on that.

Do you say: *or*   *Do you say:*

☐ I'm glad you finally got that job done.

☐ I admire the way you use your time to complete jobs like …

☐ I'm glad you(finally..)

☐ It was very thoughtful of you to …

☐ I'm glad we have (finally) gone out to dinner.

☐ I enjoyed eating out so much. Thanks for taking me there.

☐ Thanks for the meal.

☐ You're a wonderful cook. Dinner was delicious.

Note: Remember, you are automatically a negative communicator if you don't say anything when you could express appreciation in a positive manner.

In view of this little exercise, how would you classify your communication style? Is it more positive than negative? Is it more negative than positive? *Your goal should be to become as sincerely positive as possible.* When this happens you will be amazed at the changes that will take place in your mate.

Note: Do not be manipulative. This is why I said to be *sincerely* positive. And remember! You can be sincere even though you may have to force yourself emotionally to be positive. The more you practice, the easier and more natural it will become. And once you are positively reinforced by your mate because you have been positive, the process will become even more natural and easy.

AS A COUPLE

An Initial Exercise:

Step 1—It is important that you as a couple learn how to share and exchange feelings. To achieve this goal, spend 15 minutes separately making observations in Exercise 20 of *The Measure of a Marriage Workbook*.

Step 2—Now that you have recorded your responses to these questions on your worksheets, share your answers with each other by reading what your mate has written. Then discuss your answers beginning with question 1. Then move to question 2, and finally question 3. Note differences in opinion as well as agreement. Try to discover why the differences exist.

Step 3—Analyze your communication style with your mate by using Exercise 21 in *The Measure of a Marriage Workbook*.

Step 4—Now that each of you has completed the exercise for evaluating your own communication style with your mate, evaluate your mate's communication style by completing Exercise 22 in your workbook.

Step 5—Compare *your* evaluation of your own communication style with your *mate's* evaluation of your communication style. Do so by completing the comparative worksheets, Exercise 23 in your workbook.

Step 6—Use the comparative worksheets you have just completed to analyze how you view your own communication style compared with how your mate views your communication style. Isolate areas of agreement and disagreement. Discuss why this disagreement exists and *how* you can become more sensitive and understanding in your communication with each other.

Step 7—Now that you have completed the preceding steps, turn to Exercise 24 in *The Measure of a Marriage Workbook*. There are several duplicate exercises on which you and your spouse can share and express your feelings. Follow through on this exercise for at least *seven* days. You may write in your answers and let your mate read your responses out loud if you have difficulty verbalizing them. If necessary, consult the list of positive and negative emotions that follow.

Positive Feelings	*Negative Feelings*
Pleased	Anxious
Understanding	Fear
Hopeful	Lonely
Tenderness	Uncertainty
Proud	Insecure
Closeness	Confusion
Excited	Sad
Happiness	Rejection
Contented	Angry
Confident	Bored
Acceptance	Helplessness
Grateful	Scared
Affectionate	Frustrated
Sexual arousal	Frigidity
Eager	Foolish
Elated	Confused
Calm	Apathetic

Note: It may be necessary in your marriage to continue this process indefinitely. In fact, it is a good exercise to make good marriages even better.

AS A GROUP OF COUPLES

After reviewing the biblical material at the beginning of this chapter, have your group or groups concentrate on how to become positive communicators. Again, divide your groups to include both men and women, and have each group appoint a group leader and a group recorder.

Step 1—Have each group utilize the evaluation form on pages 76,78 in the Workbook, which demonstrates positive and negative communication styles. Read through this material with the total group. Then have each small group add additional illustrations which contrast negative and positive communication.

Step 2—Have each group recorder share several of the group's illustrations.

Step 3—If there is time following the group reports, allow for any questions or comments regarding the process the group has gone through.

Couple Assignment

Ask each couple to work through the couple project outlined in the section for couples, using Exercises 20,21,22,23 and 24 in *The Measure of a Marriage Workbook*.

Suggested Listening Assignment: Secure a set of Dr. Ed Wheat's two cassette tapes entitled *Love Life* (available in your local Christian bookstore). Dr. Wheat makes excellent suggestions regarding how to restore lost feelings in your marriage.

Note

1. Adapted from Mort Katz, *Marriage Survival Kit* (New York: Farnsworth Publishing Co., 1974), p. 39.

CHAPTER 13

Meeting Each Other's Sexual Needs

No concept is clearer in the Bible than the fact that men are designed by God to meet a woman's sexual needs, and vice versa. For many people this sets up a tension. Historically, human beings have not done too well at resolving it, primarily because they are unaware of God's total perspective on marriage as revealed in the Bible. And, if they *are aware* of His divine guidelines, they refuse to follow them. Unfortunately for us we cannot ignore God's laws without suffering the consequences. Though the initial results of disobedience may be emotionally rewarding, the ultimate results, even in this life, are always disappointing and often devastating.

To this point in our study we've been looking at God's *total* perspective on marriage. This is vital because it is impossible to comprehend sexual function and to be a satisfying as well as satisfied sexual partner unless we have this enlarged perspective. All the sex manuals in the world will not solve sex problems and improve sexual relations on a long-term basis—

- unless the husband and wife are in the process of becoming one emotionally and spiritually;
- unless they have "left father and mother" emotionally and spiritually;
- unless they are learning to love as Christ loved;
- unless they are experiencing mutual submission;
- unless they are learning to love at both the action and feeling levels;
- unless they are learning to understand each other not only as male and female but as unique individuals.

It is only as a husband and wife practice these principles in marriage that they can enjoy sexual expression as God intended. These divine guidelines provide the foundation that causes sexual enjoyment in marriage to endure and improve. Furthermore, they also enable a husband and wife to keep subtle selfish desires from destroying what God intended to be a mutually satisfying experience.

Before discussing specific ways we can become better sexual partners, let's look at what God says first about moral purity and then about meeting each other's sexual needs.

Moral Commitment

Once two people marry, God's laws protect that marriage. It has been that way from the beginning of creation. God made these laws absolutely clear when He thundered His commandments from Mount Sinai (see Exod. 20:14,17).

"You shall not commit adultery." The world at large

has never accepted this law. It is often a common practice for a married man to engage in sexual relations on a regular basis with women other than his wife.

One evening my wife and I were having dinner in the home of a young man (an American) and his wife who had been born and reared in another culture. The conversation turned to the life-style in her country, particularly relative to sexual mores. When I quizzed the young woman about some specific behaviors among married men and how it would affect their marriages, she responded, "Oh, wives in our culture are very tolerant of their husbands."

In essence she was expressing a fact that has been prevalent for centuries in many parts of the world that have not been significantly influenced by Hebrew/Christian values. In reality, she was saying that these women had very little choice, especially if they wanted to survive economically and socially. It is a part of the cultural system for a man to have more than one woman in his life and wives can do little but accept it as a reality.

In fact, in some parts of the first-century culture, wives could actually have been sentenced to death by their husbands for overtly rebelling against their free-wheeling and permissive life-styles. When Paul and others began preaching the gospel of Christ in the first-century pagan culture, these New Testament Christian leaders encountered some of these conditions. But along with the message of salvation, they taught a new ethic—actually an old ethic—relative to marriage. According to the will of God, a Christian husband and wife were to be loyal to each other sexually. There were to be no intimate relationships outside of their marriage.

"*Be . . . the husband of one wife.*" When Paul wrote to Timothy who was in Ephesus and to Titus who was in

Crete, he stated the qualifications for spiritual leaders in the church. In both passages of Scripture, being the "husband of one wife" stands out at the top of the list (1 Tim. 3:2; Titus 1:6).

What did Paul mean? Actually, the phrase "husband of one wife" can also be translated "man of one woman." In fact, this phrase may express Paul's original meaning more adequately. You see it was very common for a man living in the New Testament culture to have not only a wife but other girls he visited regularly for sexual gratification. There was frequently the prostitute at the local temple. Also, he may have had access to a slave girl who was considered a part of the household. In most instances, his wife was well-aware of his extramarital involvements. The other girls were for fun and games. Her place was to care for the house and to bear children and rear them. And there was actually very little she could do about the situation. She had few alternatives in her culture. It was a fact of life.

But the message and impact of Christianity brought change. In fact, from the beginning of time God planned for a man to have only one woman in his life and He planned for a woman to have only one man in her life. Though He allowed Old Testament personalities to violate this divine plan it was not within His perfect will. And whenever the plan *was* violated, it caused jealousy, fostered disunity, brought heartache and created other difficulties. This is abundantly illustrated in the life of such Old Testament characters as Abraham, Jacob, David and Solomon.

"Every one who looks on a woman to lust for her" commits adultery. The message of Christianity not only reinforced God's initial plan but established an even

higher standard of morality. When confronting the Pharisees regarding the relationship between a husband and wife, Jesus told them that to actually look on a woman and to lust after her was the same—in God's eyes—as already committing adultery in the heart. In other words, it was not necessarily the *act* of sexual intercourse that was adultery, but also the very *plan* to engage in this activity (see Matt. 5:27,28).

Don't misunderstand. Jesus was not saying that every time a man (or a woman) is tempted sexually it is sin. Unfortunately, Jimmy Carter, when he was candidating for the presidency of the United States, seems to have misunderstood the difference between "lust" as Jesus used the word and "temptation." You'll remember the much publicized comment that he made regarding the fact that he probably commits adultery in his heart every day, referring back to Jesus' statement in Matthew's Gospel. Understandably, *Playboy* and other pornographic magazines had a heyday over the statement. What Mr. Carter should have said and hopefully what he meant, to be biblically accurate, was that he is probably *tempted* every day. And to be tempted per se is not committing adultery of the heart. Adultery as Jesus defined it is when a man or woman actually look *and* plan to engage in a sexual act with someone other than his or her marital partner. The moment a person moves in that direction, the intent to engage in a sexual act becomes adultery in God's eyes.

Every Christian man and woman must be on guard against this kind of behavior. Looking—particularly prolonged looking and thinking—can easily lead to lust as Jesus defined it. Temptation can quickly become sin. We're all tempted if we're human at all. This is particularly true for men who are usually more visually oriented than women. And living in a culture that uses every means possible to tap these natural capacities creates many situations every day that are tempting. However, we need not sin against God or our marital partners. We need not lust. With God's help we can refocus our thoughts. And part of this divine plan in marriage is that sexual needs are to be met regularly within the bonds of marriage.

Engaging in Regular Sexual Relations

The Bible clearly and forthrightly teaches that regular sexual relationships are designed by God to be a natural and normal part of marriage. The apostle Paul probably spoke more specifically in this regard than any other biblical author. When writing to the Corinthians he stated: "Let the husband fulfill his duty to his wife, and likewise also the wife to her husband. The wife does not have authority over her own body, but the husband does; and likewise also the husband does not have authority over his own body, but the wife does. Stop depriving one another, except by agreement for a time that you may devote yourselves to prayer, and come together again lest Satan tempt you because of your lack of self-control" (1 Cor. 7:3-5).

To understand the reasons why Paul in this instance was so outspoken about sex and marriage, we must understand some historical and cultural factors. The city of Corinth was noted even in the pagan Roman world for its low morals. During Paul's day it was a large and growing city with a population well over 100,000 people. However, its population was mobile, consisting of traveling businessmen, sailors, and government officials. Illicit sexual behavior was rampant.

To add to Corinth's moral degradation, religious prostitution was a part of its cultic practice. History records that in New Testament times at least 1,000 priestesses were employed in religious prostitution and operated out of the temple of Aphrodite. Readily accessible and always available, they provided any kind of sexual experience any man (or woman) wanted—day or night.

It was in this environment that Paul preached the gospel of Jesus Christ on his second missionary journey. Rejected by many of his fellow Jews, he turned to the pagan Gentiles in that city. Luke records that "many of the Corinthians when they heard were believing and being baptized" (Acts 18:8). Consequently, those who made up the church at Corinth were mostly pagan people, many of whom were converted to Christ out of a life of prostitution, adulterous relationships, homosexuality, and a variety of criminal acts. In fact, Paul makes this very clear in his first letter to the Corinthian Christians when he said: "Do not be deceived: Neither the sexually immoral nor idolaters nor adulterers nor male prostitutes nor homosexual offenders nor thieves nor the greedy nor drunkards nor slanderers nor swindlers will inherit the kingdom of God. *And that is what some of you were*" (1 Cor. 6:9-11, *NIV*).

Ascetic Practices

There was yet another problem in Corinth. There were some religious philosophers who were teaching ascetic practices which included the doctrine that it is better not to marry; consequently abstaining from *all* sexual activity. This philosophy also influenced these new Christians in Corinth. Some of these believers evidently erroneously syncretized Paul's teaching on morality with this pagan practice. And since most of these Christians were no doubt already married, they attempted to practice sexual abstinence within the marriage state, thinking it would make them more acceptable to God. Perhaps their previous immoral life-style caused them to overreact to Paul's teaching on morality. Furthermore, some of these pagan philosophers probably began to proselytize these new Christians.

Paul faced this problem by acknowledging the unmarried state as good and proper *if* a person felt this was his gift from God (see 1 Cor. 7:7-9). And this would be especially true if a person felt he could maintain a life of moral purity as a single person living in the midst of a very immoral environment (see 1 Cor. 7:1,2). But then Paul made it very clear that God designed marriage as a legitimate context in which men and women could and should express sexual feelings openly, freely and without a sense of guilt. Furthermore, Paul pointed out to the Corinthians that since their questions involved men and women who were already married, they were in no way to withhold sex from their marital partners. If they did, Paul warned, they would be setting the stage for Satan to tempt one or the other into an illicit sexual affair.

We see then that the Bible is very practical in the area of sex. In essence, God is saying that people *do* have sexual needs. Furthermore, marriage is the place for these needs to be met. And each marital partner is responsible to make sure those needs *are* met. If they should decide to abstain sexually for a time, it should be agreed upon by both, but only on a temporary basis and for spiritual reasons. Note however that Paul is not correlating the *absence* of sex as being a means per se to more holiness. Rather, abstaining temporarily would simply allow more concentrated time for prayer.

The Universal Principle

Inherent in Paul's instructions to the Corinthians, who were facing some particular problems in their own culture, is a universal principle that applies to every marriage since the time of Adam and Eve. When a man and woman choose to be joined together in holy matrimony, they take upon themselves a special responsibility to meet each other's sexual needs. Paraphrasing Paul, since their bodies now belong to each other, they are not to ''withhold'' sex from each other.

We must quickly add, however, that it is important to interpret this injunction in the light of other God-given directives and principles in Scripture which relate to marriage and which have been discussed in previous chapters. Paul's exhortation to the Corinthians, if taken out of the total context of Scripture, can be used selfishly and insensitively. And used in this way it can literally destroy a marital partner emotionally, and eventually the marriage itself.

The Circle of Biblical Love

The principles outlined in our previous chapters can be summarized by once again looking at a biblical definition of love (see fig. 1, p. 94). Most references to love in the New Testament do not refer to sexual expression per se. Rather, most refer to *agapao* love—doing what is *right* and *best* for someone, even if it involves negative feelings. Closely aligned with *agapao* love is *phileo* love—responding to someone's needs affectionately and with positive emotions, but always within the guidelines of *agapao* love. For the most part, it is God's will that *agapao* and *phileo* love overlap. But the Bible clearly assumes that there are times when we must do things for someone because it is right, not because we necessarily desire to do so.

This poses a problem when it comes to *erao* love, which involves physical and emotional involvement with another person sexually. Men particularly and generally cannot function sexually without erotic feelings. Unfortunately, however, a man can experience these erotic feelings purely at a selfish level and with any woman who is sexually available. Putting it simply, it is easy for a man to engage in erotic "love" outside the circle of biblical love (see fig. 1, p. 94). The history of female prostitution affirms this point.

In some respects, women have the same capability, but not to the same extent as men. This is why most biblical injunctions regarding moral purity are directed at men (see Exod. 20:17; Matt. 5:28; 1 Tim. 3:2; Titus 1:6). It is a fact of life, generally speaking, that men *are* more visually and erotically oriented when it comes to sex. They are more easily aroused, more physically oriented and more vulnerable to temptation. Every modern-day advertising agency is well-aware of this reality.

Women, on the other hand, are more emotionally oriented. Though they are very capable of being intensely erotic, they usually respond sexually to a man who provides them with security, who understands their deep feelings, who is sensitive, tender and compassionate. Their extramarital affairs are normally precipitated because they are angry, lonesome, insecure or generally unhappy and unfulfilled.

Note: Men are also vulnerable when these emotional states occur. However, a man may also choose to engage in extramarital sex simply because he has a physical need. This is not to say that some women may not do the same thing. But it is usually the exception, not the rule.

What does all of this mean in a marriage where both the husband and wife are committed to *Christian* values? The following chapter is designed to answer this question.

CHAPTER 14

An Exercise in Developing Sexual Love

Getting to know each other sexually in a marital relationship is one of the great adventures God has designed for husbands and wives. Though creativity in this area of a couple's life must be sensitively developed within the context of both *agapao* (action) and *phileo* (feeling) love, it nevertheless provides in itself a lifelong challenge. Like any activity in life, sexual relationships can become routine and meaningless for any couple. This chapter is designed to help you keep this area of your life interesting, challenging and mutually satisfying.

AS AN INDIVIDUAL

How well do you understand your mate as a sexual being? The following questions and explanations will help you answer this question. Notice that there is a section for wives as well as a section for husbands. Since men and women differ in their sexual makeup, it is important to understand these differences.

As a Wife
How well do I understand my husband's sexual nature?

Most men are quite consistent in their sexual makeup. There are exceptions, of course, but generally when you understand one man, you understand them all. Following are some key insights to help you understand the average husband:

- Sexually, he is visually oriented.

- He can be sexually aroused almost instantaneously.

- His sexual drive is closely related to the ebb and flow of glandular fluids.

  Note: A sexually active man cannot suddenly turn off his sexual desire. It has now become a spontaneous physiological process. Once he has become used to regular sexual emissions, prostate fluid is produced accordingly.

- A man's ego is closely aligned with what his wife thinks about him sexually. For example, a man whose wife demonstrates negative attitudes toward his genitals feels intensely rejected as a total person.

How aware am I of my husband's sexual temptations?

- Most women who dress provocatively arouse a man sexually. Because the average woman in the average office in today's work-a-day world dresses provocatively, the average husband—even the Christian husband—is, to a certain extent, sexually stimulated nearly every day—and by more than one woman.

• Most advertising today, whether it is in the newspapers, magazines, TV or radio, is designed to arouse a man sexually. Since we live in a media-oriented world, it is almost impossible for the average man to avoid some kind of erotic stimulation on a regular basis.

• The degree of arousal in the average man varies, depending on several factors. But one of the most significant factors relates to the extent of his sexual fulfillment with his wife and particularly the regularity of sexual release.

Note: A man who gives himself over to lustful behavior as a way of life is never satisfied sexually. However, even a man who attempts to abide by God's standards faces regular sexual temptations, and experiences continual sexual needs.

How understanding am I of my husband's temptations?

Some women resent their husband's sexual nature. Remember that the average *Christian* husband feels guilty already regarding his weaknesses in this area of his life. To feel resentment and lack of understanding from his wife only adds to his own feelings of self-condemnation and guilt. In fact, this kind of attitude often accentuates his vulnerability to other women who *do* understand his nature, accept it and use it to their advantage.

How available am I to my husband sexually?

• Because you do not feel sexual desire does not mean your husband does not.

• Demonstrating "unavailability" does not diminish your husband's sexual drive; in fact, it may increase it.

• When your husband reads your "unavailable" signals and withdraws, it does not mean he has forgotten what he feels.

• A wise wife learns how to meet her husband's sexual needs even when it is inconvenient for her personally (during pregnancy, menstrual periods, etc.).

• When it is necessary to abstain totally, a wise wife learns how to say no without making her husband feel rejected.

What can I do to make myself more physically attractive?
   Remember: Most women do not have to undergo physical surgery to become more attractive. Remarkable changes can result from some do-it-yourself projects:

• Avoiding excessive weight

• Bathing regularly—especially before lovemaking

• Using cosmetics effectively

• Dressing appropriately for the bedroom.

What can I do to become a more creative lover?
   Note: Most people (men included) do not become creative lovers naturally. It takes thought and practice. Following are the great inhibitors in this process:

• Negative attitudes toward sex

• Inappropriate information

• Lack of information

• Thinking only of oneself.

Remember: God has designed marriage for one man and one woman. Beyond that He does not lock us into sexual forms. The very nature of both men's and women's physical and emotional makeup makes sex one of the areas of life for the greatest opportunity for creative exploration.

What can I do to set the stage for a pleasant environment for lovemaking?

The physical environment is important to a man. An unattractive bedroom or even poor housekeeping habits generally affect a man's feelings about sex. However, also remember that the emotional environment is just as important (if not more so) than the physical environment. Nothing is more disappointing to a man than negative attitudes in a beautiful bedroom.

Do I really know and understand what my husband likes and dislikes about our lovemaking? Do I make it easy for him to talk about it?

As a Husband

How well do I understand my wife's sexual nature?

It's important to realize that individual women vary far more in their sexual makeup than the average man. On the one hand, a small percentage of women have a high degree of natural sexual desire. On the other hand, a small percentage of women have a low degree of natural sexual desire. However, the majority of women fall somewhere in the middle. The facts are that many women can live comfortably (from a purely physiological point of view) without engaging in intimate sexual relationships. In this sense they differ noticeably from men.

Don't misunderstand. This does not mean women cannot and do not enjoy sex—even those with a low sex drive. It does mean, however, that their nature is different. If a man does not understand this, he can be very threatened. Furthermore, his expectation levels regarding his wife and himself become very unrealistic.

Following are several things to remember about the *average* woman.

• Whereas men are visually oriented, women are more oriented to what they sense and feel.

• Whereas the man is normally quickly aroused (even at a distance), a woman is normally aroused gradually and in a context of understanding, sensitivity and appropriate physical touch and stimulation.

• Whereas a man's sexual drive is correlated with the ebb and flow of his own body fluids (internal stimulation), a woman's sexual drive is correlated more significantly with external stimuli; namely, a warm accepting and understanding relationship with her husband.

Note: Many women experience degrees of difference in their sexual response depending on their menstrual cycle. However, the phenomenon is far different than male secretionary processes and how they affect sexual desire and arousal.

• Whereas a man's ego is closely aligned with his sexual performance, a woman's sexual performance relates more to her sense of pride and psychological need to be an adequate sexual partner.

What can I do to help my wife be more responsive sexually?

Since a woman's sexual response is usually triggered differently than a man's, careful attention should be given to the following:

• Don't expect your wife to be ready to engage in sex just because you are.

• Don't be threatened by her initial lack of desire.

• Think of ways to make sexual response more natural and easier for your wife. Following are some suggestions:

1. Remember that sexual feelings in a woman can begin to be aroused a long time before sexual intercourse—actually many hours before. This is often caused by sharing loving and tender feelings. This causes a woman to feel understood, secure and accepted.

2. Demonstrate your love to your wife unconditionally and consistently. In other words, don't compartmentalize sexual activity. Make it a part of numerous expressions of love.

Note: Some men only say "I love you" and show affection and do nice things for their wives only when they are interested in sex. This is a turn-off for many women. They feel bribed and used.

3. Plan lovemaking at a time when your wife is physically and emotionally fresh.

Note: A long day with the kids in a closed environment is not very conducive to stimulating a sexual response. Be understanding about these circumstances. Plan ways to circumvent these problems.

• Learn to know your wife's physical and psychological makeup as an individual woman. What pleases her? What kind of physical stimulation aids her in being sexually satisfied?

Caution: What may please your wife on one occasion may not on another. Furthermore, what pleases other women may not necessarily please your wife. Remember too that a woman is not as consistent in her response to certain stimuli as men. Don't let this confuse you or threaten you. Take it as a challenge and learn to know the many moods of your wife and her uniqueness as a woman.

Do I know and understand what my wife is feeling?

This is basic to feminine sexual response. Feelings of resentment, anger, insecurity, fear, etc., are all great inhibitors in causing a woman *not* to respond sexually.

Listen to your wife's feelings. Encourage her to share how she feels. Accept those feelings. Try not to take personally her negative feelings toward you as a husband. These are normal and natural. Though it is sometimes painful, remember that she will love you for it.

How can I be more tender toward my wife?

Mort Katz in his *Marriage Survival Kit*[1] suggests the following will help you develop this quality in your marital relationship:

- Tenderness is asking your wife what she is feeling.

- Tenderness is asking your wife what she means.

- Tenderness is telling your wife that you understand how she feels.

- Tenderness is telling your wife you are glad for her happiness when she is happy.

- Tenderness is telling your wife you are sorry for her pain when she's hurting inside.

- Tenderness is hugging your wife apart from sexual relationships.

- Tenderness is holding your wife gently when she's hurting.

- Tenderness is sharing your happy feelings with your wife.

- Tenderness is letting your wife know what you enjoy and appreciate about her.

- Tenderness is hanging up your clothes neatly.

- Tenderness is taking out the garbage.

- Tenderness is paying the bills.

- Tenderness is helping your wife with her household responsibilities when she asks for help.

- Tenderness is tuning into your wife's true feelings.

How can I become more physically attractive to my wife?

It is true that men are far more easily aroused sexually through what they see, but women find it more difficult as well to be aroused by a physically unattractive husband. The same basic suggestions given to wives also apply to you in making yourself physically more attractive.

- Get rid of excessive weight.

- Bathe regularly.

- Smell good.

And remember: Don't let it threaten you if your wife is not as sexually aroused by your physical manner as much as you are aroused by her feminine mystique.

AS A COUPLE

Warning! As you begin this process as a couple, your greatest challenge is being sensitive in the communication that lies before you. You're venturing into the most vulnerable area of your inner being. Be honest and yet kind and gentle. Remember too that if you do not measure up in these areas as you think you do or as much as you want to, it will be a great opportunity for developing both understanding and skill as a sexual partner. Though you may be initially threatened, great dividends can eventually come.

Note: If you reach an impasse in communication, you may need to seek help from an objective third party who is skilled in marital counseling.

Step 1—Complete the ''Evaluation Scale for Wives'' and the ''Evaluation Scale for Husbands,'' Exercise 25 in *The Measure of a Marriage Workbook.*

Step 2—Complete the evaluation scales in Exercise 26 in *The Measure of a Marriage Workbook.*

Step 3—Fill in the comparative forms, Exercise 27 in *The Measure of a Marriage Workbook.*

Step 4—Together isolate areas of agreement and disagreement on the comparative forms. Note that a one-point variance on a five-point scale may be significant.

Step 5—In addition to areas of disagreement, also note obvious areas of low understanding. Use these areas to go back and read the information that corresponds with these areas on pages 129-137 in this book, *The Measure of a Marriage.*

Together read through both sets of questions and explanations. Flip a coin to see who goes first.

As a Wife (if you're first): Read out loud to your husband the section designed for you and entitled "As a Wife." Following each question and the explanations, stop and ask your husband if he agrees with the author's observations and suggestions.

As a Husband: Read out loud to your wife the section entitled "As a Husband." Following each question and the explanations, stop and ask your wife if she agrees with the author's observations and suggestions.

Step 6 : Conclude this process together by participating in a positive interaction exercise suggested by David and Vera Mace in their excellent book entitled, *How to Have a Happy Marriage*.[2]

Sit facing each other and hold hands if you are comfortable in doing so. Tell each other some of the things about each other that you really appreciate.

Instead of a back and forth dialogue, decide who will go first, then take only one turn each. Look into each other's eyes while you talk, and address each other directly by name. Do the exercise in a reflective, unhurried way, with pauses wherever you like. During your turn, think of a number of qualities in your partner and share them slowly one by one, beginning each with "I love you because . . ."; or "I like you when . . ."; "Another thing I especially like about you is . . ."; or similar words that come naturally to you.

Take plenty of time with this exercise, and talk about it afterwards—how you felt, how you reacted to what was said to you. Furthermore, once you have gone through this experience, do it again from time to time—not often enough to make it routine, but as something to be reserved for special occasions.

AS A GROUP OF COUPLES

After reviewing the biblical material in chapter 13, divide the group into smaller groups. This time go back to the previous organizational structure. Have women with women in groups and men with men. Have each group appoint leaders and recorders.

Step 1—Before the individual groups go to work, read out loud the questions and observations in the first section of this exercise on pages 130-137.

Step 2—After you read the material out loud, instruct the groups to do the following:

Husbands' Groups: Respond to the section entitled "As a Wife," beginning on page 130. Ask for any comments they would like to make regarding the author's material. What additional questions would they ask and what additional observations would they make?

Wives' Groups: Respond to the section entitled "As a Husband," beginning on page 133. Ask for any comments they would like to make regarding the author's observations. What additional questions and explanations would they like to make?

Step 3—Have each group recorder share with the total group, avoiding repetition.

Couple Assignment

Following the group process, ask each couple to go home and personalize this group project in their own marriage by working through the projects designed for couples in this text and in *The Measure of a Marriage Workbook*, Exercises 25, 26 and 27.

For Further Reading: Read *Intended for Pleasure* by Dr. Ed Wheat and his wife Gaye Wheat (published by Fleming H. Revell). Dr. Wheat is a family physician and in this book he and his wife write very specifically regarding techniques that can improve your sexual relationship.

Dr. Wheat has also prepared two cassette tapes entitled *Sex Techniques* and *Sex Problems* (available from your local bookstore). Dr. Wheat will provide you with three hours of intimate personal sex counsel to enrich your marital life.

Just a Beginning

Though we've reached the end of this *book,* it is really just a beginning. Growing in a marriage relationship must be continuous and ongoing. In fact, it would be well for you to actually start over again and work through all the projects once more. You'll discover that your life together can deepen indefinitely.

Better yet, share the process with someone else. As a couple start a marriage enrichment class for other couples. Guide them through the projects designed for a group of couples, which will in turn launch them into the couples' projects—which you'll want to go through again yourself.

Notes

1. Adapted from Mort Katz, *Marriage Survival Kit* (New York: Farnsworth Publishing Co., 1974), p. 61.
2. David and Vera Mace, *How to Have a Happy Marriage* (Nashville: Abingdon Press, 1977), p. 126.